WITNESSING SADISM IN TEXTS OF THE AMERICAN SOUTH

Looking at works by Carrie Mae Weems, Toni Morrison, Emily Dickinson, Flannery O'Connor, Dorothy Allison, Carson McCullers, and Zora Neale Hurston, Claire Raymond uncovers a pattern of femininity constructed around representations of sadistic violence in American women's literature and photography from the late nineteenth and twentieth centuries. Dickinson's poetry is read through its relationship to the Southern Agrarian critics who championed her work. While the representations of violence found in Carrie Mae Weems's installation *From Here I Saw What Happened and I Cried*, Morrison's *Beloved*, Dickinson's poetry, O'Connor's "A View of the Woods" and "A Good Man Is Hard to Find," Allison's *Bastard Out of Carolina*, McCullers's *Ballad of the Sad Café*, and Hurston's *Mules and Men* are diverse in terms of artistic presentation, all allude to or are set in the antebellum and Jim Crow South. In addition, all involve feminine characters whose subjectivity is shaped by the practice of seeing acts of violence inflicted where there can be no effective resistance. While not proposing an equivalence between representing violence in visual images and written text, Raymond does suggest that visual images of violence can be interpreted in context with written evocations of violent imagery. Invoking sadism in its ethical sense of violence enacted on a victim for whom self-defense and recourse of any kind are impossible, Raymond's study is ultimately an exploration of the idea that a femininity constructed by the positioning of feminine characters as witnesses to sadistic acts is a phenomenon distinctly of the American South that is linked to the culture's history of racism.

For my cousin, Emma "Goo" Rogers

Witnessing Sadism in Texts of the American South

Women, Specularity, and the Poetics of Subjectivity

CLAIRE RAYMOND
University of Virginia, USA

ASHGATE

Published by
Ashgate Publishing Limited
Wey Court East
Union Road
Farnham
Surrey, GU9 7PT
England

Ashgate Publishing Company
110 Cherry Street
Suite 3-1
Burlington, VT 05401-3818
USA

www.ashgate.com

British Library Cataloguing in Publication Data
A catalogue record for this book is available from the British Library

The Library of Congress has cataloged the printed edition as follows:
Raymond, Claire, 1967–
Witnessing sadism in texts of the American South : women, specularity, and the poetics of subjectivity / by Claire Raymond.
pages cm
Includes index.
ISBN 978-1-4094-5105-1 (hardcover : alk. paper)
1. American literature—Southern States—History and criticism. 2. American literature—Women authors—History and criticism. 3. Women photographers—United States—History. 4. Photography—United States—History. 5. Sadism in literature. 6. Sadism in art. 7. Violence in literature. 8. Violence in art. 9. Women—Identity. 10. Racism—Southern States. 11. Southern States—In literature. 12. Southern States—In art. I. Title. II. Title: Women, specularity, and the poetics of subjectivity.
PS261.R37 2014
810.9'975—dc23

2013033643

ISBN: 9781409451051 (hbk)

MIX
Paper from responsible sources
FSC www.fsc.org FSC® C013985

Printed in the United Kingdom by Henry Ling Limited,
at the Dorset Press, Dorchester, DT1 1HD

Contents

List of Figures

Acknowledgements

I am grateful to Sarah Corse for encouraging me to write this book. The topic isn't fashionable or easy and Sarah's enthusiasm for the project has been crucial. I also thank Alison Booth, who read the first draft of the project, and whose astute early critique shaped the book in fundamental ways. The Excellence in Diversity Fellows program at the University of Virginia provided a grant, and invaluable support in numerous ways, for the writing of this book. I am especially grateful to Dorothe Bach, of the EDF program, for her many kindnesses. Kenny Marotta made incisive comments on the manuscript midway through its journey, and I am very grateful to him. My students at the University of Virginia engaged the material from this book, taught in various courses, with fresh and intelligent insights: I am grateful to all of them. In particular Aleshia Dunning, Adwoa Owusu, Anna Kushner, and Shantell Bingham, students in my *American Ghosts*, and *Women Photographers & Feminist Aesthetics* courses, gave their hearts to the material, and their brilliant insights reshaped the way I saw it. My former student, Conley Lowrance, was so good as to read through the manuscript with the care, intelligence, and consummate grace he brings to all he does. Carrie Mae Weems is our American Picasso: I am thankful to her for permission to reprint her photographs in this book. As always my gratitude to Ashgate's Ann Donahue: she is the key.

Introduction
Sadism and Specularity: Mirroring Femininity and Sadism

The cover image for this book, drawn from Carrie Mae Weems's *Louisiana Project* (2003), visually summarizes the terrain of this study. For Weems's photograph represents women watching each other watch, dramatizing the spectative and specular qualities of this putative feminine gaze. The heavy and dark space that looms above the two women, and the indications that the women do not watch each other out of love and devotion but rather, more complexly, view each other through the historical lens of race, and perhaps racism, suggest a back story of violence. The women, in Weems's photograph, are not violent to each other but they interact through a gaze that acknowledges the history of violence and does not seek to cover the scars of that violence. In this study of representations of sadistic violence—violence inflicted on a victim who cannot meaningfully defend herself—and representations of a feminine witness, the back story of cruelty in the traditional South becomes the front story, the story on the proscenium. In this book, I read texts that represent the humiliation, rape, and murder of feminine characters, set in the South. The emphatically staged quality of Weems's photograph coheres with my project, insofar as I am interpreting codes and ethics of the act of representation. Representations of feminine witnesses to violence form a code I seek to ravel in this study of a few texts that represent the traditional South. For in the witness to sadistic violence inheres memory, and the memory of the violation of the feminine body is that discomfiting place from which we are wont to turn away. This feminine witness figure, as I will contend, is by no means always benign. Sometimes, the woman watching another woman being violated is pleasured by that scene of violation. This problematic borderland where gender, representation, and violence intertwine in the poetics of subjectivity is the terrain of the book that follows.

The figure of the *martyr*, from the Greek μάρτυς—one who witnesses suffering and in witnessing comes to bear on his body the marks of what he sees—is deeply embedded in Christian iconography.[1] René Girard argues that while the original Greek meaning of the word was simply that of witness, Christianity brought into common use the idea of bodily suffering, in particular bodily suffering because of injustice, as the primary meaning of the word *martyr*.[2] In the book of Acts, for

---

1 "Martyr," *The Oxford English Dictionary*, 2nd ed. (New York: Oxford University Press, 1989).

2 René Girard, *The Scapegoat* (Palo Alto: Stanford University Press, 1986), 22.

example, the idea of testifying to the point of death is made central to the claims of Christianity. Etymologically, *martyros* is linked to the Sanskrit term for memory: what is inscribed, through the body, into the mind.[3] The concept of *martyros* has been invoked in discourse as the sacrificial use usually of male bodies. But in this study I will shift ground to investigate the representation of bearing witness to violence when both the figure of the watcher and the violated body represented are feminine or transgender, not masculine.

I will distinguish between the cultural work of the image of the martyred or afflicted masculine body and that of the martyred feminine or transgender body, tracking how the act of witnessing suffering marks and is marked through the representation of the feminine *watcher* of the violated other. My work is grounded in close-readings of photographic and literary texts, and I approach the photography, fiction, and poetry on which I write from an interdisciplinary perspective. My interest is in tracking how the figure of the witness represented in photography, fiction, and poetry reflects the function of this feminine witness figure in culture.

Kali Tal's maverick study, *Worlds of Hurt: Reading the Literatures of Trauma*, in analyzing the cultural function of the image of the suffering body, takes a similarly interdisciplinary approach to interpreting how we as a culture read victims and heroes.[4] Tal contrasts the cultural place of male war veterans with that of female incest survivors. Tal argues, persuasively, that while the male body that survives war is often viewed as heroic, the female body that survives the brutality of incest is often viewed as corrupted, tainted, and tagged with the mark of the false witness.[5] In brief terms, one may say that *Worlds of Hurt* shows that the sexually violated female body often does not qualify for heroic martyrdom in its representation, unless that sexual violation is "backed" with the narrative guarantee of the rape victim's death.[6] Developing from Tal, I point out that the guarantee of veracity, in representations of violence against women, often comes

---

3 Friedrich Nietzsche framed his notion of memory on just such suffering, arguing that ethics have implicitly depended upon the capacity to impose physical pain to assert the structure of guilt, in *Beyond Good and Evil* (1966; repr., New York: Random House-Vintage, 1989).

4 Kali Tal, *Worlds of Hurt: Reading the Literatures of Trauma* (New York: Cambridge University Press, 1996).

5 Tal's introduction to *Worlds of Hurt: Reading the Literatures of Trauma* (4–5) persuasively makes this case for gender differential, but it takes a full reading of her strangely demanding and broad-ranging book to gauge the depth and force of her argument about the gender-biased cultural reception of the suffering body.

6 For example, observe the awesome popularity of Alice Sebold's syrupy *The Lovely Bones* (Boston: Little, Brown, 2002), a rape and murder story made into a movie. Had the represented rape victim survived, we may guess her status as quasi-angelic girl may not have garnered its cultural hold. Even Sapphire's brilliant *Push* (New York: Alfred A. Knopf, 1996) proffers the figure of death through its closing invocation of HIV-AIDS as the destination of the martyred daughter. One could make the case that *The Lovely Bones* and *Push* turn on the idea that their raped and ultimately killed-by-rape young protagonists are innocents because they die. The question of how intractable is our lack of willingness to

from a witness who is not the victim: someone else watching the suffering female body testifies to this suffering. By contrast, the heroic male body of the war veteran is often granted direct voice.

Martyros, testimony, is a metaphor written on the body. In the following study, I focus precisely on the distinction between representing the experience of the feminine or transgender *inhabitant of* a suffering, martyred body, and representing the figure of the feminine *witness to* a martyred body. It is a difference, I will argue, that indicates and configures the cultural contours of femininity. In this study, the concept of the *martyros* is the nodum that pulls together representations of the witnessing of suffering: the witness is at risk, at risk of being harmed by what she sees and also at risk of sadistically enjoying the violence she is forced to see.

My concern in this study is with the feminine *martyros* as a figure that stands ontologically between victim and violator, and stands semiotically as a sign, or marking, or testimony, inscribed through the act of watching another suffer violation.[7] Masculinity, in the West, allows for a fusion of the suffering body and the witness. But traditional tropes of femininity divide the roles of the *martyros* who both knows and suffers: in representations of violence, one woman suffers, another woman watches. The woman who suffers violation, in particular sexual violation, is silenced or erased, unless she becomes a posthumous speaker.[8] And yet the woman who watches rather than receives violence notably is produced as a witness figure in photography and literature created by women (or, in the example of photographer Carrie Mae Weems's series, *From Here I Saw What Happened and I Cried*, re-produced by a woman).[9] This witness is a figure that watches and reports the violation of the other feminine, or transgender, body.[10] This feminine

---

mourn for the fate of, say, a raped prostitute, a woman not considered innocent, haunts the problematic of interpreting the cultural place of the female victim of sexual violation.

7 Jacques Derrida interprets the way words watch themselves in "Signature, Event, Context," and in this book I am expanding this notion to consider also the way that images watch themselves, in the context of photography. Jacques Derrida, *The Margins of Philosophy*, trans. Alan Bass (Chicago: University of Chicago Press, 1982), 307.

8 I have covered the ground of the workings of the posthumous speaker in women's writing in a previous book, *The Posthumous Voice in Women's Writing from Mary Shelley to Sylvia Plath* (Aldershot, England; Burlington, VT: Ashgate, 2006). There I made the claim that the posthumous speaker witnesses herself suffering from the vantage of having not survived a trauma intact, and yet having retained, uncannily and eerily, her ability to speak about the trauma.

9 Carrie Mae Weems, *From Here I Saw What Happened and I Cried* (Museum of Modern Art, New York, August 30, 2006–April 9, 2007).

10 As I expand on later in this book, for readings of the specific texts in this book, I interpret *transgender* characters as characters diverging from normative masculinity: feminized characters, in that sense. The definition of transgender, I realize, does not mean simply veering from the masculine but I hope that my reasons for emphasizing the transgender figure as a departure from normative masculinity will be justified as the book proceeds.

witness figure, one who watches violation forced onto the body of another woman, or transgender person, strikes me as an inadequately theorized figure in feminism.[11] A goal of the current study is to theorize that figure: the character whose representation in text, whether visual or verbal, figures a watcher of another woman's suffering. This witness that watches does not necessarily come to the aid of the violated other woman. She does watch the violation and, through this witness figure, the representation of violence is rehearsed.

Chandra Talpade Mohanty has written about the tendency of Western feminists to project female vulnerability and a capacity for bodily suffering onto the "other" of the so-called Third World woman. Mohanty's "Under Western Eyes" paradigmatically makes the case that Western feminists seem to take pleasure in assigning to non-Western woman the role of the suffering body.[12] But Mohanty still radically splits and divides the Western gaze from the body of the suffering, feminized other; indeed, this distinction forms the very crux of her classic essay. My interest, however, is in texts in which the feminine witness is not socially "other" or different from the victim whose suffering she is dramatized as watching.

To explore the depiction of this feminine witness figure, I reconsider the representation of sadistic violence in key works of photography and literature by American women contending with the Civil War, the antebellum, or the Jim Crow South: Carrie Mae Weems, Toni Morrison, Dorothy Allison, Carson McCullers, Flannery O'Connor, Zora Neale Hurston, and Emily Dickinson.[13] I have chosen them as this study's focus because each of them has achieved canonical status as photographer, novelist, short story writer, or poet, and each has produced at least one significant work that represents the drama of a feminine character or figure who watches violence. The grandmother in O'Connor's "A Good Man is Hard to Find"[14] who watches the murder of her family, or the beautiful woman shown in profile bracketing Weems's *From Here I Saw What Happened and I Cried*,[15] or the former slave Sethe in Morrison's *Beloved*,[16] or the incest victim's young mother in

[11] Elizabeth Spelman's *Fruits of Sorrow: Framing Our Attention to Suffering* (Boston: Beacon, 1997) is an exception. Spelman offers a brilliant reading of compassion and the way it circulates between women. Spelman makes clear that compassion is often a tool of oppression, for example, when inflicted by white women on enslaved women in the nineteenth century.

[12] Chandra Talpade Mohanty, "Under Western Eyes: Feminist Scholarship and Colonial Discourses," *Feminist Review* 30 (1988): 61–88.

[13] I include Zora Neale Hurston in this list, even though the book *Mules and Men*, on which I focus, does not deploy the witness function in a way parallel to the other works under consideration. But a section of *Mules and Men* focuses on a character called Big Sweet, whose transgender identity, and violent death, are of interest to this study. Zora Neale Hurston, *Mules and Men* (New York: Harper Collins, 2009).

[14] Flannery O'Connor, "A Good Man is Hard to Find," in *Flannery O'Connor: Collected Works* (New York: Library of America, 1988).

[15] Carrie Mae Weems, *From Here I Saw What Happened and I Cried.*

[16] Toni Morrison, *Beloved* (New York: Knopf, 1987).

Bastard Out of Carolina,[17] like the speakers in some of Dickinson's more violent lyrics, share in common the status of being feminine characters represented in the act of watching sadistic violence enacted on the bodies of feminine or feminized others.[18] I include in this consideration the pivotal role of the martyred transgender body, insofar as the transgender body, in the texts of the traditional South, represents a divergence from the socially constructed masculine body.

Not surprisingly, given the role of the American antebellum South as the Gothic space of the American psyche (I echo here the claim made by Gwendolyn DuBois Shaw), Weems, Morrison, Allison, McCullers, O'Connor, and Dickinson can be linked through their works' invocation of and interaction with the residue of the antebellum South. I include in my study a focus on Dickinson's violent poetry because her poetry was written during the Civil War, and importantly, was written by a poet who, despite her New England identity, owes her rise to twentieth-century canonicity to the impetus of the Southern Agrarian critics Allen Tate and John Crowe Ransom. I am not arguing that Dickinson *is* a Southern poet; rather, I suggest that her posthumous status tellingly owes much to Southern critics. I will not be the first to argue that Dickinson's most violent poetry is properly read as Civil War poetry. The reflection on the racism that spurred that war links her work to the later productions of Weems, Morrison, Allison, McCullers, and O'Connor. My approach to Dickinson's work contends with the way that Dickinson's rise to canonical fame occurred through the auspices of the Agrarians, Tate and Ransom. Tate and Ransom are largely responsible for transforming Dickinson, posthumously, from a poet who had been read as a delicate curiosity to a major national figure. Dickinson's links to Southern culture, then, merit probing.

Weems and Morrison, women born and raised outside of the South and therefore not Southerners, unmistakably reference the antebellum South in their respective 1990s and 1980s works, *From Here I Saw What Happened and I Cried* and *Beloved*, by invoking very specific motifs of antebellum racist sadism, and by drawing on the cultural remembrance of slavery.

Both Weems and Morrison invoke the ghosts of the bodily economics of antebellum enslavement. They are included in my study, then, because *From Here I Saw What Happened and I Cried* and *Beloved* conjure the South and the persistence of its racism. Flannery O'Connor, in her brutal short stories "A View of the Woods" and "A Good Man is Hard to Find," unlike Weems, Morrison, Allison, and Dickinson, presents a feminine watcher of sadism who does *not* survive. Still,

---

17 Dorothy Allison, *Bastard Out of Carolina* (New York: Dutton, 1992).

18 The grandmother, in O'Connor's "A Good Man is Hard to Find," in addition to watching her family be slaughtered is also killed herself, but the fact that she is killed last, after watching every one of her children and grandchildren be killed, coupled with the fact that after these murders she turns to the murderer and calls him "one of my own babies" situates the grandmother as the type of ethically ambiguous witness figure in which I am interested. Some of the witness figures studied in this book are more ethically ambiguous than others, but all of these witness figures have struck at least some critics as ethically problematic.

a study of representations of sadism in American women's literary and visual arts referencing the South would be incomplete without a consideration of O'Connor's murdered witnesses. O'Connor's complex legacy as a writer whose letters evince racism but whose short stories deconstruct racism differentiates her from Weems and Morrison, whose lives, like their works, show profound commitment to anti-racist activism. Importantly, however, in the patterns of her representations of violence in the rural South, O'Connor's short stories work against the grain of her racist personal letters, and strip away the illusions of normalcy and propriety that attended racism in the Jim Crow South. Dorothy Allison's autobiographical coming of age novel, *Bastard Out of Carolina*, likewise lays bare the tropes of sadistic misogyny that may ultimately be linked to the culture of racism that flourished in the Jim Crow South, the setting for *Bastard Out of Carolina*.

The ravages of what art historian Andrea Liss, in discussing Weems, aptly refers to as the "patriarchy of slavery" are recorded in the works of Weems, Morrison, O'Connor, McCullers, Allison, and Dickinson recurrently through the striking and disturbing representational trope of a feminine character watching another feminine character be sadistically assaulted. The densely hierarchical system that builds the Gothic basement of the American psyche is the psychic landscape of my study: the artists on whom my study focuses produce their works representing violence through repeated depictions of the fact and the residue of the history of slavery in the American South. The following study, then, uses the South to explore a template for what might be wider-reaching patterns of feminine witnessing, women witnessing the violation and destruction of other women. My intent in focusing the study on the South also reflects my personal background as a Georgia native. It is terrain that I know from the inside, from my own history, and terrain that has import in the broader American imagination.

Picture This

Depictions of the suffering feminine body appear as a recurrent gesture in American women's literature and photography that references Southern slavery. Indeed, the sadistic discourse of enslavement flowed into notions of femininity in the antebellum South. A rallying cry for the Confederacy during the war was to protect and preserve the sanctity of Southern, white womanhood.[19] But the apparent, and heavily inscribed, fault line between the iconography of white femininity and the forced placement of the African American woman as the antithesis to white womanhood—in the sense that the nineteenth-century cult of true womanhood

[19] See W. J. Cash, *The Mind of the South* (New York: A.A. Knopf, 1941), and Janet Coryell, Thomas H. Appleton, Jr., Anastasia Sims, and Sandra Gioia Treadway, *Negotiating Boundaries of Southern Womanhood: Dealing with the Powers that Be* (Columbia: University of Missouri Press, 2000), and, along similar lines, Donald E. Hardy's "Politeness in Flannery O'Connor's Fiction: Social Interaction, Language, and the Body," *Style* 44, no. 4 (2010): 524–48.

emphasized an idea of sexual purity from which it categorically excluded non-Caucasian women—must be kept in mind when theorizing depictions of violence against women of different races.

In the nineteenth-century South, under the laws of slavery, it was considered legally impossible for a white man to rape a black woman: the law argued that an enslaved woman could not be raped because she could not be chaste, categorically, even if she was not yet a woman but only a little girl.[20] Focusing solely on the vicious racism evident in this difference in the history of cultural interpretations of white, African American, and Native American women, however, can leave under-theorized the ways that these cultural inscriptions of womanhood, distinct in concept and in act, could and did merge in violent inscription onto the bodies of feminine subjects of all races. That is, the gendered sadism concocted in the South to forward the goals of racism could also be turned against the bodies of white daughters, as habits are wont to repeat themselves in the acts of oppressors. The fictional, poetic, and photographic works addressed in this study record and reflect this reality of sadism as a tool coined in racism but at times expressed unilaterally against women *tout court*. This project tracks the way that some women writers and photographers of the nineteenth and twentieth centuries stage the performative act of watching sadism, when the witness and the victim are both figured as culturally alike.

The depiction of white women's violence against African American women does not surface in the specific texts that I am studying, even though historically this form of violence frequently occurred. But my interest in a gendered reading of violence does not stem from a lack of concern for the ways that women violate each other. On the contrary, I seek to more fully consider the dynamics of how women watch other women's violation by focusing on texts in which both violated and watcher are of the same race and class. By controlling for the variables of race and class, I allow my study to emphasize the function of gender in violence, rather than the particular kind of racist othering that generates Mohanty's exemplary and important work.

For example, Toni Morrison's novel *Beloved* stages key scenes in which the figure of a feminine watcher who is African American views, or hears about, the sadistic treatment of another African American character. Here, the difference is between being the watcher and being the watched; it is not a difference between races and not a difference between social classes. We cannot entirely use Mohanty's theory of racist pleasure in the suffering other when we read *Beloved*, insofar as most scenes in the novel depict African American characters witnessing the suffering of African American characters. To fully read *Beloved*, we need to theorize the difficult borderlands in which the watcher in the novel, Sethe, as *martyros*, bears suffering in the sense of representing suffering's inscription onto her body and mind. This emphasis on complex form holds true in general in my

---

20 See Jennifer Wriggins, "Rape, Racism, and the Law," *Harvard Women's Law Journal* 6 (1983): 103–41.

study. In tracking the imaginative landscapes of violence and witnessing, I am also tracking the effects and codes of representation.

Of course, representation is itself a kind of witnessing. An extreme example of the risk of the watcher surfaces in *Beloved* when Sethe kills her daughter, destroying the girl she calls her "best thing."[21] Through her role as watcher of sadism, Sethe also wounds herself—and the novel makes clear that Sethe's role is scopic, wounding, and salvific. In this regard, it is worth keeping in mind that if we, the audience, are not denoted watchers of these scenes of violence, we are connoted watchers: we inhabit the ethical prism of the text. As Kali Tal argues in her introduction to *Worlds of Hurt*, readers may themselves be re-inscribed when they read texts depicting trauma.[22] In the verbal and visual texts under consideration in this book, there are at least two audiences: an audience written or imaged in the text, and an audience perceiving the text after the fact, from the outside that yet is never entirely outside, looped into the performative act of a literary or photographic text. When Sethe, the enslaved mother, kills her daughter, the mother's act of violence is a performative gesture intended to visually ward off the sadistic slave master who has arrived to claim his quarry. The audience-function is represented in Morrison's novel as neither innocent nor safe.

The complex evocation of audience in the works under consideration in my study mirrors the complicated ontology of the victims in these works. Playfully condensing victim and author into one nodus, Flannery O'Connor's "A View of the Woods" assigns to the murdered and erotically beaten little girl the name Mary, O'Connor's own first name.[23] O'Connor's short story offers to its audience (as evinced in O'Connor's letters, the author's understanding of culture suggests that she almost certainly wrote with a white audience in mind) a spectacle of eroticized sadism in which the victim is white. Indeed, the cultural similarities between the reading audience invited to have a view of the woods and the little girl whose beatings and murder take place on the stage of these same Georgia pinewoods suggests that O'Connor deploys the moment of witnessing sadism in a rhetorical strategy that conflates rather than separates audience and victim. In "A View of the Woods," the victim's gaze is explicitly dramatized and contested—the victim claims a view of the woods in which she ultimately is murdered—while the gaze of the witness, the grandfather, ultimately generates murderous action. In both Morrison's *Beloved* and O'Connor's "A View of the Woods," a violent slippage between the role of witness to sadistic violence and victim or performer of violence is critical to the dramatic development of the story.

---

21 Morrison, *Beloved*, 306.

22 Tal, *Worlds of Hurt*, 16.

23 Here, the author is dead in a way rather different from Barthes's influential thesis, but congruent with Barthes's theory of the relationship between text and audience. See, Flannery O'Connor, "A View of the Woods," in *Flannery O'Connor: Collected Works* (New York: Library of America, 1988); Roland Barthes, "The Death of the Author" (1968), in *Image, Music, Text*, ed. and trans. Stephen Heath (London: Fontana, 1977).

In these texts, the act of watching is dramatized and set parallel to the act of representing: audience and author are implicated in the violent pleasures of the text. Here, I think it is important to note that Carrie Mae Weems—the only photographer I am considering in this study—re-photographed the images that make up her controversial installation piece *From Here I Saw What Happened and I Cried*. In this series, Weems's re-imagings and inscribed text retell the story of the enslaved people whose images she recasts in a superlative reclaiming of the African American voice inscribed by nineteenth-century white, male photographers.

In other words, the shift from the role of one who silently watches violence to the role of the one who describes, depicts, *or*, in some cases, enacts, violence, is the transformation charted in the texts considered in this study, although each text I consider depicts a different transformation. My attempt, in this study, is not to construct a universal theory of the feminine witness but to adumbrate differences and similarities within and between textual instances, to suggest points of common resonance; I am tracing templates for understanding the feminine act of watching another woman being violated, analyzing text, photographic and written, for the places text illuminates the social field.

On Sadism and Cruelty

I am studying texts that depict sadistic violence in this book, but my definition of sadism is slightly different from received notions of the sadistic. To give fair warning, this book is not about sadomasochistic play but instead about violence that destroys the victim. Theories of sadistic violence have tended to create a gender divide: the feminine falls into the place of the violated and masculinity into that of the violator.[24] One of the motivations of this study is to complicate that gender designation and look beyond traditionally defined roles of masculine sadism/feminine masochism. I want to interrogate the very complicated ethical position of women who watch the violated body or bodies of other women by considering examples in which a feminine character regards another, violated, feminine character. The watcher may or may not attempt to help that violated woman; in this study the definitive mark is the representation of the feminine watcher of violence, but the meaning of this representational mark varies.

My usage of the term *sadism* also diverges from Freudian notions of sexual pleasure through sadomasochism. I do not invoke erotic play when I use the term *sadism*. Rather, I refer to the spectative, visual aspect of acts of cruelty that

[24] I do recognize that there is a rich and varied history of commentary and debate on masochism. And yet as Michelle Massé long ago made clear in *In the Name of Love: Women, Masochism and the Gothic* (Ithaca: Cornell University Press, 1992) our culture tends to consider masochism a feminine trait, even as Freud theorized masochism as a male disorder. See also, E. Jones, L. Trilling, and S. Marcus, *The Life and Works of Sigmund Freud* (New York: Basic Books, 1961).

are inflicted on the helpless body of a non-agreeing other. The word sadism in this study is defined as *violence inflicted onto the body of a person who cannot meaningfully defend herself or refuse the act of violence enacted against her*—violence that is a vehicle of visuality, performed for the pleasure of the sadist's eye. Moreover, my attention is on the representation of the act of witnessing sadism. I am emphasizing the spectative force of sadism as such, bearing down on the question of how sadism connects to the witnessing and/or spectatorship of violence. Ultimately I argue that the distance between witnessing, watching, and enjoying violence is a fine line indeed and one that ought not be obscured by the ideological supposition that women do not enjoy watching other women be violated. In some of the examples I study, I find feminine watchers of violence who are created as figures that work against the replication of violence, who witness with pain, to bend Blanchot's notion of thinking with pain. And in some cases I argue that the feminine witness figure acts as an audience for violence: a watcher who takes pleasure in seeing another woman's violation. In this sense, my study has to be read chapter by chapter because I do not make one argument that each chapter supports. Rather, I focus my study on one line of inquiry—that of the relationship between representations of sadism, gender, and watching—that each chapter engages, and each with different results.

I have chosen to focus the study on literature and photography insofar as the works I am studying lay claim to modes of witnessing, lay claim to the cultural place of the gaze, even as they draw on different disciplinary traditions and different notions of the work's connection to history. For example, Morrison initiates her novel *Beloved* with an inscription dedicated to the "sixty million and more" victimized in the era of American slavery.[25] It is a novel positioned by the act of witnessing: written to witness and to be witnessed, a gesture not without controversy. Carrie Mae Weems's series *From Here I Saw What Happened and I Cried* was created in response to Weston Naef's invitation that Weems participate in the Getty exhibition *Hidden Witness*, an exhibition Naef conceived of to explore African American history through photographic traces, an exhibition that makes explicit the representation of the witness function as well as implying that representation is a form of witnessing.[26] Also claiming an explicit agenda, Flannery O'Connor made clear, in interviews and essays, that her goal in writing fiction was to bear witness to Christianity: to force her audience to see the violent necessity of repentance, and the violence often necessary for repentance. Emily Dickinson's

---

25 Naomi Mandel, "'I Made the Ink': Identity, Complicity, 60 Million and More," *Modern Fiction Studies* 48, no. 3 (Fall 2002): 581–613. Mandel's essay veers from my interpretation in that I would think that Morrison writes *Beloved* not only to say that no act of commemoration or mourning will suffice but also to say that before *Beloved* there were no real efforts to publicly mourn and commemorate those victimized by American enslavement.

26 Weston Naef, *Hidden Witness: African American Images from the Dawn of Photography to the Civil War* (Los Angeles, The J. Paul Getty Museum, 1995).

poetry frequently invokes the stance of witness (not to mention martyr), with the poems' speakers repeatedly claiming the role of the one who sees that from which others turn away.[27] Dorothy Allison's *Bastard Out of Carolina* invokes as its central motif the desire of the abused child to have an audience watch her abuse, while Allison has personally addressed issues of child abuse and gender-based violence.[28] *In Bastard Out of Carolina*, the abused child's fantasy in desperation becomes not the fantasy of rescue from the abuse but rather a longing that the beatings and molestations be witnessed by others who suffer in watching the horrors visited on the child's body. The photographs, poems, novels, and stories under consideration in this study, then, are texts that dramatize, privilege, analyze, and question the representation of the role of the female witness.[29]

The witness to sadistic violence is a central figure for Morrison, Weems, O'Connor, McCullers, Allison, and Dickinson, and one that arguably these authors, and certainly Weems the photographer, use for activist purposes. To theorize this figure that performs the witnessing of suffering, I will draw on the work of Slavoj Žižek,[30] who usefully frames Jacques Lacan's "Kant Avec Sade."[31] In conjunction with an extended reading of Kant, I return to Elaine Scarry's seminal theorization of the fissure between suffering and symbolic discourse.[32] I will as well bring to bear Arthur C. Danto's theorizations of ethics in representing violence, drawing on Danto's theorization of photography at the edge.[33] Unlike earlier feminist theorists of sadism, such as Deborah Horvitz, I will trouble and complicate the gendering of sadism, arguing that only in conceptualizing the fraught ethical space of feminine witnessing can we begin to unpack the claims that feminism must make towards moral justice. Maurice Blanchot's *The Writing of Disaster* is an important reference point for my study insofar as Blanchot, here, begins to unpack

[27] Developing from Faith Barrett and Cristanne Miller's *"Words for the Hour": A New Anthology of American Civil War Poetry* (Amherst: University of Massachusetts Press, 2005), I will show that the poems Emily Dickinson wrote during the Civil War dramatize topoi of racism and its inherently sadistic bent, presenting Dickinson as a witness to her era, despite her lived habit of reclusivity.

[28] *Dorothy Allison's Life Informs her Art*, Dorothy Allison interviewed by Alison St. John, prod. Pat Finn, KPBS, April 27, 2011.

[29] My inquiry into the substance and form of witnessing is structurally like Dominick La Capra's investigation of the possibility of a "middle voice" regarding historical representations of trauma, but with the crucial difference that I am concerned specifically with the gendered aspects of witnessing. See *Writing History, Writing Trauma* (Berkeley: Parallax, 2001), 27, 36.

[30] Slavoj Žižek, *The Sublime Object of Ideology* (New York: Verso, 1989).

[31] See Jacques Lacan, "Kant with Sade," in *Écrits: The First Complete Edition in English*, trans. Bruce Fink (New York: W. W. Norton & Company, 2007).

[32] Elaine Scarry, *The Body in Pain: The Making and Un-making of World* (Oxford: Oxford University Press, 1987).

[33] Arthur Coleman Danto, *Playing with the Edge: The Photographic Achievement of Robert Mapplethorpe* (Berkeley: University of California Press, 1996).

the extraordinary ontological instability of the category of trauma.[34] *The Writing of Disaster* argues for the recognition of the impossibility of complete recovery from violence. While his focus has been subsumed under trauma studies, I will take Blanchot's lead and extend the theorization of violence in the direction of theorizing the limits of atonement by witnessing.

It is my hope that my book will not only be read as trauma theory but also as a book about violence and the limits of representation. I choose to focus on sadistic violence, as opposed to simply violence, because I want to emphasize the structure of power and the importance of watching that circulate in the acts of violence the representations of which I am studying.[35] This book, then, explores the master-slave dialectic as a social event rather than interpreting Hegel's master-slave dialectic in psychoanalytic terms. If Judith Butler influentially defines the master-slave dialectic as an interior psychic drama,[36] I suggest that it reflects social structure first. This is not to say that the relationships between master and slave in the American South, the history that haunts the images on which I focus, did not produce psychic lives brutally imbricated by power. Rather, I wish to draw attention to the blunt corporeal reality of the physical manifestations of power, and point to the way that power firstly manifests, in instances of violence, not as interior mark but as exterior force. In that sense, my work in this book is also activist in that I hope to point out, through careful readings of textual instances of witnessing violence, the way that violence must be read *before trauma*. I object to the way that trauma studies often presume a privileged untouchability for the space of violence, allowing violence an ontological privilege and coding trauma as ancillary. My turn away from interpreting the psychopathology of the victim, then, is in the interest of keeping focus on the evitable nature of cultural sadism. In particular, my interest in this book is to look at how manifestations of power gather physical momentum around the transfer point of gender: the dialectic in which this study suspends itself is reading gender and race as power relations.

My argument turns on the fulcrum of the representation of witnessing violence enacted by the actor in the cultural position of "master" against the body of another actor who is rendered largely or completely powerless by placement in the cultural position of "slave" (or, as I will suggest, "daughter"), when that witness is in some sense allied with the victim by dint of gender. A simpler way to put this claim would be that I am writing a study of representations of masculine violence against feminine bodies *as seen by* other feminine watchers. The definition of sadism that this study uses stipulates that the victim is one whose victimization functionally

---

34 Maurice Blanchot, *The Writing of the Disaster*, trans. Ann Smock (Lincoln: University of Nebraska Press, 1986).

35 Michel Foucault's notion of the panoptic structure of power, the function of the gaze in punishment, in modernity has some relevance to this work. See, Michel Foucault, *Discipline and Punish: the Birth of the Prison* (New York: Random House, 1977).

36 Judith Butler, *The Psychic Life of Power: Theories in Subjection* (Palo Alto: Stanford University Press, 1997).

deprives her of voice: the witness embodied in displaced textual matter—visual or verbal moments of communication—may express what the victim might have wanted to express. Or, she may not. The witnessing function, then, is fragmented by definition.

The witness function, in representation, lays bare the way that relational power aggregates desire around the perpetrator of violence: the perpetrator's desire is expressed, not the victim's desire, for it is the victim's desire that is suppressed or destroyed by violence. It is precisely the witness function deployed in literary and photographic texts under consideration in this study that gives the lie to theorizations of feminine masochism.[37]

The troubled boundary between the realm of the representational and that of "true" history surfaces paradigmatically in Carrie Mae Weems's photographic series *From Here I Saw What Happened and I Cried.*[38] The series is built in part of re-photographs of images that were originally daguerreotypes of enslaved African Americans. In re-photographing, inscribing, and installing these images, Weems establishes an uncanny confluence of fiction and reality in the realm of the witness, whose act of bearing witness resembles what, in *Beloved*, is called "rememory."[39] The images that constitute *From Here I Saw What Happened and I Cried* were originally intended to document and exploit, but Weems's handling of them pushes them into the arena of the visual art installation that rebukes the original intent of the nineteenth-century anthropologist who produced the daguerreotypes.

Standing before the series *From Here I Saw What Happened and I Cried* in an art gallery, the witness enters the uncanny, liminal space between genres, a liminal space also reflected in Toni Morrison's dedication for *Beloved*—for Morrison references real, historical, kidnapped Africans and enslaved African Americans, in sharp juxtaposition to a novel that is a magical re-working of historical material,[40]

---

[37] Helene Deutsch, "The Significance of Masochism in the Mental Life of Women." *International Journal of Psychoanalysis* 11 (1930): 48-60.

[38] Indeed, one might well connect Weems's practice of "re-photographing" enslaved people in the series *From Here I Saw What Happened and I Cried* with *Beloved*'s neologism of "rememory," a force of memory so powerful it alters the physical landscape in which the event took place. The land itself bears "rememory" not just people, implies *Beloved.* In addition, in Weems's *Sea Island Series*, the beautiful and sad witnesses to the violent ravages are feminine objects, the round, deflated airy ball, the spring with its measured holes you can see through, the tipped crosses (martyrs to martyring, a re-telling of real history through a lens), the lovely mailbox open with the bicycle tire leaning its head beside, the open door, the closed praise-house, and circles and wheels everywhere. Or are these in fact symbols of the violated? Their status as represented objects places them as photographic signifiers one step removed from suffering.

[39] Morrison, *Beloved*, 41.

[40] The case of the enslaved "Medea" made headlines in mid-nineteenth-century Ohio, when a young enslaved fugitive woman named Margaret Garner murdered her own child to prevent the daughter from growing up in slavery. Morrison rewrites the story of Margaret Garner in *Beloved.*

a mode of both magical realism and historical fiction. If the echoing position of the author or artist behind the work cannot be entirely elided in readings of the reception of the work, in reading the literary and photographic work of African American and white writers and artists side by side, my interest remains in the works' representations of witnesses and victims. However, I am alert to some uncanny conjunctions between variant modes of witnessing. As Dominick La Capra eloquently states: "Trauma brings about a dissociation of affect and representation: one disorientingly feels what one cannot represent; one numbingly represents what one cannot feel."[41] One could re-write his sentence by replacing the word *trauma* with the word *violence*. In other words, violence disturbs the representational axes that are part of witnessing and can themselves be witnessed.

Expiation and the Iron Eye

Judith Butler, in the *Psychic Life of Power*, treats Nietzsche's concept of bad conscience, noting how the violent suppression of desire becomes itself desire, inasmuch as the punitive quality of the law covers the function of the desirous urges of the punisher, the judge, and enforcer.[42] But Butler interprets Nietzsche along distinctly late twentieth-century lines as a theorist of psychic interiority. Indeed, against the grain of earlier feminist studies, it is my argument that we may make a wrong turn to theorize as primarily internalized and psychic the social problem of powerlessness.[43] Instead, my study places focus on the pleasure the victimizer takes in violating the other and the pleasure the victimizer takes in silencing or suppressing the victim's testimony of her violation. The pleasure of suppression is laid bare, exposed in the writing of Allison, Dickinson, O'Connor, Morrison, McCullers, and in the photography of Weems. In the representations

---

[41] La Capra, *Writing History, Writing Trauma*, 42.

[42] Judith Butler, "Hegel's Unhappy Consciousness," In *The Psychic Life of Power* (Palo Alto: Stanford University Press, 2007).

[43] Late twentieth-century and early twenty-first-century texts theorizing sadism include Deborah Horvitz, *Literary Trauma: Sadism, Memory, and Sexual Violence in American Women's Fiction* (Albany: State University of New York Press, 2000); Ann Jones, *Problem Novels: Victorian Fiction Theorizes the Sensation Self* (Columbus: Ohio State University Press, 2007); Michelle Massé, *In the Name of Love*; Marianne Noble, *The Revenge of Cato's Daughter: Dickinson's Masochism* (Baltimore: Johns Hopkins Press, 1998); Gail Mason, *The Spectacle of Violence: Homophobia, Gender, and Knowledge* (London: Routledge, 2002); Richard J. McNally, "What is Psychological Trauma?" in *Remembering Trauma* (Cambridge, MA: Belknap Press of Harvard University Press, 2005): 78–104; Dori Laub, "Truth and Testimony: The Progress and the Struggle," in *Trauma: Explorations in Memory*, ed. Cathy Caruth (Baltimore: Johns Hopkins University Press, 1995): 151–8; Cathy Caruth, *Unclaimed Experience: Trauma, Narrative, and History* (Baltimore: Johns Hopkins University Press, 1996); and Patricia Yaeger, "Consuming Trauma; or, the Pleasures of Merely Circulating," in *Extremities: Trauma, Testimony, and Community* (Urbana: University of Illinois Press, 2002).

under consideration for this study, the witness figure reflects the pleasure of the victimizer in chilling stillness in recognition of the risk that the witness, in her relative powerlessness, will not be able to alter the conditions of violence. As Anne Coughlin notes in "Representing the Forbidden," the very act of depicting sadism draws the writer into the space of taboo, where she herself occupies the liminal domain of witness, marred or damaged by what she witnesses. The authors and photographer whose work is the focus of my study mine a risky terrain, showing what sadism looks like and what it does to the victim and the victimizer.

Expiating violence by reproducing images of violence—in photography, fiction, poetry—has been queried by theorists of violence and trauma. *Beautiful Suffering*, for example, suggests that only in accepting the possible beauty of images of violence can we ethically pay respect to the sacrifice of the victim depicted. Survivor testimony of violence rarely indicates that victims want to be put on display *by others*, whether in photographs or biographical, literary documentation.[44]

While Melanie Boyd, provocatively, has argued that victims of sexual abuse are more the products of cultural constructs of trauma than subjects who have been traumatized (an argument that rehearses early twentieth-century beliefs that incest was only traumatic if it became exposed publicly), my understanding of the problematic ethics of the representation of sadism would tend to reject the belief that testimony in itself damages more than the event.[45] It strains credulity to think that giving testimony of trauma damages *more* than the original trauma, especially insofar as the logical criterion for the damaging effect of testimony is the power of the original trauma. I am, then, keen to theorize how the tactics of the rhetoric of representing sadism that these authors and photographer deploy are tactics in which the sadism of patriarchy and racism is exposed through a kind of devil's bargain between victim and witness, in which the feminine witness and the feminine victim do not merge but violently aggregate the quality of symbol and speech on the side of the witness. This violence of representation allows the original sadistic act (such as the beating of the granddaughter, Mary Fortune, in "A View of the Woods") to be exposed, yet also silences the possibility of the victim's testimony.[46] In other words, the expiation achieved when a feminine character witnesses another woman's violation occurs through the two feminine characters' or figures' coalescence into rhetoric: one speaks while the other is proleptically

---

44 The politics of confession, of "breaking the silence," while themselves fraught and contradictory even so recognize the importance of the victim making a decision regarding revelations. See, Jane E. Brody, "Supportive Steps After a Sexual Assault," *The New York Times*, December 20, 2011.

45 Please see Renee Heberle and Victoria Grace, *Theorizing Sexual Violence* (London: Routledge, 2009).

46 Teresa de Lauretis, "The Violence of Rhetoric: On Representation and Gender," in *Gender/Sexuality Reader: Culture, History, Political Economy*, ed. Roger N. Lancaste and Micaela Di Leonardo (New York: Routledge, 1997).

removed from the field of speech. A prime example of this rhetorical tactic would be the close of Morrison's *Beloved* in which the very footprints of the victim are elegized in their disappearance, by the invocation of the refrain "This is not a story to pass on."[47]

In this study, I am looking for the story of American sadism and the traces it leaves interpreted in photographic and literary texts. Even as the history of slavery functions as a memory site for the American psyche, it also performs, in the texts I consider, as the formal template for sadism. That is, slavery functions as a social metaphor, or collective representation, of powerlessness in the American psyche, which is of course not to suggest that the practice of enslavement was not also a practice of corporeal sadism. Here, I want to clarify further why I am diverging somewhat from Freud's definition of sadism.[48] My intervention into women's representations of physical and psychological violence (enacted by a masculine privileged figure onto the body or mind of a victim who categorically is represented as feminine) aims to expose the absolute inequity of power inherent in sadism, violence in which the victim cannot fight back. Silencing the victim, the violence is depicted as occurring solely for the pleasure of the violator, for whom, as O'Connor's character Misfit puts it, "ain't no pleasure but in meanness."[49] And the witness, the feminine watcher of violence, is ambiguous ethically: in some instances this feminine character seems to take pleasure in watching another woman be violated, in some instances she watches in numb, horrified powerlessness but later gains the power to speak on behalf of the sacrificed other.

This problematic of pleasure, pleasure that Michel Foucault in *The History of Sexuality* identified as the bastard child of philosophy, haunts the texts depicting sadism that I am explicating.[50] Foucault points out that in philosophical discourse we theorize desire but rarely pleasure. And yet the problem of sadism is linked to pleasure in that very often the only explanation possible for the violence is the pleasure experienced by the violator. Sadism is never enacted in self-defense.

Unlike sentimental art that simplifies violence, the witnessing femininity in the texts of this study indicates that the sadistic coil of racism and misogyny in the antebellum South, its residue, is so persistent because of the sadist's drive for pleasure. By contrast, the pleasure of representing violence in the literature and photography that I am considering in this study would seem to be the pleasure of expiating violence; and yet can the two kinds of pleasure be so easily dissociated? The authors and photographer in this study lay bare violence that not only harms

---

[47] Morrison, *Beloved*, 321, 322.

[48] See Sigmund Freud, *Three Essays on the Theory of Sexuality*, trans. James Strachey (1966; rev. ed., New York: Basic Books, 2000).

[49] O'Connor, "A Good Man Is Hard to Find," 152.

[50] Michel Foucault, *The History of Sexuality, Volume I: An Introduction*, trans. Robert Hurley (New York: Vintage-Random House, 1979). See also, Suzanne Gearhart, "The Taming of Michel Foucault: New Historicism, Psychoanalysis, and the Subversion of Power," *New Literary History* 28, no. 3 (1997): 457–80.

psychologically but also erases social identity, an ending of all possibility of pleasure for the victim. But what about the possibility of the witness's pleasure in watching victimization? And should we interpret the act of representation as always signified by and signifying of the act of witnessing? That is the razor's edge on which the ethics of witnessing balance.

The question of how pleasure might attend texts that purport to critique violence is a complex knot to tease out. In readings of Dickinson, Morrison, McCullers, O'Connor, Allison, and Weems, I trace differential responses to witnessing violence. I emphasize again that I do not offer one monolithic interpretation of the feminine witness figure; instead, I look individually at each different representation. The question of how they facilitate aesthetic pleasure—the pleasure of the audience in response to words or image—while condemning the violence represented in their visual or verbal text, indicates a fine line between pleasure in establishing oneself as witness of the suffering other and a kind of self-sacrificial grief in absorbing the other's suffering into one's words or photographs. In my readings of these texts, in the chapters that make up this study, I argue variously that some texts perform activist work while others problematically leave unresolved the question of the pleasure of witnessing. I do not shoehorn the authors and photographer under consideration into one monolithic theory of feminine witnessing. Instead, I note the importance of this figure of the feminine witness in all the works of this study.

I will diverge, then, from Marianne Noble, Jessica Benjamin, and Michelle Massé, all of whom theorize masochism, in that I am *not* reading for representations of masochism.[51] While these feminist critics offer exemplary studies of the connections between gender and perceptions of masochism, my study of sadism draws from Rhonda Hammer's work on what she calls "family terrorism," in that I interpret sadistic violence as its own phenomenon, not answered by a willing masochist. Indeed, my definition of sadism is violence that is met by the desire to resist, the desire to refuse to be made a victim. For example, when Morrison describes Sethe's humiliation on learning that schoolteacher is studying Sethe's "animal characteristics," Morrison does not suggest that Sethe enjoys this humiliation.[52] Instead, Morrison depicts Sethe's extraordinary will to resist victim status. Brilliantly, hauntingly, Morrison's *Beloved* shows that even as Sethe fights to resist victimization for herself, the key to that resistance is the sacrificial murder of her daughter.

Morrison's late twentieth-century novel is representative of a kind of canonical femininity that creates itself as feminine by representing watching violence without flinching. A story of feminine witnessing watches sadism in the performative sense but it does not posit a female actor of sadistic violence. As Deborah Horvitz

---

[51] See Marianne Noble, *The Masochistic Pleasures of Sentimental Literature* (Princeton: Princeton University Press, 2000) and Jessica Benjamin, *The Bonds of Love: Psychoanalysis, Feminism, and the Problem of Domination* (New York: Pantheon Books, 1988).

[52] Morrison, *Beloved*, 226, 294.

argues, in avowedly essentializing terms, "women feel and express rage ... and the difference lies in the link, for the men, between inflicting pain and [gaining pleasure]."[53] But this idea that masculinity is contiguous with sadistic pleasure is problematic precisely because it erroneously frames femininity as victimization. Even if the victims in this study of the representation of violence are feminine, it is not my conclusion that the essence of femininity is to be victimized. Instead, my intervention will be to trace ways that Morrison, Weems, Allison, O'Connor, McCullers, and Dickinson represent violence as a gender-effect that is imbricated and created by a culture that interweaves misogyny and racism, paradigmatically.

If feminine characters and figures in these works are *not* posed as sadistic actors, the works do operate through a kind of metaphysics of gender in which pleasure is never accorded to the victim. This metaphysics entails the representation of the disturbing aesthetic moment of a feminine character, or figure, watching sadism, for the feminine watcher of sadism both is part of representation and also observes representation. She functions as a disturbing textual moment of regress, a *mis en abyme* structure expressive of anxiety, and also possibly subversion.

For example, Morrison's *Beloved*, while largely critically well received and foundational to Morrison's canonical placement in literary studies, was also critiqued on the grounds of presenting scenes of excessive suffering.[54] What's interesting about this critique is that, in *Beloved*, violence is embedded in the gaze of steely-eyed Sethe. Sethe reports, hears, and audits not only her own suffering—enslavement, rape, and beating—but also that of Paul D., and that of her daughter, the un-named Beloved. "'Red...me and Beloved outdid ourselves with it,'" says Sethe, indicating elliptically that she saw her infant daughter bleed to death, and indeed caused this death for what becomes clear were scopic motives—so that the sadist schoolteacher might be frightened enough of what he has seen to back away.[55] If she is heroic, Sethe is heroic by dint of her ability to see sadistic violence and not collapse in response to what she sees, a dubious gift.

This very divergence from sentimentality is marked by Morrison's steely formal control, which can be interpreted as a type of narrative distancing.[56] Distancing, or even dissociation, typifies the feminine witness function that my study traces.[57] Weems, for example, deploys pastiche, visually repeating, in a kind

---

53 Deborah Horvitz, *Literary Trauma*, 132.

54 Stanley Crouch, in "Literary Conjure Woman," *The New Republic* 194 (1987): 43, complains that *Beloved* "reads largely like a melodrama lashed to the structural conceits of the miniseries."

55 Morrison, *Beloved*, 232.

56 M. A. Travis, "Beyond Empathy: Narrative Distancing and Ethics in Toni Morrison's *Beloved* and J. M. Coetzee's *Disgrace*," *Journal of Narrative Theory* 40, no. 2 (2010): 231–50. Travis makes just this argument about narrative distancing in *Beloved* in "Beyond Empathy." Formal complexity includes but also goes beyond the trope of narrative distancing.

57 La Capra appears to argue that all representation of trauma involves dissociation (*Writing History, Writing Trauma*, 40).

of stutterance, earlier photographers' work as a mode of critiquing the ideology embodied in that work. Morrison's use of magical realism, along with narrative evocations of psychic distance or dissociation in *Beloved*, makes impossible a sentimental response to the novel's possibly melodramatic diegesis. We cannot wish, in proper sentimental fashion, to save the life of the baby ghost who haunts the novel because Morrison never makes clear whether this ghost-function really is a ghost or rather a mother's intense grief manifesting as psychosis. The harsh prism of Morrison's novel is faceted to show that we cannot, no matter how much we grieve, repair the damages of the sadistic system of patriarchal slavery.

In the works of Weems, O'Connor, Morrison, McCullers, Allison, and Dickinson, complex and shifting codes of disrepair make the conceit of sentimental resolution impossible. My study aims to query through these signal texts how the feminine figure watching sadism marks a blind spot of feminism, the uncomfortable terrain in which women watch frozen as other women are violated, or, in some cases, *enjoy* watching other women be violated. Horvitz raises the question, in *Literary Trauma*, of why in her survey of literary representations of trauma she does not uncover a feminine character that performs sadism. Indeed, Horvitz shapes her study by asking why we have no female character that correlates with male protagonists' commission of sadistic acts. Horvitz places emphasis on the active manifestation of sadism, and persuasively tracks a gender differential. But her emphasis on trauma—the impact of sadism on the victimized—rather than a direct emphasis on the articulation of strategies representing sadism is just the focus I want to shift or overturn. By placing emphasis not on trauma but on witnessing, I also reveal, in some cases and not in others, a type of feminine pleasure in watching the suffering feminine other.

Reaching back to invoke Elaine Scarry's magisterial work *The Body in Pain*, I want to shift the ground from Horvitz's and Griffith's focus on the victim to an engagement with the act of representing the witness to the perpetrator of sadistic violence.[58] In the perpetrator is the poison of the anti-ethical, the act that seeks to annihilate the other. As Scarry makes clear, violence silences the one violated. But, interestingly, the watcher of suffering seems to have her tongue loosened by this position of bearing witness, and her ethical position is often ambiguous and always challenging.

---

58 Jennifer Griffiths, "Uncanny Spaces: Trauma, Cultural Memory, and the Female Body in Gayl Jones's 'Corregidora' and Maxine Hong Kingston's the 'Woman Warrior.'" *Studies in the Novel* 38, no. 3 (2006): 353. This shift of paradigm is important in ethical terms because in literary and photographic representations of violence we are sometimes permitted to see the structure of sadism. By retaining focus on the violent actor, a focus manifested through the character of the witness, sadistic structures can be laid bare. This exposure of the sadistic structure specifically—of the patriarchy of racism—requires a focus *not* on the victim but on the perpetrator. In the works that I consider in this study, just such an emphasis on representing the act of seeing the sadist is articulated.

Chapter 1
Empathy and Risk: Photography, Writing, the Softest Voice

There is a risk in the tactic of revealing the sadistic substructure of patriarchal racism. At risk, in this venture, is the very articulation of the figure witnessing the victimization of the other: indeed, she seems to be given the story to tell, or image to show, in exchange for entering a fragmentary moral badlands. In representing the witness watching the victim, Weems, Morrison, O'Connor, McCullers, Allison, and Dickinson's works walk a performative tightrope—performing violence for an arguably still patriarchal audience while also critiquing that violence. But it is the power of the critique afforded by representation of violence that interests me most. Morrison's Sethe, in *Beloved*, bemoans her capacity for clear sight—her capacity to see sadism and still not lose her mind. She asks why her mind won't fold into what she imagines would be the comforting nullity of madness.[1] Even Sethe's desperate and apparently mad act of slitting the throat of her baby, Sethe herself understands as a reasonable response to the scopic logic of the sadism of enslavement. It decrees that Sethe can only stop schoolteacher's sadistic program by being more sadistic than he is, out-hurting the hurter. Importantly, this evocative claim (of *out-hurting the hurter*) does not refer to Sethe physically attacking the man who "owns" her, schoolteacher. It refers to her understanding of the power of the visual image, the gruesome tableau of slaughter with which she greets schoolteacher when he arrives to force her back into slavery.

Sethe performs in front of schoolteacher the only act of violence more extreme than his desire: the slaughter, as sacrifice, of an innocent infant. By performing in front of schoolteacher the visual excess of his desire for violent sadistic pleasure, Sethe stops him, briefly but crucially, from performing sadism. Morrison's description of the act of a mother murdering her infant daughter functions as both commentary on and meta-performance of sadism. That is, just as Sethe acts violently to turn back the sadist, so also Morrison performs written descriptions of sadism extreme enough to turn back the residual pressure of racism that persists generations after slavery.

If Morrison makes clear that Sethe does not enjoy her capacity to clearly witness sadism through *rememory*, a process of acute, painful re-articulation of sadism, Horvitz, in *Literary Trauma*, turns to Jessica Benjamin's very problematic belief that "'domination is anchored in the hearts of the dominated,'" reviving

---

1 Morrison, *Beloved*, 81.

Benjamin's argument that domination is a "two way process."[2] Benjamin and Horvitz contend that victims of sadism, although traumatized, also are actively in complicit, tacit agreement with their torturer. But the literary and photographic representations of sadism on which I focus in this study make clear that the victim of trauma is anything *but* willing. Sethe, for example, is depicted as passionately driven to escape this role of victim. Likewise, Dickinson's violent poems depict victims seeking a space—usually posthumous—in which they can at last escape suffering. Dickinson's poems of course do not deal with death in fact but with a *topos* called death in which the speaker gains a private secure place, safe from sadism. In the frame of the texts interpreted in this study, the complicity of the victim hypothesized by Benjamin would seem to be illusory. Indeed, the effort to escape victimization drives the representations considered in my study.

For example, in Dickinson's poem "I never lost as much but twice, / and that was in the sod," the trajectory of the speaker's abjection is intertwined with her objection, her protest.[3] The speaker loses to "God" in the poem, and Dickinson scandalously uses "God" to signify a sadistic and masculine enforcer of death and burial. This transmutation of the accepted, standard-usage meaning of "God" (typically signifying benevolence, absolute goodness and life) is given no explanation in Dickinson's poem. The poem depicts a space in which cruelty and suffering occur *de facto*, unexplained. Suffering in the poem is inflicted on the speaker for the pleasure of the poem's designated locus of power, "God." Dickinson's enraged speaker stands above the grave that represents metonymically her unjust suffering and rages against the systematic domination inflicted on her by "Burglar, Banker, Father." The content of her rage is its context: the unexplained, unjustified fact of the speaker's abject position, her repetitious losses.

Here, Dickinson's "poor" speaker subjects to scathing revelation the unjust terms of her victimization. However, her victimization significantly is not primarily suffering inscribed onto her body but instead suffering inscribed onto the body of *another* that she witnesses. Dickinson's speaker here describes with mathematical precision the equation of her sadistic deprivation. Imposed by a patriarchal force, enacted along the axis of her body's vulnerability, her proximity to the grave, a mechanism of loss drives the poem. Significantly, the speaker in this poem is not the primary victim, in the sense that she is the one who buries others: hers is not the buried body. Rather, the buried other, rendered humiliatingly into "sod," is the representation of embodied victimization in the poem. Here, the thin line between the witness and the victim is very thin indeed, for the speaker in Dickinson's

---

2 Horvitz, *Literary Trauma: Sadism, Memory, and Sexual Violence in American Women's Fiction* (Albany: State University of New York Press, 2000), 133.

3 All references to Dickinson's poetry indicate *The Poems of Emily Dickinson: Reading Edition*, ed. R. W. Franklin (Cambridge: Belknap Press of Harvard University Press, 1998). Following standard practice, I refer to the poems by the numbers Franklin has assigned them. The poem cited is Fr 49.

poem takes no pleasure in the suffering of the other. Her suffering is simply the experience of the other's suffering.

And yet Dickinson's speaker is an implicitly upright figure contrasting with the even more abject embodiment of those dead others she mourns. The speaker is liminal—feminized insofar as she differentiates herself from the overwhelmingly powerful and masculine "Burglar, Banker, Father," and she is also feminized in that socially, in the poem's world, she is powerless and "poor." Here is the representation of a feminine character who is socially abject but is not an abject body—she is not buried and made "sod." The speaker is made to suffer by the masculine force codified as "Burglar, Banker, Father," specifically because she sees the suffering of the other inflicted by this trinity. The speaker is at once impotent and omniscient, capable of reaching the "door of God" but once at that door, able only to beg.

Dickinson creates the speaker by deploying the rhetorical strategy of describing a sadistic father, radical insofar as Dickinson could only expect a male audience (despite female readership) to determine the critical reception of her work; indeed men did determine the critical fate of Dickinson's poetry, as I will explore later in this book. In choosing this extended metaphor of death as sadistic father ("God" as sadistic dealer of death) Dickinson codifies and represents a structure of sadism as a given, unexplained, of the world the speaker inhabits. As Horvitz argues, "when the dominant culture is patriarchal and racist the psychodynamic of sadism is most often enacted with white men in the role of the oppressor with women of color as well as white women in the role of victim."[4] But Dickinson's poem, like Morrison's *Beloved*, O'Connor's "A Good Man is Hard to Find," Weems's *From Here I Saw What Happened and I Cried*, and Allison's *Bastard Out of Carolina*, deploys a third figure, neither white male sadist nor female victim, but feminine witness, a witness that chillingly reports the system in which the vulnerable other is turned into "sod," humiliated or destroyed, by the powerful sadist. The witness reveals the annihilating quality of sadism, but this feminine character also erupts into a place of ambiguous, ethical determination, fissuring the comforting paradigms of sentimentality. She is "poor" and enraged, yes, but the quality of detachment that permeates the poem informs an ethical problematic that the following study seeks less to resolve than to illuminate and elucidate.

Ethics, After Nietzsche

What might be the ethical parameters of such witnessing as these artists deploy, such womanly witnessing of sadism, linked by image and evocation to the antebellum South and its residue? In this study I am less concerned with tracing the history of American slavery and Jim Crow (other works superlatively accomplish that task) than I am with tracking the ethical problematic of the representation of

---

4 Horvitz, *Literary Trauma*, 131.

sadism generated by that system.[5] If the works on which this study will focus have in common references to slavery and the aftermath of slavery in the American South, I want to sound out the echo of that connection by unpacking the formal gesture shared between, for example, Weems and O'Connor, a gesture of shocking the audience with horrifying images, images that the two artists link to the event and the residue of slavery and its sadism in the antebellum South.

Weems, Morrison, O'Connor, Allison, McCullers, and Dickinson invoke by direct and indirect citation the connection between the history of slavery in the American South and the performative act of women watching sadism. But they do not, strictly speaking, unearth new knowledge about slavery. Instead, they deploy the symbolic of slavery as rhetorical code for sadism (which in itself reflects that sadism was historically very frequently the treatment the enslaved received at the hands of the enslavers). O'Connor's "A View of the Woods," for example, culminates in a young girl being brutally beaten to death by her grandfather precisely because he does not see her as racially "pure"; that is, entirely stemming from his bloodline. O'Connor's brutal short story exposes the regress to incest logically promulgated by racist policies against what was, in Jim Crow, called miscegenation.

"A View of the Woods" not only raises questions about the old man's erotic pleasure in beating his granddaughter but also throws into relief a key problematic of watching sadism, that such watching may generate desire to act sadistically: early in the story, before he himself becomes the beater, the effeminized, powerless grandfather helplessly watches his son-in-law beat the granddaughter. Finally, at the story's close, the grandfather steps into the role of the beater. The grandfather is feminized when he watches the little girl being beaten and feels powerless to stop her father from beating her.[6] But when the grandfather becomes the beater, he is drawn by O'Connor as a bull-like figure, a bully, a figure terrifyingly claimed by masculinity.

The Image of Beating the Child

Freud's essay "A Child is Being Beaten" differentiates just such categories: the body of the one who is being beaten, the body of the one who beats, and the gaze

---

[5] Contemporary histories of slavery and Jim Crow are numerous. They notably include Grace Elizabeth Hale, *Making Whiteness: The Culture of Segregation in the South, 1890–1940* (New York: Pantheon Books, 1998); Donna Franklin *Ensuring Inequality: The Structural Transformation of the African-American Family* (New York: Oxford University Press, 1997); and Erskine Clarke *Dwelling Place: A Plantation Epic* (New Haven, CT: Yale University Press, 2005), which was reviewed by Steven Hahn, "Divine Rights," *New Republic* 234, no. 4 (2006): 28–33, as "one of the finest studies of American Slavery ever written."

[6] O'Connor, "A View of the Woods," 531.

of the one who watches the beating.[7] The resolution of the trauma of violence, for Freud, is to release oneself from masochism by refusing to inhabit the subject position of the beaten. But the problem with such a relational solution is that in a system like the patriarchy of slavery it is not always possible—structurally, socially—for the feminized subject *to refuse* to be beaten. Weems, Morrison, Dickinson, McCullers, Allison, and O'Connor reflect this site of the impossibility of refusal in their work by dramatizing and deploying the representation of the act of watching sadism. The solution to the problem of sadistic systems of racism and misogyny would seem to begin by representing the structure of the system, even as exposing this structure to sight as an act of representation carries the risk of replicating the system, repeating sadism as representation, as description, as image.

Consider this question of representation as reiterated through the lens of Lynne Tirrell's analysis of ethics and context in art in her essay "Aesthetic Derogation."[8] Tirrell raises the possibility of the power of "words and images to create or to reinforce a social reality that is morally contested."[9] While I agree with Tirrell that the aesthetic context is a privileged space, it is also important to note that the very ethical ambiguity illuminated in Tirrell's essay attends the work of the artists in this study. Diverging from Tirrell, I do not necessarily treat aesthetic context as an *exception* to ethics. While Catharine MacKinnon has been criticized for what is considered her unsubtle understanding of what representation is, her argument that depicting acts of erotic denigration *could* be ethically problematic cannot be disputed out of hand unless we believe that representation is an act outside the register of ethics, set apart from ethical concerns.[10]

For, clearly, some acts of representation are considered ethical or anti-ethical gestures. For example, consider the depiction of icons in Eastern Orthodox worship as a case in which the very act of creating and viewing the icon is believed by the faithful to be ethically correct, insofar as, for the Orthodox Christian, worship must be enacted through veneration of the icon, which is a sacred representation by virtue of being extant and being seen. Or, on the opposite side, pro-Nazi propaganda was surely a representation that no one now would argue occurred outside the realm of the morally reprehensible. If some representations fall clearly within the domain of ethical arbitration, then one cannot call simplistic Mackinnon's theory that representation can be interpreted as an act to be judged ethically, regardless

---

7 Sigmund Freud, "A Child Is Being Beaten," *The Journal of Nervous and Mental Disease* 56, no. 4 (1922): 405–6.

8 Lynne Tirrell, "Aesthetic Derogation," in *Aesthetics and Ethics: Essays at the Intersection*, ed. Jerrold Levinson (Cambridge: Cambridge University Press, 2001), 284–314.

9 Tirrell, "Aesthetic Derogation," 284–5.

10 For commentary on MacKinnon see, for example, Ann J. Cahill's essay "Sexual Violence and Objectification," in *Overcoming Objectification: A Carnal Ethics* (New York: Routledge, 2011).

of whether one agrees with her choice of which images constitute violent acts in their effect as representation. My approach in this book is to consider the act of representing violence as itself a gesture that falls within the field of ethical concern and debate. It may not fall in a fixed and predictable way; regardless, the act of creating and consuming representation falls within the purview of ethics.

I have chosen to focus this study on work, such as Weems's, that has achieved cultural prestige precisely because mine is a study concerned with ethics. And as Tirrell makes clear, we cannot interpret art as inhabiting ethical space unless we first interpret art as inhabiting a space of cultural power. In this study, then, I choose artists and writers who are arguably, if contentiously, considered central to our culture, at least in their status within their fields. The photographers and writers on whom this study focuses are women who have to varying degrees resisted the marginal status accorded the feminine in our culture (even as their work is not, in the main, interpreted as queer, they queer the traditional sentimental trappings of the feminine). My definition of sadism, as the annihilation of the capacity to speak and be meaningfully heard, makes central the way in which the antebellum South rendered impermissible, inaccessible, impossible the *topos* of agency and voice for the victim feminized by racist violence. In that sense, the capacity to give imagery and voice through representation of witnessing scenes of sadism functions as resistance in the work of the photographer and authors on whom this study focuses.

This evisceration of subjectivity, this eradication of the victim's project of identity, compels the creation of representations of witnesses in the works I discuss. This witness-function sometimes is a character distinct from the victim and sometimes represents a split gaze describing a formerly victimized status. Tirrell's unpacking of the ethics of violent language in literature can help us navigate the way that text and image intertwine in the works investigated in this study. For the repetition of images of sadism is undercut by context—O'Connor's character of the grandmother in "A Good Man is Hard to Find," for example, watches her entire family be slaughtered by the sadistic "Misfit" and drily notes the gendered politesse that surrounds each of their sequent murders as the Misfit separates the men and "ladies," lest they see each other in the untoward physical positions of the disemboweled.[11] But when the grandmother attempts verbally to undo the loss of her progeny by claiming to the man who has murdered them that he is her "own baby," the project of recuperation is either shattered or saved, depending on how one reads O'Connor, in whose work violence can be seen as salvific or proof of human depravity.[12] In "A Good Man is Hard to Find" O'Connor places a frame, or in Tirrell's phrase, "giant quotation marks," around the image of sadistic violence.[13] Such an interweaving of stark evocation and sharp curtailment typifies the texts in this study.

---

11 O'Connor, "A Good Man Is Hard to Find," 148.

12 O'Connor, "A Good Man Is Hard to Find," 152.

13 Tirrell, "Aesthetic Derogation," 306.

The borderland role of the feminine witness complicates the relationship of the viewer and the viewed. Eric Rosenberg, writing on trauma, frames a compelling look at connections between trauma and representation. Drawing from Cathy Caruth's work on trauma, Rosenberg argues that what is traumatic resists, definitively, assimilation into narrative, producing a kind of stutterance or post-traumatic repetition, which Rosenberg qualifies as banal.[14] But Rosenberg's impeccable definition of trauma yields interesting results if we shift perspective to consider it from the ethical prism of the sadistic agent, for with this shift the question emerges of precisely whose narrative cannot assimilate sadism. The most traumatized victim *has no internal narrative*, as Morrison's character Sethe makes clear when she refers to those who have lost their minds due to suffering sadistic abuse. Morrison gives us the ruined character of Beloved to signify that for those most victimized by the patriarchy of slavery there was no possible recuperation of narrative for the victim in her own voice. The figure of Beloved—as ghost, as child possibly raped, as child murdered, a victim par excellence—has become pieces that from her own perspective cannot be reassembled. Sethe, the iron-eyed witness, can assemble narrative; Beloved, the victim, cannot.

But in *Beloved*, what of schoolteacher, the sadist? What is his ability to recuperate narrative from the fracturing force of his violations of Sethe? Here, Rosenberg's concept of assimilation takes on a chilling second meaning because schoolteacher can and does assimilate, codify, write down, *narrativize* the itinerary of his sadism. Indeed, schoolteacher enjoys listing his cruelties. Without question the main task and act of schoolteacher is to narrativize trauma, to write in the book with the ink Sethe makes the story of her destruction. Schoolteacher's book demonstrates Laura Mulvey's claim that "sadism demands a story," insofar as his book elaborately theorizes and preeminently gives narrative force, plot, and rationale for the pleasure he takes in degrading the enslaved.[15] The claim that the resolution of trauma lies in narrative, then, is deeply problematic. It appears instead that sadism is pleasured by narrative—demanding a story.

The victim of violence, unlike the sadist, may not demand a story. Rather, she may demand recognition of the rupturing and nonsensical force of the moment when sadism was inflicted upon her body. The iron-eyed witness, developed as a key character in the works interrogated in this study, oscillates between answering the victim's desire to express the rupture that sadism forms (in psychic life, in bodily harms) and possibly feeding the sadist's pleasure in narrative. Importantly, Morrison uses fractured speech in key stretches of *Beloved* to comment on the falsity of attempting to narrativize trauma from the perspective of the victim, while Weems visually performs stutterance in printing re-photographed photographs.

---

[14] Eric Rosenberg, "Walker Evans's Depression and the Trauma of Photography," in *Trauma and Visuality in Modernity*, ed. Lisa Saltzman and Eric Rosenberg (Hanover, NH: Dartmouth College Press, 2006), 31.

[15] Laura Mulvey, "Visual Pleasure and Narrative Cinema," in *The Sexual Subject: A Screen Reader in Sexuality* (New York and London: Routledge, 1992).

They refuse the sadist's desire for system and story. Weems and Morrison refuse to give the story that sadism demands. Dickinson's enigmatic poems also notoriously refuse coherent narrative, while O'Connor's apocalyptic story lines effectively shatter the form of the short story of which she, ostensibly, was a master. Allison's story maintains a coherent narrative but it explodes a character—Pearl—in its central section, while McCullers closes *The Ballad of the Sad Café* with a forfeit of narrative, in the immolated figure of the defeated trans-gender hero/heroine, Miss Amelia, and more elliptically in the evocation of the song of the chain-gang.[16]

In each text considered in this study, then, narrative resolution is strikingly troubled. The problematic links between sadism and narrative indicate the difficulty of describing such violence. Rosenberg raises the idea that in representations of violence there also inheres a retreat from violence, drawing from Michel Foucault the idea that "language in its being is that softest of voices, that nearly imperceptible retreat."[17] As Rosenberg interprets photography as a kind of language, Weems's photographic series *From Here I Saw What Happened and I Cried* can be read as a sentence. Indeed, Weems implies this reading in the graphic inscription of the series' title across the images beginning and ending the series, inscriptions that read together form a sentence.

Might I, then, interpret the representations of violence considered in the following study as a retreat from violence, a step back from violence, a *topos* of "displacement?"[18] The idea of a nearly imperceptible "retreat" from violence that inheres in the writing about violence is obviously problematic but also profoundly alluring and, for some of the works covered in this study, deeply true. For the careful depiction of the figure of the witness of sadism is correctly limned by Foucault's phrase of a "nearly imperceptible retreat." This gesture of seeing violence through the displacing strategy of double-witnessing (first the witness as character, second the character as representation) takes up and dismantles the sadist's desire for performing as powerful actor; it displaces him. But even in displacing the sadist, simply by giving representation to him, legible narrative modes also preserve him.

The link between the sadist and his victim is strengthened *through* representation. To perform any representation of sadism is to rehearse the sadist's pleasure, and this fact includes picturing or describing the victim's suffering.[19] Argues Rosenberg, "Despite all attempts to blunt trauma by aesthetics or abstraction, these very modes of representation or embodiment, of exposure, only serve to carry and at times betray it."[20] Any replication of sadism, however intended, may risk serving the sadist's pleasure.

---

16 Carson McCullers, *The Ballad of the Sad Café* (New York: Bantam Books, 1951).

17 Rosenberg, "Walker Evans's Depression," 33.

18 Rosenberg, "Walker Evans's Depression," 34.

19 See also, Mark Reinhardt, Holly Edwards, Erina Dugganne, et al., *Beautiful Suffering* (Chicago: University of Chicago Press, 2006).

20 Rosenberg, "Walker Evans's Depression," 40.

Only by turning from narrative, avoiding the sadist's pleasure in the accomplishment of seeing his violence rehearsed, can the victim of sadism properly reveal the harm she has sustained. And notably Weems's *From Here I Saw What Happened and I Cried*, Morrison's *Beloved*, McCullers *Ballad of the Sad Cafe*, O'Connor's "A Good Man is Hard to Find" and "A View of the Woods," Allison's *Bastard Out of Carolina*, and Dickinson's violently cryptic lyrics do fracture narrative, though they do not so utterly explode its demands as to be nonsensical throughout. From this borderland space of creating text, visual or verbal, that remains legible while pressuring legibility to its edge (a risk that rewarded Dickinson with a lifetime of non-recognition) emerge tactics of representing sadism as that which almost fractures the witness through whose figure representation takes shape.

If trauma is formal, as Rosenberg correctly claims, it may be because sadism is formal.[21] Sadism depends on the formal mark of power that annihilates an "other" who cannot resist annihilation, because of the social binds misogyny and racism place on her behavior. The retreat from sadism that the representation of witnessing sadism enacts is one that does not refuse the formality of sadism but may, in some instances, erode its claims by laying bare the structure of injustice that supports the patriarchy of racism. But how can race and gender matter so much to questions of representing violence and spectatorship? Is it impossible not to read in Foucault's description of language as "the softest of voices" a gendered claim?[22] If I close by suggesting that the feminine witnessing typified by the kind of witness of sadism that this study engages is one of the "softest voice[s]," I complicate the gendered implications of that claim. Toni Morrison, Flannery O'Connor, Dorothy Allison, Emily Dickinson, Carson McCullers, and Carrie Mae Weems sound out a retreat from direct representation as a form of resistance to the gendering, or silencing, force of sadism, pressuring the boundaries of culturally legible representation.

The ethical problematic presented by representation of the feminine witness figure is the complex gesture of retreating from (but just how far from?) the subjectivity of the victim.[23] Invoking this chill witness figure, there is an ineluctable movement away from the fracture of violence: the witness describes sadism in a performance for audience. This distancing from the victim also risks a pleasure less than ethical: relief that in the space of text we are not going to encounter or engage the victim's subjectivity, relief that we will not be asked to inhabit the mind of the victim. And there is the risk of sadism's hierarchical economy asserting a disturbing equation by which the description of sadism achieved through the

---

21 Rosenberg, "Walker Evans's Depression," 45.

22 Michel Foucault, "The Thought of the Outside," in *Aesthetics, Method, and Epistemology*, vol. 2 of *Essential Works of Foucault, 1954–1984*, ed. James Faubion, trans. Robert Hurley et al. (New York: The New Press, 1998), 168.

23 Mieke Bal dilates on the problem of being a watcher of others' suffering, finding that any pleasure in the aesthetic force of the scene of violence is suspect. Reinhardt et al., *Beautiful Suffering*.

witness character serves to displace from the feminine witness character the threat of degradation, at the expense of more firmly placing the mark of degradation onto the victim she witnesses.[24]

Here, the victim-function in representation serves to anchor the aesthetic in a disturbing economy: the witness figure owes its performative capacity to the victim's utter loss of voice, her subjectivity's erasure. The vortex of sadism, as I have defined the term, renders the victim incapable of meaningful protest. The witness figure risks making use of the victim figure's abjection: the risk is that the witness gains power in witnessing not by denuding the sadist of power but by making a troubling compact with the victim. The victim figure provides aesthetic momentum that builds a beautiful or honorable space for the witness figure. The ethical no-man's land in which the witness figure is placed ineluctably is part of the problem of facing sadism through the act of representation, insofar as the witness figure gains power by delineating another's absolute loss of power.

That the texts under consideration in this study respond to and shape an American paradigm of sadism is a fact to revisit, a subterranean national aesthetic. The revisiting—to expose and condemn—of the residue of sadism persisting from the patriarchy of slavery is itself a necessity, an ethical imperative. The witness character through which sadism is represented as an event, always scopic, not surprisingly is a gendered figure. And yet interpreting this figure is not best performed through a reading attentive only to gender, but rather through a reading aware of the problematic connection between power and ethics, a reading in which feminine does not necessarily mean female but rather signifies the relational powerlessness of the feminine in the antebellum and Jim Crow South.

The texts on which I focus respond to an imperative of witnessing, in representation, even as the path to such response calls for nearly impossible balancing acts between vision and blindness, speech and refusal to speak, and between knowledge and the refusal to claim what one would prefer not to know. Weems, Morrison, Dickinson, O'Connor, Allison, and McCullers show us what we might rather not see and, in creating works that give pleasure in this painful art, they play at the edge of the aesthetic. Just this gesture of playing with the edge becomes a gesture by which the artist or writer acknowledges her national identity by discursively limning its pain. The question lingers of the pleasure of seeing and reading sadism. I will argue that the representation of feminine characters watching sadism functions variably as unacknowledged capitulation to *and also*, at times, powerful resistance against entrenched cultural structures of sadism.

---

[24] As suggested in Laura E. Tanner, *Intimate Violence: Reading Rape and Torture in Twentieth-Century Fiction* (Bloomington: Indiana University Press, 1994).

Chapter 2
Projects of Identity in Carrie Mae Weems's *From Here I Saw What Happened and I Cried*: The Crucible of Witnessing

American photographer Carrie Mae Weems (born 1953) has built a career on the premise of art as activism. She makes explicit her claim to the role of the artist who addresses and recuperates the wound of racial injustice. Following in the footsteps of great documentary photographer Roy DeCarava, Weems's early series of photographs of her family of origin, *Family Pictures and Stories* (1981–82), is a beautifully wrought series of images exploring her African American family's love for and joy in each other. This early series exemplifies what bell hooks, in "Carrie Mae Weems: Diasporic Landscapes of Longing," has called not a post-colonial but an anti-colonial approach—an approach that centers the gaze on African American subjects not as after-effects of colonization but as human beings valorized and honored: in short, a gesture of anti-racist activism expressed in art.[1] The slightly later series, *Ain't Jokin'* (1987–88), ups the volume on Weems's direct attack on American racism. Critic Abigail Solomon-Godeau interprets Weems's use of the tactics of "taunting" as an act of re-territorialization, interpreting Weems as an artist from a minority or marginal culture by aligning Weems's status with that of Franz Kafka—an artist from a minority culture whose current canonicity, cultural centrality, is now inarguable.[2]

It is from Solomon-Godeau's correct positioning of Weems as a canonical figure—a photographer who has become eminent among American photographers of her generation—that I will approach Weems. Indeed, her status as a canonical photographer, as an artist represented in the permanent collections of museums such as the Museum of Modern Art (MoMA), provides a pivot for my exploration of Weems's representation of sadism in *From Here I Saw What Happened and I*

---

1 bell hooks, "Carrie Mae Weems: Diasporic Landscapes of Longing," in *Inside the Visible: An Elliptical Traverse of 20th-Century Art in, of, and from the Feminine*, ed. Catherine de Zegher (Cambridge: MIT Press, 1996), 173–80.

2 Abigail Solomon-Godeau, "Taunting and Haunting: Critical Tactics in a 'Minor' Mode," in *Women Artists at the Millennium*, ed. Carol Armstrong and Catherine de Zegher (Cambridge: MIT Press, 2006), 371–402.

Cried (1995–96).[3] The artist's cultural position of eminence is important to my reading of this series.

In interpreting Weems's representations of subjects who are shown as visual markers of suffering and in some cases debasement, I depend on a definition of the meaning of the word "sadism" that differs radically from psychoanalytic usage. Whereas, for Freud, sadism is primarily defined as a sexual perversion, as discussed in my introduction, I shift this definition to emphasize a "delight in cruelty," the secondary definition of sadism, with emphasis on a delight in *watching* cruelty. That is, for the purposes of my study, I shift the definition of sadism from its psychoanalytic framework and instead interpret the word in terms of ethics. The definition of sadism with which I will be working, then, is that of pleasure in inflicting, and watching the infliction of, humiliation and/or pain onto a subject who cannot meaningfully defend herself. I never use the term *sadism* to indicate mutually agreed-upon erotic play, but instead invoke the term to describe the edge of an ethical problematic, the position of the actor who inflicts suffering on a victim completely unable, because of social or physical constraints, to meaningfully respond in self-defense. Whether or not there is yet an erotic torque to this relation is not my concern here, insofar as the trajectory of the desire of the sadist is not, in the terms laid bare by Weems's *From Here I Saw What Happened and I Cried*, playful.

In considering the ethics of representing sadism, as I have above defined the term, Weems's spectacular series, *From Here I Saw What Happened and I Cried*, presents several key points of crisis of interpretation, and it is the goal of this chapter to work through the crises presented by Weems's powerful work. Weems's eminence as an American photographer, despite her status as a member of minority culture, is significant because the current culturally privileged position of her work summons us to ask what it is that she offers—in representing the violence and sadism of racism—that happens to find an acceptable fit within dominant trends in art criticism. The biographical fact of Weems's membership in a minority culture, read as an aspect of her artistry that causes Solomon-Godeau to compare Weems to Kafka, is both essential to my reading of Weems and also insufficient: essential insofar as Weems's frequent use of the gesture of installation pieces poses and emphasizes the question of the artist's embodied contact with the work, and insufficient insofar as Weems's ascendance to canonical status asks its

[3] Weems's important retrospective, *Carrie Mae Weems: Three Decades of Photography and Video*, shown February 2nd through May 19th at the Portland Museum of Art, the city of Weems's birth, and traveling in 2014 to the Guggenheim Museum in New York City, cements her reputation. Moreover, as a 2013 MacArthur Fellow, Weems has garnered the well-deserved title of "genius." See, *Carrie Mae Weems: Three Decades of Photography and Video*, edited by Kathryn E. Delmez, with essays by Kathryn E. Delmez, Henry Louis Gates, Jr., Franklin Sirmans, Robert Storr, and Deborah Willis, and published by Yale University Press October 30, 2012.

own questions.[4] My interest is in pursuing the question of how Weems has resisted marginal status.

Of Carrie Mae Weems, Eddie Chambers aptly notes, "Weems has built an enviable reputation as being one of the most interesting contemporary artists whose practice focuses unflinchingly on what we might possibly refer to as racial narratives."[5] Following Chambers, I want to look at Weems's work not to contest the intensity, necessity, and brilliance of the way she builds her anti-racism, humanist platform, but to consider the violent terms of humiliation depicted in some of her images. I want to consider these images through the way that Weems positions a feminine viewer of that violence.

In its intertwining of minority and canonical status, gender and sadism, Weems's series on which I will focus, *From Here I Saw What Happened and I Cried*, is a tough and essential case in point. The series was developed upon invitation from the prestigious Getty museum, as Weems was tapped to participate in an exhibition curated by Weston Naef called *Hidden Witness: African Americans in Early Photography*. Weems's contribution brilliantly troubles the very premise underlying *Hidden Witness*—the idea that photography may provide a clean ethical frame for viewing otherwise hidden sadism or trauma. Weems's *From Here I Saw What Happened and I Cried*, as an answer to Naef's invitation, complicates received notions of the ethics of witnessing through aesthetic representation. *From Here I Saw What Happened and I Cried* proceeds by constructing images of violence seen by a feminine witness. And it is important to emphasize and not lose track of the fact that her 1995–96 series originated specifically upon Naef's invitation that Weems present evidence of witnessing. The very inception of the series revolves around questions relating to the ethics of witnessing through aesthetic representation. This point of origin for the complex conceptual weave of seeing and bearing witness is central to my interpretation of the series insofar as the series is an installation of re-photography, rather than original photography, purposely dramatizing the problematic of representation, through reconfigured re-presentations, making explicit the act of representation. Viewing the series, we must see anew what once was seen differently.

From Here I Saw What Happened and I Cried is a series of 34 "found" photographs that Weems has re-photographed and significantly altered—tinting,

---

4 In her 2012 film, *Lincoln, Lonnie and Me: A Story in Five Parts*, Weems addresses those questions when she closes the film with the evocation of a ghost figure, portrayed by the artist herself, refracted through Pepper's Ghost Technique. This ghost figure threatens her presumably mostly white middle-class audience with dismemberment and ruin, stating that "Revenge is a Mother-Fucker." In other words, she refuses the position of complicity. Carrie Mae Weems, *Lincoln, Lonnie and Me: A Story in Five Parts*, LOOK3 Festival of the Photograph, Charlottesville, Virginia, June 16, 2013.

5 Eddie Chambers, Review of *Carrie Mae Weems*, by Carrie Mae Weems (Café Gallery Projects, London), *Art Monthly* 288 (2005): 30.

cropping, framing, and inscribing with verbal text.[6] Some of the photographs in this series, the ones upon which I will focus my reading, were long housed in the archives of Harvard's Peabody Museum (Figures 2.2 and 2.3). These photographs were originally taken as part of a mid-nineteenth-century anthropological study in which enslaved father-daughter pairs were photographed (by daguerreotype) in a grievous effort to "document" their supposedly subhuman physiognomy. Anthropologist Louis Agassiz and photographer Joseph T. Zealy together were responsible for the mid-nineteenth-century production of these photographs that were intended as tools of scientific enquiry. Herein surfaces already an aspect of the complex ideological underpinnings of photographic documentation, a problematic that Weems's series for *Hidden Witness* magisterially invokes. Weems's re-photographing of the daguerreotypes of enslaved Americans raises the following question: what, exactly, did Zealy and Agassiz's daguerreotypes, before Weems's altering of the images, document? With the mid-nineteenth-century anthropological lens that drove Agassiz removed, we surely no longer interpret the photographs, preserved in Harvard's Peabody Museum, as documenting the brutal claims of racism to lodge in physiognomy.[7] That is, in Weems's retake of these daguerreotypes, the photographs' original documentary intent is now obviated. But there are traces that remain: a history of racism, linkages between early anthropology and racism, and also the forceful residue of insisted upon personhood that yet gleams in the eyes of the humiliated objects of study, whom Weems witnesses by re-photographing.

The haunting gesture of Weems's re-presentation of the Peabody Museum photographs in *From Here I Saw What Happened and I Cried*—photographs that do not make up the bulk of her series, but, for me, form the ethical crux of the series—has not escaped criticism. Some prominent scholars have raised questions focusing on the ethics of Weems reprinting these disturbing images at all. In a conference paper at Duke University, Cherise Smith raised the question of whether by re-presenting these photographs of slaves at their moment of debasement—the moment at which the human being is forced to appear as an object of study for the anthropologist (the scientist who, in the case of these photographs, was conducting his study specifically to prove his subjects subhuman)—Weems does not in fact

---

6 In addition to its physical home at MoMA, parts of the series can be viewed at the following sites: http://www.moma.org/collection/browse_results.php?object_id=45579, and http://carriemaeweems.net/.

7 Weems also deploys these images in her *Sea Islands Series*, "declar[ing] a centeredness with her installation for an audience posed for a visual experience. She frees these captured icons and she reinvents their purpose by declaring them her images with their inclusion into the framework of the gallery installation as art objects." William T. Dooley, introduction to *In These Islands: South Carolina and Georgia* (Tuscaloosa: University of Alabama, Sarah Moody Gallery of Art, 1995), 10, quoted in Willis, "Photographing Between the Lines: Beauty, Politics, and the Poetic Vision of Carrie Mae Weems," in *Carrie Mae Weems: Three Decades of Photography and Video*, ed. Kathryn E. Delmez (New Haven: Yale University Press, 2012), 38.

violate certain ethical codes, codes that would urge us to protect the dead from humiliation.[8]

Smith's conference paper effectively recants her glowing interpretation, in "Fragmented Documents." At the conference at Duke, Smith critiqued Weems's gesture of exposing these humiliated photographic subjects. Likewise, Andrea Liss, in an early and overall positive review of the original Getty exhibition, raises the question with regard to Weems's *From Here I Saw What Happened and I Cried* concerning "how to represent the victim without re-victimizing the victim."[9] But surely the problem here is more complex than re-victimization. For the difficulty inheres in the ethical knot of how representation, particularly in the case of Weems's installation re-presenting images of the dead, may be said to re-victimize the dead.

Weems herself has voiced ambivalence about the series, which was so admired by the First Lady, Michelle Obama, as to elicit for Weems an invitation to the White House.[10] Weems states that the series makes her cry, a striking fusion of her role as artist and as witness, a statement that comes close to answering the question of who is the "I" in the sentence, "And I Cried" that closes the series.[11] Weems states further that the series made her painfully aware of the power difference between the photographer, who has photo-power, and the photographic subject, vulnerable in her/his embodiment.[12] This series, of all her work, is the only one of which Weems claims "I cannot live with it," a statement that could be interpreted to mean she feels guilt over having produced the series, though Weems goes on to explain that she means she cannot have images from the series in her house, where she lives.[13] This series is also Weems's signal use of the technique of re-photographing.[14]

The Peabody Museum daguerreotypes, the re-photographs of which constitute part of Weems's installation, were taken some 150 years before Weems's installation was created, and the enslaved Americans whose images the Peabody Museum kept

---

8 Cherise Smith, "Rethinking Carrie Mae Weems's Historic Appropriations" (address delivered at the conference Pictures and Progress: Early Photography and the Making of African American Identity, Duke University, Durham, NC, March 2–3, 2007).

9 Andrea Liss, "Facing History" review of *Hidden Witness: African-American Images from the Dawn of Photography to the Civil War*, *Afterimage* 23 (1995): 22.

10 http://carriemaeweems.net/ (accessed June 30, 2013).

11 Carrie Mae Weems, Carrie Mae Weems and Deborah Willis: INSight Conversation, LOOK3 Festival of the Photograph, Charlottesville, Virginia, June 13, 2013.

12 Weems, Carrie Mae Weems and Deborah Willis: INSight Conversation. The term photo-power is from Geoffrey Batchen's *Burning with Desire*.

13 Weems, Carrie Mae Weems and Deborah Willis: INSight Conversation.

14 Weems argued vociferously with Robert Frank to retain permission to reprint a Frank photograph from *The Americans*. She suggests that part of the reason she has begun to recreate iconic images, using actors, rather than re-photograph them, is to avoid further arguments of this kind. Weems, Carrie Mae Weems and Deborah Willis: INSight Conversation.

in its files are no longer alive to be re-victimized in a straightforward sense. In a strictly physical sense, those who suffered the humiliation of Agassiz's "study" are now beyond further harm. It seems imperative, then, that we re-explore, adjust, and tighten our notion of how re-victimization can be enacted against the dead through reproduction of the images of the dead. Can re-victimization be spectral, purely performative, strictly textual? For example, the young woman across whose chest Weems places the text "You Became a Scientific Profile" cannot now walk in and see the image of herself in the Getty or MoMA (where the series is owned in the museum's permanent collection). This nineteenth-century woman cannot confront her own image and feel rage, shame, grief, or desire for vengeance—whatever we might imagine ourselves feeling were we her.

And yet, confronted specifically with this image, we are caught by the possible repetition of debasement of the, now public, mistreated feminine figure (Figure 2.2). I am interested, in particular, in Liss's response to this young woman's image, as well as to another image in the series of a young woman offering her sex, across which Weems has inscribed the text "You Became Playmate to the Patriarch," insofar as Liss instinctively brings these women back to life—invoking their former inarguable status as victims and verbally moving to protect them from re-victimization.

And Eddie Chambers, in his review of Weems's work exhibited at Café Gallery Projects in London, states that "a significant number of the more racist images ought really to be set to one side and not given periodic kisses of life—even if such resuscitation takes place by an African American artist under the guise of a knowing and artistic deconstruction and engagement with the U.S.A.'s racist past."[15] The spectacle dimensions of sadism—not only enacted on the vulnerable body, but also enacted through the gaze—carry a unique ethical freight (again, I am here using the term sadism to indicate cruelty inflicted in a context of absolute relational vulnerability). The ethical problematic of how representation inscribes violence is raised not only by Weems's *From Here I Saw What Happened and I Cried*, but also by the complex critical responses to Weems's work. Cherise Smith's objection to this series is made solely on ethical grounds. What Smith, Liss, and Chambers uncannily share, despite their diverse sophistication as critics of visual objects and culture, is a slide into interpreting these representations—photographs retaken, cropped, framed, tinted, and inscribed, objects functioning on the representational axis *par excellence*—as not only vivid but somehow alive, available to be re-victimized, given a bad kiss of life: revenants of representation.

Weems's work is vulnerable to such hypothetical accusations of sadism not only as history and documentary, but also as aesthetic mark. For implicit in the complaints of Smith, Liss, and Chambers against *From Here I Saw What Happened and I Cried* is a critical gesture of holding Weems responsible for the production of revenants: as if, vampire-like, Weems drew the lifeblood of her art from these wounded innocents (the enslaved Americans represented in Agassiz

15 Chambers, Review of *Carrie Mae Weems*, 31.

and Zealy's daguerreotypes), and in so doing, made them revenants, gave them an unhallowed, unasked-for second life. Chambers states that Weems has worked under a "guise," as if Weems should not be trusted—a masked woman, a sadist, a dominatrix wearing a guise herself. This image of Weems as a masked dominatrix presiding over the victimized images of the enslaved fathers and daughters who were already victims of Zealy and Agassiz is profoundly troubling. Weems's gaze, for these critics, comes into unholy alliance with the gaze of those who first documented the "photographic subjects" whom she reprints.

In other words, Chambers interprets Weems the artist as having a responsibility not, as he explicitly states, in her role of presenting images from the Peabody Museum to the public, but rather more, as he intimates, for *looking at* the photographs of enslaved Americans and *not turning away*, and also not allowing her audience to turn away. In the view of Chambers, the most ethical stance would be not to look at all at these images, images that unquestionably humiliate their subjects. In looking, Chambers implies, Weems becomes a sadist: a "guise" or mask crosses her face as she holds her gaze on these sadistically produced images. Indeed, in revealing, by reproducing, what might be seen as the origins of documentary photography (i.e., "scientific" documentation through photography), Weems bears down on the ethical problematic of the gaze at the heart of the conceit of documentary photography.

Cherise Smith has beautifully traced the originary complexity of documentary photography, with regards to the African American community, writing on Weems's indebtedness to and departures from DeCarava.[16] Crucially, one must interpret Weems's *From Here I Saw What Happened and I Cried* as already itself posing a critique and simultaneous intensification of the claims of documentary photography. The series critiques the very notion that what Zealy and Agassiz set out to "document" was ever in any sense real—in fact, it was utterly ideological. The problematic of documentary photography—that it presumes a reality when that very subtext may always already in fact be ideological—is revealed in Weems's installation. To be sure, the series documents the savagery of an earlier ideology, even as the photographs that Weems represents were also thought, in their day, to be "documents."

However, I am less interested in querying the difficulties and ambiguities of the status of documentary photography—the question of just how deceptive the conceit of photography as documentation is—and more concerned with questions around gender and the gaze raised by Weems's controversial series. In particular, I want to intervene in received notions of the passive, heteronormative, presumptively feminine gaze by reconsidering how the figure of a woman watching violence plays through both the conceptualization and the reception of Weems's offering for the *Hidden Witness* exhibition. That is, regardless of the complex

[16] Cherise Smith, "Fragmented Documents: Works by Lorna Simpson, Carrie Mae Weems, and Willie Robert Middlebrook at the Art Institute of Chicago," *Art Institute of Chicago Museum Studies* 24 (1999): 244–59, 271–2.

reengagement of documentary that most certainly occurs in Weems's installation, the aspect of this contretemps to which I want to point is the fact that the series is framed within the visual field of a feminine watcher—a fact ironically brought forward by critics instinctively interpreting Weems as a character in her own series, a masked dominatrix coldly surveying suffering "photographic subjects" (to borrow the phrase from Weems's own taunting inscription in the series). To rephrase with an emphasis on the nexus of gender and watching, the problematic figure of a woman watching sadism plays through Weems's *From Here I Saw What Happened and I Cried* in ways that both surpass and support the series' interrogation of the documentary genre.[17]

As I have suggested in quoting Liss and Chambers, part of the complex reception of this series seems to be viewer discomfort with images of others' humiliation—not simply because those images are re-photographed by Weems, but more so because recorded in the images is *the history of their being seen by Weems*. The record of this moment, of Weems herself seeing the images, is recorded in the tinting, cropping, framing, inscribing, claiming with text that marks the representations. Weems's gender, in particular, seems to trouble Chambers, who envisions Weems erotically kissing the images she reprints—when, in fact, the series is not in the least erotically titillating. By implication, in presenting these re-photographed photographs, Weems makes very clear that she saw them, was able to continue looking at them, and could look at them with an eye steely enough to allow her not only to re-photograph, but also to remake the images.

The gesture of locating the anthropological daguerreotypes in the Peabody Museum that inaugurates the completed installation articulates Weems in the role of the witness, responding quite directly to the charge of the *Hidden Witness* exhibition. One imagines Weems's first encounter with the images at the Peabody, their very residence in that bastion of scientific history itself a troubling allegory of the persistence of memory across generations.[18] As witness to the images of sadism recorded in the photographs created by Zealy for Agassiz (the one whose gaze precedes that of her audience), Weems's burden is inflected by gender. Insofar as Weems selects, re-photographs, tints, blasts text across, and generally reclaims the images, she as a woman who looks—an artist known socially and professionally as a woman—centers the installation. Weems's earlier *The Kitchen Table Series* (1990), for example, articulated her apparent identification of a confluence of the claims of femininity and the possibility of representing gender by representing

[17] I call "sadism" the humiliation and debasement pictured in Zealy and Agassiz's daguerreotypes because I am working with a very specific definition of sadism: violence done against a subject who cannot defend herself in any meaningful way, and who will not be defended by the culture in which her victimization occurs.

[18] Indeed, if Celeste-Marie Bernier reads the Peabody photographs as "ancestor" portraits, the imagined first encounter between Weems and these debasing images becomes poignantly charged—even if Bernier draws on the term ancestor as allegory. See her *African American Visual Arts: From Slavery to the Present* (Chapel Hill: University of North Carolina Press, 2009).

the gendered gaze. While not autobiographical, *The Kitchen Table Series* does unmistakably instate a feminine gaze—an entity given a representational status of the real in the context of that powerful floating signifier, the kitchen table. To argue as I do that Weems, in the installation of *From Here I Saw What Happened and I Cried*, enacts a feminine gaze is not an argument that would seem at variance with the artist's practice and conceptualization of gendered ways of seeing.

Indeed, a womanly watcher—a feminine figure who witnesses and watches—not only is implicit in the series' construction but also explicitly is placed in Weems's *From Here I Saw What Happened and I Cried* series. The piece is framed by George Specht's colonialist 1925 photograph (for *National Geographic*) "Nobosodrou, Femme Mangetu." This blue-tinted, reprinted, photographed, feminine profile is positioned by Weems to regard, as a witness, the red-tinted images within the series: to figuratively stand as the "I" who "Saw What Happened" and "Cried." At the inauguration of the series, this profile image looks towards the series of reprinted red-tinted photographs; and the same profile in mirror looks back across the series at its close. The Specht profile tinted blue is marked as the cool witness figure, the cool customer who claims to be crying (as a point of fact, for the words "And I Cried" are written across the second image) but looks anything but tearful. With the words "From Here I Saw What Happened" on the first image and "And I Cried" on the second image, in duplicate the Specht profile re-photographs gaze towards each other across the field of red-tinted debasement and grief contained in the other images of the series. These profile images bookend the series, enclosing the humiliated subjects contained in the photographs that are tinted red. This gesture of the witness, instantiated by the re-photograph of Specht's work, ethically anchors the series, mournfully recuperating the woman's elegant beauty.

That this witness, figuratively performed by the Specht image, is a woman is not incidental to Weems's project. For much of the worst humiliation imaged in *From Here I Saw What Happened and I Cried* is humiliation recorded visually on the body of a woman. Notably, A. M. Weaver argues that Weems "tells her stories from the perspective of a black woman, indeed she herself is *invariably* [my italics] the protagonist in her private/public dramas—it is always her life, her voice, her body that represents the scope of human reality."[19] Deborah Willis likewise observes that "For more than three decades, Weems has focused her lens on her own body and used her writings to extend the conversation."[20] Willis, who has made clear the importance of the explicit witness figure of the artist in Weems's later work, goes on to claim that even when Weems is not pictured in her own work she is, almost mystically, evoked by the images she photographs or re-photographs.[21]

19 A. M. Weaver, "Carrie Mae Weems: History and Dreams," *Aperture* 197 (2009): 24.

20 Willis, "Photographing Between the Lines," 33.

21 Willis, "Photographing Between the Lines." Willis is particularly interested in the "witness figure" that Carrie Mae Weems develops in series such as *The Louisiana Project*, and extends into later series, series in which Weems is unquestionably present, placing her body, as Willis argues, as a marker for witnessing.

How are we to interpret Weems's offering for the *Hidden Witness* exhibition in the context of such insistent, almost privative, gendering as is recorded, according to Weaver, in Weems's work? That is, how shall we interpret, in particular, Weems's depiction of the humiliation of enslaved women framed within the elegant and emphatically not enslaved gaze of the Specht photograph—the woman titled "Nobosodrou," who is herself, it must be made clear, a photographic subject? Is Weems, as Weaver suggests, the real subject of this series? And, if so, which figure is she? The humiliated enslaved person in a photograph by whose caption she is called Delia? Or the elegant Nobosodrou?[22] Weaver's claim seems to founder on this difficult series—a series that breaks apart and reveals the violence implicit in the conceit of the witness, not to mention the more subtly and insidiously violent strictures of femininity. My suggestion, developing from Willis, is that although Weems is not present visibly in these re-photographed images in *From Here I Saw What Happened and I Cried*, instead Weems invokes a provocatively feminine "I" who *should* see and *should* cry. Weems's gaze is the eye that contains the series and this eye is articulated in the act of re-photographing daguerreotypes originally taken by nineteenth-century white men. Her resistance to their gaze is in developing the trope of witnessing.

Witnessing Saartje

The enslaved women photographed and stored as specters in Harvard's Peabody Museum are humiliated in their womanhood specifically, as Shaw points out in her work on Kara Walker that also contends with these nineteenth-century images.[23] Their breasts bared forcibly by the anthropologist studying them and the youth in their eyes snuffed, these women bear comparison with the so-called "Hottentot Venus"—treated humiliatingly by late eighteenth-century natural scientists de Blainville and Cuvier—insofar as the late eighteenth-century natural scientists may be interpreted as precursors to nineteenth-century anthropologists.[24] As Anne Fausto-Sterling explicates, the humiliation of Saartje Bartman, known pejoratively as the "Hottentot Venus," in the name of science was humiliation focused on gender—the scientists were bent on measuring her genitalia to compare it to that of women of European descent (Fausto-Sterling's article does not mention which women of European descent were measured to contrast with Bartman,

---

22 For an unaltered image of "Delia" from the Zealy and Agassiz daguerreotypes, please see Gwendolyn DuBois Shaw, "The 'Rememory' of Slavery: Kara Walker's *The End of Uncle Tom and the Grand Allegorical Tableau of Eva in Heaven*," in *Trauma and Visuality in Modernity*, ed. Lisa Saltzman and Eric Rosenberg (Hanover, NH: Dartmouth College Press, 2006), 162.

23 Please see DuBois Shaw, "The 'Rememory' of Slavery," 173.

24 Anne Fausto-Sterling, "Gender, Race, and Nation: The Comparative Anatomy of Hottentot Women in Europe, 1815–1817," in *Feminism and the Body*, ed. Londa Schiebinger (Oxford: Oxford University Press, 2000), 203–34.

although Sander Gilman does unpack this question).[25] The natural scientists "studying" Bartman were hoping to prove, along the same lines as Agassiz a generation later, that women of African descent were categorically hyper-sexual in their physiognomy. Not surprisingly, this reification of ideology in scientific praxis could only be circulated through symbolic violence. The enslaved women whose photographs Weems found in the Peabody Museum, like Bartman, were humiliated in gendered terms, examined by nineteenth-century anthropologists who exemplified not outsider beliefs, but rather the core ideology of their day that expressed itself in the sadistic act of turning a woman's body into a field of scientific enquiry. De Blainville, Cuvier, and Agassiz can be interpreted as sharing in common an attempt to prove that enslaved women were properly, in Darwinian terms gaining popularity at the time, meant to be enslaved, and sexually misused. This Darwinian notion of biological hierarchy finds its sadistic underpinning revealed in Agassiz's "study," upon which Weems powerfully comments, and has important and disturbing precedents.

But in what specific ways does Weems's *From Here I Saw What Happened and I Cried* comment on Agassiz and his documentary project? The gender valence of the women's humiliation, it may be argued, is central to Weems's work of commentary. As she notes, "from the very beginning, I've been interested in the idea of power and the consequences of power; relationships are made and articulated through power."[26] If the enslaved women pictured in Agassiz's productions bear the burden of social debasement, the women are also pictured as bearing a burden of sexual debasement. We remember that these are daughters photographed with their fathers, even as Agassiz makes explicit his interest in studying the genitalia and breasts of his subjects. All the while, framing these women in Weems's series is another woman—the not-enslaved woman whose elegant profile may work on the visual register to recuperate the raw damages revealed and represented (and revealed only in representation) in the ghastly and ghostly red-tinted pictures Weems created for the core of the series (Figures 2.1 and 2.4).[27]

If Smith pointedly argued at Duke that, in bringing to our gaze the photographs of these humiliated women, Weems humiliates them all over again—an act that Smith has come to see as unconscionable, breaching the implicit contract between

---

[25] Sander L. Gilman, "Black Bodies, White Bodies: Toward an Iconography of Female Sexuality in Late Ninetieth-Century Art, Medicine, and Literature," in *"Race," Writing, and Difference*, ed. Henry Louis Gates, Jr., and Kwame Anthony Appiah (Chicago: University of Chicago Press, 1986), 223–61.

[26] See, Dowould Bey, "Carrie Mae Weems," *BOMB* 108 (Summer 2009): 60–67.

[27] The open question of whether the red tint signifies blood or ghostliness, or some other force, suggests the way that Weems's work encourages and interrogates audience engagement. One of my students suggested that the red tint marks a racial divide, reading for white audiences as the color of rage and haunting and for African American audiences as the color of blood-inheritance and mourning. Shantell Bingham, spoken communication, Women Photographers and Feminist Aesthetics, ARTH 3559, University of Virginia, April 2013.

artist and visual object—I revisit here the argument of whether documentary imagery itself is inherently violative to its subjects. To approach Weems's series, one should first ask the question: can the project of documenting violence dilute violence, or only strengthen its echo, as it is rehearsed in the act of viewing the image of violence?

Anne Fausto-Sterling, for example, argues in her essay on Bartman that her decision not to reprint images of Saartje Baartman stems from a desire not to re-victimize Baartman. Fausto-Sterling argues that there is something inherently unethical in showing a late twentieth-century audience visual images from the "scientific" study of Bartman at the close of the eighteenth century. What is interesting here is not simply the emphasis placed by Fausto-Sterling on the humiliating discourse inscribed onto Baartman's body, but also the twist that Fausto-Sterling puts in play with her claim that to show these images again is to work in concert with de Blainville and Cuvier.

For Fausto-Sterling does not refuse to reproduce the visual record of Cuvier's study simply because it intrinsically, in the study's very existence, humiliated Bartman, but because Fausto-Sterling is implicitly concerned with the risk of a sadistic bent in a contemporary audience. That is, she appears to be concerned that reproducing the images of Bartman produced by de Blainville and Cuvier not only would humiliate Bartman in the esoteric sense of debasing the dead, but could also provide her contemporary audience with titillating pleasure—a sadistic moment of pleasure translated from Cuvier and de Blainville's racism and misogyny to the possible racism and misogyny of Fausto-Sterling's contemporary audience. Fausto-Sterling takes as a given the sadism of Cuvier and de Blainville, but also raises the disturbing possibility that her reading audience shares in this sadism, inherits this nation-building discourse of misogyny and racism. It is very much Fausto-Sterling's project to expose and dismantle the sadistic racism and misogyny within what she aptly calls the development of the ideology of the nation. She fails, however, to fully theorize her mistrust of her contemporary audience.

We can only assume that Fausto-Sterling has herself seen the images of Saartje Bartman that she refuses to reproduce on ethical grounds. For Fausto-Sterling, Bartman could be "re-victimized" (to use Liss's phrase) if the representation of her humiliated body scientifically studied to be degraded were exposed to someone in Fausto-Sterling's contemporary audience who would take a pleasure in Baartman's humiliation similar to that of Cuvier and de Blainville. Fausto-Sterling, then, posits herself as an ethical witness: one who can see the humiliating, sadistic images of Bartman and not participate in the sadistic pleasure of the gaze. And yet she seems wary of this privileged ethical position; so wary that she fears her audience cannot be trusted to sustain it. The question remains, however: why does Fausto-Sterling not question her *own* possible sadistic pleasure in gazing at the humiliating images of Baartman which she refuses to reproduce?

The approach of de Blainville, Cuvier, and Agassiz and Zealy could scarcely be more ideologically similar. Yet where Fausto-Sterling makes the decision not to reproduce images of Bartman while maintaining for herself an unquestioned ethical high ground, Weems's entire project inheres in the re-photographing *for audience* the painful images of enslaved, stripped women. And if Fausto-Sterling seamlessly claims an ethical high ground that no one (to my knowledge) questions, Weems clearly makes herself vulnerable to charges of unethical pleasure in gazing on and using for her art the debasing images of enslaved daughters. I am fascinated and somewhat disturbed by the racial torque of this difference: is it possible that no one questions Fausto-Sterling's moral high-handedness simply because she is white, or, to echo the discourse of scientism, because she is a scientist? It bears remembering that even as she refuses to reproduce graphic visual images of Baartman, Fausto-Sterling unquestionably does represent the "Hottentot Venus" in the exceedingly graphic written text of "Gender, Race, and Nation."

Yet if, as I argue, Zealy's and Cuvier's humiliation and ideological disfigurement of their subjects' images is very similar, Fausto-Sterling and Carrie Mae Weems differ in their responses to the viewing of these records of sadism. Fausto-Sterling, a scientist, Ivy League professor, and author of *Sexing the Body*, and Weems, an activist and artist, diverge radically in their theories of viewing visual records of humiliated women. Is it important, and does it matter that the author of *Sexing the Body* is white while Weems identifies herself as African American? In the context of their respective works, "Gender, Race, and Nation" and *From Here I Saw What Happened and I Cried*, neither scientist nor artist directly dramatizes her own claims on race—though, as I will discuss, Weems's racial identity may be read as implicit subtext for her production of her series. Yet a radically different theory of viewing is advanced in these two works that, from the vantage point of the later twentieth century, approach eighteenth- and nineteenth-century racism and misogyny very similarly. Fausto-Sterling tells us as audience that we cannot be trusted to look at visual records of sadism (i.e., visual images of the sadism inflicted on Bartman), while Weems's *From Here I Saw What Happened and I Cried* is structured without question around the act, or acts, of probing the meaning of seeing: she *demands* that we look. Moreover, Weems's is a series in which the "I" who witnesses is figured as a woman (the image of Specht's photograph) who stands as figurative representation for Weems's notion of the witnessing role of women, or possibly only of African American women.

Weems, it appears, trusts her audience not to be sadists themselves, possibly because the series is shaped and shaded by a powerful structuring of feminine witnesses who act as guides to the audience.[28] Weems as implicit first witness, and the blue-tinted Specht profile photograph as implicit witness who never leaves the series, who is positioned always as witness, tell us, as audience, to look and to cry.[29] Weems argues that looking at traces, records, of sadism is imperative: it is

---

[28] Carrie Mae Weems, *Sea Islands Series*, in *Carrie Mae Weems: Bodies of Work*, http://carriemaeweems.net/galleries/sea-islands.html (accessed July 1, 2011).

[29] It is important here to recall that Weems's earlier *Sea Islands* series showcases and intensely troubles notions of female connection across racial boundaries: an image from the *Sea Islands* series places the figure of a white woman sadistically "overseeing" an African American woman. Indeed, interrogating the scopic metaphor of slavery with its "overseers" clearly informs Weems's renovation of the gaze in this work.

part of our relationship to the dead, to the past—an act absolutely ethical, but not without costs and risks. Weems anchors the aesthetic virtuosity of her work, her commanding artistry, on this risky venture of honoring the dead by revisiting their real humiliation.

Ernest Larsen sees Weems as just such a risky watcher, an artist who interposes herself into places of risk, who aligns and identifies herself with the "lost subjects of history."[30] But Larsen then draws back and qualifies this identity, stating instead that Weems "attempts communion" with the enslaved and the dispossessed.[31] This shift between identifying with the enslaved as opposed to "attempting communion" with the enslaved alerts us to the difficult ethics of Weems's series. Weems presents photographs of humiliated, enslaved women either on the assumption that the audience will recuperate these enslaved women's identities, seeing dignity and valor in their ability to bear injustice and survive, or with an invitation to the audience to collude in sadistic pleasure—viewing the enslaved women's debasement in the reprinted photographs and, from that watching of their suffering, gaining sadistic pleasure. This possibility of pleasure is the center of Cherise Smith's discomfort with the series.

While Weems cannot present images of the deceased enslaved women in order to recuperate their own lives (which are, of course, already gone), she can use these images to tear the scab off the wound of American racist misogyny, in particular the wound of the fusion of racisms and sexisms. Weems's witness function, embedded in *Hidden Witness*, cannot incite audiences to act to save the very subjects described in their suffering and humiliation. For Weems places sadism across the divide of mortality: we cannot reach the original victims and cannot save them since they have long ago died. To be sure, that fact is structured into the act of witnessing performed by Weems. Gazing at *From Here I Saw What Happened and I Cried*, we look at the images of the stripped, enslaved young women knowing that they did not escape Zealy and Agassiz—the daguerreotypes are evidence, records of this not-achieved escape. The Peabody Museum photographic images are records—proof—of sadism's spectacle inasmuch as they embody the sadistic impulse as gaze, records of sadism. Through its temporal positioning, then, this series is less explicitly activist than Weems's later *The Louisiana Project*,[32] a series that agitates for change *now*. However, Weems may be attempting something different from straightforward activism in *From Here I Saw What Happened and I Cried.* A tone of insuperable mourning attends the series, an act of weeping ("I Cried") inscribed into and made permanently and inextricably part of the series—a mourning that no activism can quite measure or resolve.

The change that could have prevented Agassiz's cruel anthropological use of the bodies of the enslaved women whose photographs Weems culled from

[30] Ernest Larsen, "Between Worlds," *Art in America* 87, no. 5 (1999): 128.

[31] Larsen, "Between Worlds," 128.

[32] Carrie Mae Weems, *Carrie Mae Weems: The Louisiana Project*, ed. Erik Neil, Susan Cahan, and Pamela R. Metzger (New Orleans: Newcomb Art Gallery, 2004).

Harvard's Peabody Museum is completely beyond the power of Weems or her late twentieth- and early twenty-first-century audience to enact: we gaze at this series frozen before the images, and our frozen position, blocked by the always already given imposition of 160 years separating us from Agassiz's victims, stages us in an ethical badlands. When I teach this series as part of my undergraduate course on twentieth-century women photographers, students often see rage in the eyes of the enslaved woman across whose collar bone Weems has inscribed, "You Became a Photographic Subject" (this status as photographic subject is in no way mitigated by Weems's reproduction). My students see this young woman as a beacon of rage, a figure demanding justice, granting the photographed woman an interiority that Zealy and Agassiz attempted to wrest from her.[33] But the hard reality is that no one watching Weems's series—in a museum, a book, on a screen projected on a classroom wall—can stop or undo what Zealy and Agassiz did to their "photographic subjects." By the position in time of *From Here I Saw What Happened and I Cried*, Weems insists that to act as audience to her series is to risk entering the frozen space of watching violence when there is no way to stop the violence. This wager, of placing audiences in a tight ethical space, is surely the gambit of her series.

Weems, by putting her audience in this position of frozen watcher, replays and plays through the terms of her own feminine watching. Like Sherrie Levine's postmodern repetitions, Weems quotes Zealy's photographic records as a gesture that both comments on the postmodern aesthetic and also comments on gender.[34] Visually quoting Zealy's photographs, Weems positions herself as primary audience. Weems's role of witness—implicitly—for the recovered Peabody Museum photographs is recorded in the work produced by the act of reprinting the images. She saw them, unquestionably: in the structure of her work she is always first witness, seeing first the photographs of the debased enslaved women subjected to Agassiz's sadistic anthropology. Weems stands in the structure implicit in her series as the feminine witness to their suffering.

Femme Fatale

Critics Susan Canning and Ernest Larsen call upon physical metaphors—metaphors erotic and violent—to describe Weems's role as a woman artist who plays through tropes of witnessing. To indicate that Weems's work is not merely pretty but also mightily conceptual, Canning writes that Weems "perseveres in

[33] Aleshia Dunning, a student in my class, American Ghost, argued that Weems's gallery of enslaved people functions like the life-size outlines of women killed by domestic violence that are to be found in Ms. Dunning's mother's social work office: that is, they function as remembrance *and warning*. Aleshia Dunning, personal communication, April 2011.

[34] On Levine's work, see especially Howard Singerman, "Sherrie Levine's Art History," *October* 101 (2002): 96–121.

her seduction while kicking us all in the ass," and by this very physical (and one must say, sadomasochistic) metaphor, Canning means that Weems does not shy away from addressing issues of race and gender in her work.[35] Larsen, making a comparable point, deploys an eerily similar metaphor, writing that "what Weems is after might be typified as a come-hither look followed by a sucker punch."[36] In the language of both critics, Weems is described as femininely erotic, for Canning claims that Weems's work "seduces" while Larsen ascribes to her work a "come-hither look." Both critics, then, interpret Weems according to very traditional gender codes—as a beauty who beckons the audience with erotic ploys (*seduction, come-hither look*) only to turn on them with another erotic key, that of the sadistic mistress (*kicking us all in the ass*, *sucker punch*).

It is as if the discomforting images that Weems deploys in her installation were an embodiment of the threat of the feminine gender, the threat of the feminine gaze rapidly folded, according to the critical discourse quoted above, into the seductress—sadomasochistic, and not entirely in control of her art, swayed by an erotic torque. In both Canning's and Larsen's language, Weems is typified by her gender: "come-hither" and "seduce" as terms applied to her work slip dangerously close to sounding as if they intended to critique Weems through a lens of stereotypical gendered discourse. The "sucker punch" and the "kick in the ass" to which Larsen and Canning also attribute the power of Weems's art hardly undo the gender stereotyping of "come-hither" and "seduce." Rather, they attempt to pigeonhole Weems as a certain kind of woman: a *femme fatale*.

My argument is that even as Weems powerfully explores the nexus of gender, race, and aesthetics in her work, it is a misreading to interpret her power as invoking the femme fatale: her work does not function along these restrictive gendered codes. Perhaps Larsen and Canning attribute to Weems the quality of femme fatale because of the threat to gender clichés found in her work, particularly in *From Here I Saw What Happened and I Cried*. Weems has, implicitly, first seen the disturbing images she rephotographs in her series; and in the role of witness Weems becomes a threat to received notions of woman as empathic, emotive beyond all other qualities. Because she eschews the traditional feminine witnessing gesture of sentiment, Weems's gaze, unmistakably recorded in her work, becomes a threatening, disturbing gaze. Weems possesses, it would seem, a "come-hither look" not in the stereotypical way that Larsen implies, but rather in the sense that her art beckons us—it draws us "hither." The look Weems casts is not to elicit from us a gaze upon herself; rather, she looks in order to see, and asks her audience to do the same.

In Weems's hand, this role of feminine witness, unlike sentimental witnessing, threatens gender hierarchy. Even so, there may be ways in which it may not

---

[35] Susan Canning, Review of *Carrie Mae Weems: Projects*, by Carrie Mae Weems (Museum of Modern Art, New York), and *From Here I Saw What Happened and I Cried*, by Carrie Mae Weems (P.P.O.W., New York), *Art Papers* 20, no. 2 (1996): 50.

[36] Larsen, "Between Worlds," 123.

threaten gender hierarchy enough. To return to Larsen and Canning, in both critics' terminology, the suggestion is that we the audience are drawn to the feminine illusion, the high-value pulchritude, of Weems's work, and apparently also erotically drawn to Weems (an extension of the assumptions of gender stereotypes set in motion by phrases such as "come-hither look"). But we are also Weems's "suckers," those whose "asses" she kicks. In what sense could we possibly be so violated by Weems in the act of looking at her art?

Central to my reading of the problematic of ethical representation that anchors and inspires *From Here I Saw What Happened and I Cried* is the way that Weems makes explicit that this installation is all about the feminine gaze: "I Saw" is ascribed to the feminine figure in Specht's photograph for across her shoulders the words "I Saw" are inscribed. As I have argued, Weems produces the series by seeing: she sees first and then re-photographs, altering what she saw. She envisions, dramatizes, inscribes, and reorganizes these images, and as such, the images presented in the installation also come to function as records of her act of seeing them. Weems paradigmatically performs the act of watching. She goes to the Peabody and sees Zealy and Agassiz's scandalous anthropological record and records her own history or memory of seeing the images.

Instead of breaking down upon seeing the enslaved fathers and daughters who were Agassiz's objects of study—breaking down in the sense of putting the images away, unable to contend with them—Weems quite magnificently does contend with them. She arranges, tints, crops, inscribes, and insists that we, the public, all see the evidence of the sadistic underpinnings of nineteenth-century anthropology. She codifies and theorizes, making cool and sharp the feminine role of empathy. That is, Weems claims in the series to locate a feminine witness who "Cries," who responds with the particularly appropriate feminine weeping, but this weeping is entirely enacted on the aesthetic register—it is claimed linguistically, aesthetically, but not offered performatively. Weems distances herself from sentiment even as she makes reference to its key trope, weeping. But according to Larsen and Canning, as Weems "sucker punches" us and "kicks us in the ass," she forces her audience to see the violence recorded in the Peabody Museum photographs, even though there is nothing now we can do for these innocent victims. From whence does the metaphor of Weems forcing us to see the images arise? In Canning and Larsen, Weems's *force* is her aesthetic virtuosity—she compels us to look because of the beauty of the installation she produces. And yet surely the word beauty would be misapplied to *From Here I Saw What Happened And I Cried*; instead, it carries the power of a rather harsh sublime.

Although I disagree with the blurring of Weems's gender and her work in phrases such as "come-hither look"—a description that erroneously blurs Weems's social objectification with the effect of her art—the problematic of violence that is not incidental but inherent in the aesthetic signified by Canning and Larsen is also of crucial importance. In its formal grace, *From Here I Saw What Happened and I Cried* interacts with but does not participate in sadism. It observes sadism, and in a sense offers the pleasure of formal grace, albeit the grace of revision, in the very place of watching sadism. In reproducing Zealy's daguerreotypes, the series reveals sadism. But Weems here may not be the sadist, she may not be the one taking pleasure in rendering human beings degraded.

After the Antebellum

Importantly, Weems's series complicates the role of photographer for the artist. Weems, a photographer, takes no original photographs for this series. Instead, in this installation Weems records that she is refusing the role of original photographer. As Howard Singerman makes clear in *Art History, After Sherrie Levine*, the gesture of a woman artist re-photographing and presenting as visual quote the work of an earlier male photographer has to be interpreted along multiple axes.[37] Indeed, Singerman brilliantly claims that Levine's postmodern repetitions revolutionize art history, that is revolutionize practices of allusion, inheritance, and critique. Weems's deployment of the tactic of re-photographing, or coming "after" an original photograph, alludes to Levine's practice.[38] Weems is interested in revolutionizing not only the academy but also the way the academy intersects history *tout court*.

Weems's re-photographing in *From Here I Saw What Happened and I Cried*, however, is repetition that calls attention not to the artistry of the original but instead to the original photograph's cultural position outside art and yet inside fields of cultural power. Weems is not re-photographing the work of master photographers but of anthropologists. And yet, like Levine in the *After Walker Evans* images, in creating *From Here I Saw What Happened and I Cried*, Weems forcefully performs a gesture of questioning, troubling, veering from, rejecting, the role of originary photographer. Her choice, for this installation, to make the postmodern gesture of repetition is both a turn of gender—in this series Weems performs as the woman watching—and also a commentary on the role of the photographer. Of this decision to reproduce culpable images, Weems clarifies:

> I was trying to look at the history of photography and the way in which African Americans had been particularly depicted and inscribed through and in American photography ... I'm trying to heighten a kind of critical awareness around the way in which these photographs were intended, and then of course, the way in which they are ultimately used by me—a strategy that I hope undercuts the original

---

37 Howard Singerman, *Art History, After Sherrie Levine* (Berkeley: University of California Press, 2011).

38 Weems cites Levine as an influence for this series. And yet, we cannot say of Weems's *From Here I Saw What Happened and I Cried*, as Rosalind Krauss argues of Sherrie Levine's re-photographing practice, that she "add(s) nothing, create(s) nothing." "Bachelors," *October* 52 (Spring 1990): 58; quoted in Howard Singerman, Catherine Ingraham, Sylvia Lavin, eds., *Sherrie Levine: Sculpture* (New York: Galerie Jablonka, 1996), 10. See also Weems, Carrie Mae Weems and Deborah Willis, INSight Conversation.

intention of the maker and then gives the subject another level of humanity and another level of dignity that was originally missing in the photograph.[39]

While Levine's *After Walker Evans* images may or may not limpidly draw to the surface the problematic of economic oppression and photographic power that could be theorized in response to Evans's original images of tenant farmers, Weems's repetitions decidedly have a point to make in the field of politics, and this point is made not merely through the skillful evocation of stutterance/repetition in the face of atrocity but as well through tinting and writing text on the re-photographed images. By stutterance, here, I mean that the series establishes the trauma it performs and represents by the very lack of fluidity encoded in the gesture of re-photographing, a gesture that performs a visual stutter.

Weems is by no means naïve in her invocation of the postmodern tactic of quote and pastiche. She makes use of that tactic's attention to the commodity "art" by invoking this problematic of art as commodity across the images of enslaved African Americans. That is, Weems invests the problematic of the commodity with a different weight (different from Levine) by enfolding visually the commodification of art and the commodification of the human being, the enslaved body that was sold, the image of which Weems visually mourns. In images such as Levine's *After Walker Evans: 4*, Levine's relationship, as a woman, to the tenant farmer's wife whom Evans originally photographed, is complex, turning on questions of essentialism and self-definition. Weems, like Levine, returns, via postmodernism's troubling of the linear narrative of authorizing art, to the problem of the vulnerable subject whose identity is effaced rather than articulated by the corrosive claim of the male photographer's name, and gaze.

Weems's installation built of re-photographed images does walk a very fine line in its relationship to activism: what is the point in mobilizing images of suffering if not to save the victims? In Weems's stark insistence on the non-recoverable status of some suffering, the permanent residue and trace of some acts of sadism, she moves beyond sentimental activism and forges a space for a stronger reckoning.

But this is a risky space to create. Deploying representations of non-recoverable harm, I would counter that Weems does not, as Canning argues, kick us in the ass. She does not, as Larsen suggests, sucker punch us. But she does perform a feminine figure, herself as artist, and proffers femininity as that which watches sadism. Weems compels this feminine figure to witness by the invocation of the grammar of "I." That is, Weems creates a doubled ontological "I" who watches, a feminine "I" who watches sadism, and who is Weems and who transcends Weems. This performance opens a space for the audience witnessing, but only if we agree to watch as if we were women. In Barthes's terms, the author's death permits the life of the reader; but Weems's injunction to her audience is that we watch through

[39] Carrie Mae Weems, Interview with the Museum of Modern Art, *MoMA2000: Open Ends*, September 28, 2000–March 4, 2001, http://www.moma.org/collection/object.php?object_id=45579 (accessed March 19, 2013).

a gendered gaze, a way of watching that keeps us aware, painfully, of the social restrictions placed not only on the function of the author/photographer but also on the reader/audience.[40] The performance of the installation series *From Here I Saw What Happened and I Cried* models a woman watching sadism, a record of violence that cannot be remedied.

Framing Gender and Sadism

The Specht profile that frames the other images in the series is explicitly positioned by Weems as a woman watching those who have been violated (Figures 2.1 and 2.4). Unlike the recorded-in-humiliation red-tinted images that make up the center of the series, this blue-tinted image is granted clear subjectivity—she denotes this image by the term "I." This "I" is a feminine figure whose gaze supervises, *sees*, all the suffering and humiliation in the red-tinted images. Whether we follow A. M. Weaver's claim that "Weems herself is invariably the protagonist in her public/private dramas—it is always her life, her voice, her body that represents the scope of human reality," the watcher of violence here is feminine—represented by the photographic image of a feminine figure, a beautiful woman shown in profile.[41] Her femininity is prominently articulated, the breasts and delicate profile—a beautiful, not enslaved woman witnesses the enslaved, humiliated women whose images Weems found at the Peabody. Indeed, Weems here dramatizes the act of feminine witnessing by juxtaposing queenly composure with abjection.

What is striking about this act of feminine witnessing is that while it approaches the sentimental in its invocation of the terms of sentiment—"I Cried"—it also eschews the sentimental in its invocation of claiming the gaze—"I Saw." The feminine witness given figure in this series (the Specht photograph) brackets the scenes of grievous suffering and female debasement shown in the series, and in this bracketing role does not appear to cry and does not appear to act—the beautiful figure holds still in her cool blue remoteness, her geography of a far-away "here." The anchorage of "here" is apparently Africa, but also extends to the here-and-now of the late twentieth century when Weems was creating *From Here I Saw What Happened and I Cried.* From the vantage of a post-modern "here" Weems the artist enters the archive of the humiliation of enslaved subjects and witnesses, and then performs this witnessing by creating *From Here I Saw What Happened and I Cried* by using the visual stutter of re-photographing.

The span of years, between 1840 and 1860, that *Hidden Witness* encompasses is strictly an era of ghosts; as Shaw notes, the most Gothic period in American history.[42] Every enslaved person victimized by Agassiz is dead, beyond

[40] As Barthes suggests, the death of the author is the birth of the reader, so with Weems's risky art it seems she creates an engaged audience by risking her own disparagement for showing us such truths. Roland Barthes, "The Death of the Author."

[41] Weaver, "Carrie Mae Weems: History and Dreams," 26.

[42] DuBois Shaw, "The 'Rememory' of Slavery," 161.

recuperation. And the conceit offered by Celeste-Marie Bernier that here we see ancestor photographs can only be pushed so far: part of the sadism of slavery revealed by these images of fathers and daughters is the violence racist ideology inflicted on familial inheritance. Somewhere in America, Delia's progeny may well thrive, but that narrative's displacement is only one more aspect of the sadism of slavery (that is, it is unlikely that Delia's descendants, were they to happen upon Weems's work, would know that they are Delia's descendants). The beautiful, not enslaved African woman Weems positions as regarding the suffering, enslaved African American women, remains cool blue and remote, elegant, and in fact not crying, even as Weems inscribes the idea but not the act of crying on the image. Her cool blue remoteness communicates that she watches violence, but her gaze is too remote to alter that violence.

The non-sentimental activism that Weems achieves in this series is a great accomplishment. No visual work expresses the sadism of American slavery and racism as intensely, insistently, as Weems's pithy 34 images. But there may yet be a problematic to unpack in reading the ways that ethics map onto aesthetics in *From Here I Saw What Happened and I Cried*, this series that now holds a canonical place in MoMA's permanent collection, even as it has drawn controversy. To look further at this controversy, I turn here to consider the culturally interpreted trace effect of the female body on the work the woman artist produces.

Who's "I"?

Bridget R. Cooks approaches writing about Weems's risky tactics in representing visual violence by noting the ethical difficulty of writing about representations of violence. In writing about images of sadism, we also re-present these images ineluctably in our words. Of her own work, clarifies Cooks, "In making this essay performative, by explicitly describing and reproducing the images of Black Americans that are the subjects of these visual works, I am taking the risk of re-inscribing exploitation and historical gestures of racial hatred in order to discuss them."[43] But Cooks takes the risk because there may be no other way to confront the aftereffects of sadism, violence against a person who cannot meaningfully resist due to social, physical, or verbal barriers.

Cooks's essay, "See Me Now," is especially valuable for its inspired comparison of Augusta Savage's career with that of Weems, careers separated by 50 years.[44] Cooks illuminates the problem of reading Weems, as she is predominantly read, as a performer in her own work simply because she is an African American woman, as if this status overrode Weems's productions. Cooks points to the racial and gender bias of the assumption that Weems is always "in" her work where other

---

43 Bridget R. Cooks, "See Me Now," *Camera Obscura* 12, no. 36 (1995): 71.

44 Cooks, "See Me Now," 74–7. Augusta Savage was an eminent American sculptor of the early twentieth century. See Alan Schroeder, Augusta Savage, and JaeMe Bereal, *In Her Hands, The Story of Sculptor Augusta Savage* (New York: Lee & Low Books, 2009).

artists are not. As Cooks points out, Augusta Savage could not appear as an artist at all. Her work literally had to be cordoned off from her body, socially pulled away from the African American female body of its creator.[45] The tragedy of Augusta Savage having to hide her physical presence, having to receive awards "in the mail, or given to her apart from the ceremonies," Cooks rightly reads as an effect of racism.[46] The framing assumption of a connection between the artist and the performance of "artist" Weems complicates by presenting this connection between the body of the woman and the art she creates *as a dramatic act of gazing*. Weems dramatizes that the connection between body and art is the gaze of the artist upon the material work.[47]

In *From Here I Saw What Happened and I Cried*, unlike *The Kitchen Table Series* in which Weems appears clearly and is embodied and performs in a cinematically located feminine body, Weems displaces embodiment onto the re-presented photographs. Weems is a watcher in this series, an artist who sees and manipulates visual objectivity. Her gesture of absenting herself while performing watching violence—presenting images that record the sadistically humiliated women in Agassiz and Zealy's photographs—cuts decidedly against the grain of sentimental femininity. Weems does not here place her female body on view. She does not show herself weeping. Instead, she shows herself *seeing*. We as audience see the recorded trace of Weems's own seeing of sadism, and this knowledge makes room for a refashioning of gender codes.

And yet might this very absence of Weems's representation of herself usher the work into canonicity, making Weems no longer an up-and-coming young artist, but one who has indeed arrived? While Cooks draws on Barthes's "The World of Wrestling," arguing that the victimized object of the gaze can "look back and reverse the spectators' agency" in *From Here I Saw What Happened and I Cried*, it seems unclear to many critics that Zealy's photographic subjects are indeed reversing the spectator's agency—reversing Zealy and Agassiz's sadistic agency.[48] Instead, Weems is read by Smith, Liss, and Larsen as possibly insufficiently connected to Agassiz's victims to reverse the gaze, that is to reverse the power structure by which Zealy and Agassiz watched the enslaved Americans. Does Weems's work permit these photographic subjects to "look back" at their attackers through deployment of their rephotographed images? I want to unpack as carefully as possible the objections of these critics in order to argue that despite difficulties in this disturbing series, Weems ultimately does achieve a real ethical power in the context of her aesthetic mastery.

---

45 Cooks, "See Me Now," 75.

46 Cooks, "See Me Now," 75.

47 As Willis points out, although in the series *From Here I Saw What Happened and I Cried* Weems does not appear, in other series such as *The Louisiana Project*, *The Kitchen Table Series*, and *Roaming*, the artist uses herself as a witness figure.

48 See Roland Barthes, "The World of Wrestling," in *Mythologies*, trans. Annette Lavers (New York: Farrar, Straus and Giroux, 1972), 15–26; Cooks, "See Me Now," 70.

For Weems's grappling with sadism and representation in *From Here I Saw What Happened and I Cried* is more complex than just reversing the gaze. As Cooks makes clear, Weems's art at times has been met by a kind of "anger at the artist herself."[49] Because Weems performs a steely gaze in *From Here I Saw What Happened and I Cried*—images that reproduce representations of humiliation and degradation—the series implicitly presents Weems as the woman artist watching violence. This gaze, Weems's gaze, may not in its enactment of seeing necessarily permit the original violated victim to gaze back at the sadist. For Weems, gazing at the women in Agassiz and Zealy's anthropological photographs may or may not provide a forum in which these humiliated, enslaved women at last look back at their sadistic anthropological assaulter (in Barthes's terms, reversing the gaze). But the series does provide a forum in which Weems herself is performatively marked by the possibility of her connection to the victims in public perception. In other words, Weems takes a risk in assuming that audiences will read her re-presentation of the images produced by Agassiz as an act that permits the victim to reverse the gaze and look back at the sadist, and this risk is effectively borne on her persona as artist.

In figuring the woman watcher as the Specht photograph, Weems displaces the act of gazing onto the figure of another woman so that the series depicts the drama of one woman watching other women being sadistically humiliated, and the spectator incapable of ending this violence. The beautiful woman shown in profile in the blue-tinted images, whose inscriptions make clear that she is the witness to the suffering of enslaved women, watches endlessly as the victims of Agassiz's sadistic anthropology are endlessly displayed. It is this repeating loop of traumatic photography that at once offers us the chance to engage the sadism of slavery—in Blanchot's words, to "think with pain"—but also makes the series controversial, hard to swallow.[50]

Weems herself notes the alterity of her approach, stating that she is "interested in sort of forging another kind of information that opens up another kind of space to think about what might be offered to you."[51] This "other kind of space" stages the act of looking at violence, but without sentimental invitation to direct activism. All of Weems's art is powerful in its activist engagement, and yet the Agassiz and Zealy subjects present humiliation and degradation unique among Weems's subjects. This anthropology, with its sadistic turn, cannot be addressed by direct activism because of the temporal divide between Agassiz's victims and Weems's art. The inability to heal the damage we see in the faces of Agassiz's victims moves the series away from sentimentality: what neither Weems nor her audience can recuperate is the injury of soul done to the enslaved women whom Agassiz sadistically victimized, by the humiliation of being stripped of clothing

---

49 Cooks, "See Me Now," 73.

50 Blanchot, *The Writing of the Disaster*, 68.

51 Cooks, "See Me Now," 73.

and photographed to prove one's non-human status.[52] In other words, Weems's double-sided performance of the gaze in this series—as installation artist who sees the images she reproduces and deploys the feminine character of the blue-tinted woman in profile as witness to sadism—presents feminine gazing as that which sees sadistic violence and also stands still before it, in traumatic stutterance insofar as re-photographing images semiotically repeats an originary sign.

Ancestors and Antecedents: Of the Canon, of the Flesh

Celeste-Marie Bernier opens her book *African American Visual Arts* with an extended reading of Weems's *From Here I Saw What Happened and I Cried.* In honor of Weems's work, Bernier titles her introduction, "From Here I Saw What Happened and I Cried." As mentioned above, in sharp contrast to Cherise Smith, Bernier argues that Weems's series regains dignity for Agassiz's victims. Bernier asserts that "for viewers not blinded by racist expectations, they [the photographs from Harvard's Peabody Museum] tell tales of slave sorrow and humanity through the expressive individualism of their eyes and the forcefulness of their gaze."[53] Bernier's rhetoric excludes Blanchot's notion of "thinking with pain," insofar as anyone who criticizes Weems's series for revealing unhealed and non-recoverable suffering, in Bernier's terms, is herself racist. Bernier contends that Weems recuperates the lost dignity of Agassiz's victims—that the subjects "gain heightened dignity in Weems's hands"—because the cropping and sand-blasted text that Weems deploys reconfigures the images, to some degree covering the women's breasts.[54] While Bernier is surely correct in reading self-contained dignity in the gaze of the enslaved women victimized by Agassiz—the entrée to his "anthropological debate"—this truth may only heighten the sadism the pictures depict.

Seeing the haunted, haunting eyes of the enslaved people named "Jack," "Drana," "Renty," and "Delia" in the Peabody Museum images, we become vividly aware that they are humiliated by Agassiz's anthropological practice. The problematic of the series is found in the following question: what does Weems ask us, as her audience, to do with this painful revelation of sadism? A sadism that may merge with contemporary racism, but also diverges insofar as the explicit juridical moment of Agassiz's sadism, based in slavery, is done. If Bernier and Cooks suggest that in Weems's hands the enslaved women photographed by Zealy reverse the gaze and gaze back, this argument, I think, can only be put forward on the premise that the women already were gazing back, and this capacity to gaze

[52] In particular, Agassiz's decision to study fathers and daughters in pairs functions as sadism because of the anthropologist's peculiar desire to humiliate his subjects not only before himself, but also before each other, perverting the father-daughter relationship in a manner chillingly reflective of antebellum codes interweaving paternity and slavery.

[53] Bernier, *African American Visual Arts*, 16.

[54] Bernier, *African American Visual Arts*, 15.

back unfortunately did not undo the act of sadism lodged in Agassiz's decision to humiliate them. Just as we cannot now retrieve the real names of "Jack," "Drana," "Renty," and "Delia" (i.e., the names they had before they were enslaved, or the names they might have chosen had they not been enslaved), we cannot now punish Agassiz, except in the echo-work of cultural memory.

Weems's representation of Agassiz's victims asks us, as she asks herself, to freeze in a kind of shock before the images of Agassiz's sadism, and from that shock to develop a non-sentimental and perhaps painful approach to undoing larger networks of sadism, misogyny, and racism where they still prevail. In a sense, *From Here I Saw What Happened and I Cried* is a series that situates us where we can do nothing and we must do everything—discomforting injunctions.

Weems's response to the Agassiz photographs is to re-photograph them, a visual marker of stutterance and emblem of rage, of throwing back into the public eye the crime of slavery. In remaking the photographic records of Agassiz's sadism, Weems performs an ethical gesture of stutterance: in her hands, the sinister fluency of Agassiz's "scientific profile" and "anthropological debate" breaks down, becomes a stutter.

The images drenched in red convey violence, of course, but the images drenched in red also intimate the capacity of those who have been violated to haunt their victimizers. Here, reversing the gaze is indeed complicated; it becomes a spectral spectacle.[55] As Avery Gordon's *Ghostly Matters* makes clear, the traces of earlier acts of sadism do not vanish, but become sites of haunting, "A seething presence … the ghost is not simply a dead or missing person, but a social figure."[56] What haunting may mean in *From Here I Saw What Happened and I Cried* is the capacity of the dead to confront the living. The red-drenched ghosts, enraged, and the red-paged text Weems inscribes upon the figures, are not passive representations—even so, these ghosts cannot attack Agassiz and Zealy, as the once enslaved dead cannot attack those who owned them. These ghosts of anthropology confront us even as they cannot confront those who specifically violated them.

Who can look at these ghosts without apprehension of rage, grief, guilt or all these emotions? Weems positions her feminine figure, Specht's profile photograph, in the badlands—a public place where the feminine watcher sees sadism and, even as she textually claims to "cry," does not in fact perform weeping. We do not see the blue-tinted, elegant woman in profile weeping, even though the words "And

[55] The feminine figure of George Specht's 1925 "Nobosodrou, Femme Mangbetu" is positioned by Weems as the watcher of the violent racism represented in the 30 red-tinted reprinted images but this blue-tinted "Nobosodrou, Femme Mangbetu" may also evince racism, Specht's work vulnerable to complicity with early twentieth-century racisms. By tinting this dignified profile blue, differentiating her from the enraged red that drenches the violated subjects on whom the woman in profile gazes, Weems puts in place a categorical distinction between these figures. One is a watcher, a woman at great geographical distance from the "here" of the antebellum South. The others are the watched.

[56] Avery Gordon, *Ghostly Matters: Haunting and the Sociological Imagination* (Minneapolis: University of Minnesota Press, 1997), 8.

I Cried" are inscribed on her image. Instead, the figure and the inscription across the figure allow us to *conceptualize* weeping, mourning, to theorize the position of crying, and this leveraging of mourning as hermeneutic tool generates the possibility of vengeance through symbol as act. While the culprit anthropologist and slave owner as *pater familias* cannot be punished (since they too are dead), the vengeance of Weems's red-tinted images and their blue-tinted witness is enacted semiotically, naming patriarchy as the foundation of racism, a foundation that must be uprooted to appease these ghosts.

Archival Fracturing

I place a brief detour here to contrast Weems's use of archival material with that of Christian Boltanski's reprinting and altering of archival material from the Holocaust. The difference I would like to emphasize is that Boltanski draws from photographs that are either snapped before the victim becomes fully a victim (*before* he or she is murdered or *after* the victim has survived the death camp), while Weems's reprinting of Agassiz's anthropological victims forces us to look at those suffering humiliation *in the moment of the photograph*.[57] The difference I want to emphasize, where there are so many other differences upon which one might comment, is the timing of the photographs. Weems's reprinted images of Agassiz's anthropological victims show these women in the moment of their suffering: precisely the place and time of the image is where we see not the intimation but the fact of the victim's sadistic treatment—sadistic in the sense that they appear in the position of humiliation and also appear just as Agassiz desires. In other words the photograph not only records but also enacts violence, in these Peabody Museum images.

This difference makes Weems's handling of the archive controversial not simply for ethical reasons—the caveat placed by Fausto-Sterling on the risk that contemporary audiences might take pleasure in the re-vision of earlier centuries' sadism—but also for psychological reasons. The terrible moment of empathizing, finding one's own union and solidarity with the victim, the fullest gesture of witnessing, is called for in Weems's *From Here I Saw What Happened and I Cried* precisely because the victims (the "photographic subjects" and "anthropological debates") are shown in the moment of their suffering. The witness perhaps risks annihilation of herself if she empathizes completely with the destroyed victim. But Weems pushes us to the boundary of the ethics of watching representations of sadism. The concept of the archive as that which houses what is past is fractured by Weems's demand that we confront what is past as if it were red-hot now, visually quoting the nineteenth-century photographs to elide rather than articulate temporal difference.

[57] Marianne Hirsch, "Projected Memory: Holocaust Photographs in Personal and Public Fantasy," in *Acts of Memory: Cultural Recall in the Present*, ed. Mieke Bal, Jonathan Crewe, and Leo Spitzer (Hanover, NH: Dartmouth College Press, 1999), 12.

It bears returning, then, to the question of what kind of archive Weems taps in creating her powerful series. Since my effort in this chapter is to hew as closely as possible to reading Weems's re-presentation of the Agassiz-Zealy daguerreotypes housed in Harvard's Peabody Museum, relics of science, I should ask what kind of archive, properly speaking, does Harvard retain with these images? The images of kidnapped, enslaved African American fathers and daughters at first glance would appear to describe wholly subjugated subjects—subjugated in the position of the seen, whose gaze is without power. The gaze of Agassiz and Zealy, unified in concert, is chillingly preserved in the images enshrined as science by Harvard. To blame Weems for bringing the images to the public is to ignore that the images were *already* in the public domain, already housed, if not displayed, in a major museum before the commissioning of *Hidden Witness*, the Getty exhibition.

The images in the Peabody functioned as records, but the archival ambiguity of such records haunts the reading of any presentation of the images. For while we look at Boltanski's use of archival material to contend with the Holocaust in full knowledge that Hitler's power is over and done now, some aspects of the Peabody Museum photographs fall into a disturbingly ambiguous realm. We all agree that slavery was an evil system on a par with the Third Reich, and yet the harms of the Agassiz-Zealy images pull on cultural threads other than antebellum slavery. These images also raise questions about sadism embedded in anthropology, in the academic hierarchies of scientific progress, and in persistent tropes of racism housed by Harvard. That the Peabody Museum retained the images makes clear that Agassiz has not been erased from the record of science. Agassiz's sadistic stripping and debasing of human beings in order to prove them not human is linked not simply to slavery but also to anthropology: the archival source from which Weems drew for her series *From Here I Saw What Happened and I Cried* gives subtle and unmistakable testimony to a frightening tenacity of the racist and misogynist tenets underlying anthropology.[58]

It is tempting to read Weems, who has done graduate work in the field of ethnography, as using this series in part as a way of intervening in cultural studies. For she deploys Specht's complicatedly positioned original photograph as a kind of feminine witness, a figure almost for a feminist anthropologist: this elegant woman in profile who steadfastly witnesses and sees the suffering of the women in Agassiz's photographs, the very words of witnessing "I Saw" inscribed across her body. Weems's use of the text of witnessing, "I Saw What Happened … And I

[58] Important exceptions include currently practicing feminist anthropologists such as C. Nadia Seremetakis and Kath Weston, who focus on conducting anthropology as an exploration that, far from setting the scientist apart from the "specimen" she studies, includes the scientist as part of the study. Both Weston and Seremetakis have published studies focused on their own cultures, studies that include themselves as an "object" of inquiry. For example, see Seremetakis, *The Last Word: Women, Death, and Divination in Inner Mani* (Chicago: University of Chicago Press, 1991) and Weston, *Families We Choose: Lesbians, Gays, Kinship* (New York: Columbia University Press, 1991).

Cried," positions the blue-tinted feminine figure as a figure seeing, understanding, others' humiliations.

Weems establishes a rhetoric, a conversation, between her blue- and red-tinted figures—the cool, blue mourner, the enraged, blood-red victims—and dramatizes a geographical divide between the articulated "here" in "From Here I Saw" and the unspoken and unspeakable "there" of antebellum slavery. This place of no place, an unspeakable "here," is a haunted geography of the soul that Weems's visual and verbal text suggests was all but uninhabitable by the living. The cool, blue-tinted figure remaining in Africa, watching, keeps her distance and keeps her poise. This seeing "I" is categorically distant in the rhetoric of Weems's series. She claims to cry, but does not show tears; she watches the visual record of Agassiz's sadism and remains remote, holding her place in the intact and unbreached "here"—a troubling position of witnessing.

Like Emily Dickinson's chilling speakers who calmly describe amputations, bandaging, and stabbing (see especially poems 267, 309), Weems's cool-blue witness, in deflecting the easy resolutions of sentimentality—a figure of a woman who is clearly not crying even as she inscribes the need for crying—plays through ethical ambiguity. Who, really, is the "I" who "Cried" in this series? For whom does the Specht photograph enact displacement? The ambiguity that Weems shapes around the witness figure—an ambiguity put in place by the difference between the poised profile of the 1925 photograph and Weems's text that claims the figure is weeping—pressures the ethics of watching sadism and lays bare the difficulty of bearing witness to atrocity.

Weems deploys the reprinted image of the Specht photograph, held in its stasis as witnessing figure, in order to dramatize a third gaze, a gaze implied in Barthes's "The World of Wrestling." If Barthes envisions the body that has become spectacle turning back the gaze on the spectator, Weems intervenes in and complicates the audience's position. Our putative role should be to judge Agassiz for his sadism and to sympathize with the plight of his victims. But Weems's use of the figure of the witness displaces us and demonstrates how static and trapped in a loop of witnessing is the gaze that truly sees sadism. This very gaze becomes part of sadism, against its own will. In other words, ethically, Weems figures for us that we should not be able to leave the Getty Museum's *Hidden Witness* behind, for we should have seen that which in some way turned us to stone—becoming the frozen figure of witness, a figure that Weems structures as literally caught in an endless loop of watching suffering without being able to act to alleviate it.

To fully witness the kind of sadism underlying the type of anthropology that attempted to prove human beings were not human, what Liss aptly calls the "patriarchy of racism," and to plumb the depths of that system, it is necessary that we see sadism and also recognize that Agassiz's work was socially sanctioned in its day—indeed lauded as part of an emerging field, Darwinian mastery as the master trope of modernity. Harvard's very preservation of the images makes clear the complex embedding of sadism in the culture and aesthetic that Weems's series works to unpack.

In giving us this ambiguous rhetoric of witnessing that the series plays through, Weems signifies the problematic of femininity that sees sadism but keeps its distance. If Deborah M. Horvitz, in *Literary Trauma: Sadism, Memory, and Sexual Violence in American Women's Fiction*, draws a starkly gendered view of representations of sadism in the American canon, that distinction of woman-as-victim surely must be interrogated. Horvitz argues that in literary representations of violence, "deservedly furious, enraged women imagine their revenge against the men who oppress, imprison, beat, rape, humiliate and abandon them, but *they do not act upon it*" [emphasis added].[59] While I agree with Horvitz's assessment of the relative scarcity of representations of women enacting sadistic violence, my interpretation of the relationship between gender and representations of sadism is more complicated, as I will show.

What is initially interesting in Weems's *From Here I Saw What Happened and I Cried* is that the installation is not only between media—re-photographs with an extended prose poem inscribed across the images, sand-blasted text that works more deeply than title or caption—but also between modes, insofar as Weems represents victims who surely imagined but did not act on revenge. Horvitz implies that feminine figures or characters categorically cannot act sadistically, but she does not consider the very complicated relationship that emerges in texts in which feminine figures or characters witness sadism of which they are not necessarily the victim.

The victims in Weems's *From Here I Saw What Happened and I Cried* may very well have harbored fantasies of revenge, but we as audience of Weems's series are not privy to those fantasies. And though they may inspire our own fantasies of revenge, the question of whether the series itself acts as revenge is complicated by the consideration of what Agassiz's victims might have wanted to *do* to avenge themselves. We can be fairly sure that Delia, for example, did not think a good way to avenge herself would be to have her stripped-bare image grace MoMA's walls. Instead, the locus of revenge here is displaced from the victim and placed onto an audience in whom Weems hopes to inspire notions of social justice and cultural retributive vengeance. I believe that she does inspire us with notions of justice in this series, but it is a justice that may well exclude whatever fantasy of revenge Delia herself, for example, may have had.

Weems's installation disturbingly dramatizes the way that, just as Agassiz's sadism is enacted not only before but also through the camera, Weems's series replicates the problematic of the disembodied spectator always already present in the photograph—the photographer/audience always already beyond the reach of the "photographic subject." Weems refers to this nexus—this crossing between herself and the sadistic photographer whose work she witnesses by re-photographing and representing—when she deploys the phrase "photographic subject" across an image that she re-presents for an audience.

---

[59] Horvitz, *Literary Trauma*, 18.

Weems complicates any easy notion of witnessing and judgment we might bring to the Getty's *Hidden Witness*. Weems's justice is enacted through installation of photography as a visual tool not only of confrontation, but also of contestation. Playing with Agassiz's own terms to bring into the public eye the image of the outcast, Weems overturns Agassiz's visual rhetoric to shape the image of the dispossessed as metonym for the possibility of justice. Her series raises the problematic question of what is culturally legible as "truth." Truth is contested across the ground of science and the arts, and Weems's brilliant project, *From Here I Saw What Happened and I Cried*, performs an intervention into easy notions of truth, arguing for justice that is never based on ease.

Nakedness and Ethics

Exploring ethics of representation, Arthur C. Danto argues that "to be human is to care about how we are seen"—a sweeping claim, to be sure, but one that can be brought to bear on Weems's project of re-presenting Agassiz's sadistic anthropological daguerreotypes.[60] Without doubt, these images of enslaved daughters are unlikely to present how these women might have desired to be seen. Indeed, insofar as Agassiz's goal was to prove that his subjects were not fully human, Agassiz presents the objects of his study categorically as they would *not* want to be seen. That is, if we apply Danto's claim that "to be human is to care about how we are seen," for example, to the woman called "Delia" in Agassiz's daguerreotypes, we can say that in her humanity Delia would categorically not want to be seen through Agassiz's racist eyes—stripped of clothing, humiliated, debased.

It is notable that Danto seeks to define humanness through aesthetics, a clear and compelling departure from racist anthropological definitions of what biologically constitutes humanness and at the same time a departure also evocative of some strains of racism and eugenics (though I hasten to add that this trace meaning of the aesthetics of the human is clearly not what Danto has in mind). But Danto's gesture of invoking the primacy of the aesthetic raises a question that we can fruitfully apply to Weems's *From Here I Saw What Happened and I Cried*. Specifically, how does her reframing of these images at long last allow Agassiz's victims to be seen as they would have wanted to be seen? Does Weems's series respect the idea that "to be human is to care about how we are seen" with regard to the hypothetical though still ethically compelling wishes of the enslaved fathers and daughters whose images Harvard's Peabody Museum archived?

In "The Naked Truth," Danto offers an approach that I am going to apply to interpreting Weems's performative gaze as the installation artist who reprints images archived by Harvard. I draw on Danto because of the provocative power of his claim that "to be human is to care about how we are seen." I will close this

---

[60] Arthur C. Danto, "The Naked Truth," in *Aesthetics and Ethics: Essays at the Intersection*, ed. Jerrold Levinson (Cambridge: Cambridge University Press, 2001), 258.

chapter, then, with an extended look at how Danto's interpretation of the ethics of Peter Hujar's photograph of the transvestite Candy Darling, *Candy Darling on Her Death Bed* (1974), can help unpack the ethical questions that coalesce around Weems's *From Here I Saw What Happened and I Cried.* Although not writing on Weems's series, Danto meditates on the ethics of representing those no longer alive, and also on the relationship between the photographer and his or her posthumous subject. Claims Danto: "[F]or reasons far too deep for me to understand it is a human reflex to want to establish an image of the departed, as if death is not final if the image itself lives on in the minds of those left behind."[61] He goes on to make clear that the mere fact of being dead is no consolation for having a humiliating image of oneself circulating in public.[62] Here, the problem of Weems's unflinching gaze, recorded and performed in *From Here I Saw What Happened and I Cried*, becomes the problem of whether she merely circulates humiliating images of the dead, or enacts justice that transfigures the meaning of these inarguably humiliating images.

Celeste-Marie Bernier, as noted, argues that Weems grants dignity to the enslaved victims of Agassiz's study and Zealy's camera. But the question of precisely how Weems restores dignity to images whose creators' motivation precisely was to strip away dignity invites further scrutiny. Bernier claims that the re-framing of images alters the meanings of the photographs, and that Weems's use of inscription likewise subverts the original discourse of Agassiz's racism. No longer humiliating records of sadistic debasement, Bernier maintains that the daguerreotypes meant by Agassiz to prove slaves' subhuman status, in Weems's hands, become portraits of ancestors, preserving the true dignity of the dead, honoring the dead.[63]

The pressing nature of the question of whether the dignity of the enslaved women who appear in *From Here I Saw What Happened and I Cried* is repaired by Weems's re-use of the images reflects the intensity of the mid-nineteenth-century anthropological sadism exposed in Weems's work. Weems's connection to those whom Bernier terms ancestors matters: her connection as the artist to her subjects, how she enters into the intimate relationship of re-representing the images of their nakedness, their unutterable vulnerability, their nakedness, both physical and metaphysical. In "The Naked Truth," Danto offers an interpretation of similar ethical risks in Peter Hujar's memorial photograph, *Candy Darling on Her Death Bed.* He draws on Hujar's memorial photograph of Candy Darling as exemplary of the proper ethical relationship between photographer and subject. Danto's argument turns around the pivot of representing the dead. Danto notes that Hujar, portraitist of Candy Darling dying, "lived in the closed world of transvestites and accepted their values without question."[64] In other words, as a gay man, Hujar

61 Danto, "The Naked Truth," 265.

62 Danto, "The Naked Truth," 266.

63 Bernier, *African American Visual Arts*, 14–16.

64 Danto, "The Naked Truth," 270.

is accorded ethical propriety in photographing the transvestite Candy Darling because Hujar's embrace of transvestite culture makes him, for Danto, proximate to Candy Darling's alterity—not a stranger to the status of outcast, not an onlooker.

Weems, as an African America artist, seems to claim an analogous proximity to the enslaved "ancestors" in the Peabody Museum archive. Weems, of course, has never been enslaved, but she traces her ancestry through a Mississippi heritage that may well suggest a history of enslavement in her forebears. It is important to note here that Weems, like Hujar, chooses, in her positioning of herself as an artist, to claim the status of compatriot to the outcast. That is, while Hujar and Weems did not choose to be, respectively, gay and African American, Hujar and Weems did both choose to articulate and emphasize a public stance of identifying, respectively, with gay culture and with African American culture. With Danto, I think it is appropriate to read an artist's ethical position vis-à-vis her work in part by interpreting the artist's purposeful development of her public identity. In this way, public identity—Hujar as a non-closeted gay man and Weems as an artist who emphasizes her cultural identity as African American—becomes part of the record of the photographic enterprise, recorded and legible.

Borrowing Danto's paradigm, one would say that Weems performatively produces herself as a compatriot to Zealy and Agassiz's victims—Weems positions herself so as to "live in the closed world" of race by *seeing racism*, acknowledging the sadistic depths of American racism. This world that Agassiz's tragic subjects inhabited Weems wills herself to join, as compatriot, by invoking a very porous "I"—a transitive subjectivity that definitively can *see*. In this sense, Weems is impeccably ethical in her performance as the installation artist who exposes the depths of racism as sadism.

Danto goes on to extol the profound respect that Hujar displays for Candy Darling, and the way that this respect is recorded in the work as "authentication and a gift."[65] Hujar, argues Danto, "ha[s] deferred to the image Candy Darling would identify as her and [has] submerged his artistic will to that of the subject."[66] What is interesting here is that Weems's position as the artist who produces *From Here I Saw What Happened and I Cried* on these criteria—of respecting the subject's will—begins now to seem ambiguous. For the violated subjects of Agassiz's study cannot have identified themselves in these sadistic images—Agassiz's images cannot possibly be argued to stand for these enslaved women's projects of identity. Indeed, Agassiz's very impetus was to deprive the women of the project of identity, that is, of humanity.

And yet it may be argued that Weems, in these re-photographed and reframed images, *does* offer a kind of "authentication" to these victims of racist anthropology. For the goal of Weems's series is to expose the sadistic paradigm that produced the original daguerreotypes housed by Harvard that in turn strip their enslaved subjects of their projects of identity. In this exposure of violence against these

65 Danto, "The Naked Truth," 270.

66 Danto, "The Naked Truth," 270.

photographic subjects, one can argue that Agassiz's victims, in Weems's series, are offered some measure of "authentication and gift," a place to be seen in their human suffering—a space created by the meditative distance set in play by the artist's performative claim that introduces and generates the series: "I Saw."

In this way, we might read Weems's re-photographs by seeing, as my students usually claim to see, meditations on rage and superlative self-control in the eyes of the stripped subjects. But do such readings depend upon the gendered assumption of feminine empathy (Weems's in particular) across historical epochs and, as such, might they be suspect? What we understand of the life experience of the young woman set before Agassiz's gaze and his camera is presented in the fact of her being set before his camera in this humiliating fashion. Reading her despair, we find unjust the actions of those who tried to prove her less than human. This belated opportunity for recognition of self-sovereignty in the minds, if not the bodies, of the women Agassiz "studied" functions as the gift that Weems grants these posthumous victims. Weems may not be able, as Hujar can of Candy Darling, to reveal the enslaved women's projects of identity, but at least she can and does tilt the lens so that the fact that the women *did have projects of identity* becomes clear.

And yet part of the humiliation of Agassiz's photographic subjects is the prospect of audience. We stand as one of the formations of debasement towards which the picture is geared in its original inception. The question is: does Weems alter the mirroring function of this image enough to force us to see ourselves in it? The word *mirror* is used here purposely; we have to see ourselves in the enslaved photographic subjects if we are to follow the ethical direction of Weems's project.

Concerning the question of whether Weems "submerges [her] artistic will to that of the subject," I think there can be no question that the answer is *yes*.[67] This submerging of her artistic will is precisely the engine of Weems's installation, *From Here I Saw What Happened and I Cried.* For Weems steps away from the role of original photographer entirely, ceding her power as an original photographer and becoming one who re-photographs others' photographs. Whereas Levine re-photographs to contest outdated conceptualizations of the artist, Weems submerges her artistic will for the sake of activism against racism. But can we interpret Weems's performance as following the "will" of the photographs' subjects, a question very difficult to answer because the subject of this series is ambiguous, in some sense. Is the subject the specific enslaved victims of Agassiz's sadistic anthropology? Or is it all African Americans who were enslaved? Or is it all African Americans descended from those who were once enslaved? The guiding trope of *Hidden Witness*, the exhibition for which Weems's *From Here I Saw What Happened and I Cried* was originally created, may imply the assumption of a common inheritance, for all African Americans, from the scarring fire of American slavery. Weems's series exemplifies the ethical implications of this assumption.

Of Weems in this series, one might say that the subject to whom she submerges her artistic will is the population of African Americans violated by

---

[67] Danto, "The Naked Truth," 270.

past enslavement and continued racism. If such a subject may seem too broad to be credible, it is important to recall the original context for which *From Here I Saw What Happened and I Cried* was created: as a response to the charge of Naef's *Hidden Witness* exhibition. The enslaved victims of Agassiz's sadistic study on whom Weems turns her unflinching gaze might make us weep. But this sentimental response turns into a kind of visual stutterance: what good would our tears now do for "Delia"?

Fittingly, weeping is not performed in Weems's series; it is only indicated by the textual and visual rhetoric of *From Here I Saw What Happened and I Cried.* Tears become a coda to Weems's articulation of the claims of witnessing. "Cried" is the word that closes the series, ushering us into consideration of the injustice that Weems's series exposes, but also keeping consideration performatively dry-eyed, a kind of witnessing that diverges from gendered expectations of feminine empathy and instates a different kind of gaze—a womanly watcher who sees sadism and who freezes our gaze before the unacceptable image of violence to which there is no recourse in time. This suffering procures witness: a gaze paradoxically disinterested in victims but powerfully assertive of justice.

Coda: On the Ethics of Representation

How may a photographer, or writer, present images of victims to an audience that may believe itself to stand outside, beyond, the threat of harm, without harmfully inscribing the ontological status of abjection onto the victim represented?[68] The act of creating a representation of suffering is ethically complex, as I hope this chapter on Weems has made clear.[69] My comments in this coda do not directly invoke Weems but are inspired by her brave work. The risk, in representing a victim, of flattening the victim into an abject image may be understood as the very pivot of the rhetoric of the representation of suffering—the risk of participating in the making-to-suffer of the victim. Writers, or photographers, who represent violence

---

[68] Susie Linfield has taken up this question in *The Cruel Radiance: Photography and Political Violence* (Chicago: The University of Chicago Press, 2010). Folded into Linfield's book is a passionate debate with Susan Sontag's *On Photography* (New York: Farrar, Straus and Giroux, 1977) and even Sontag's later work, *Regarding the Pain of Others* (New York: Farrar, Straus and Giroux, 2003).

[69] Arthur C. Danto's *The Abuse of Beauty: Aesthetics and the Concept of Art* (Chicago: Open Court, 2003) meditates on this problem, for example. Others to take up the charge include Nancy Armstrong and Leonard Tennenhouse in *The Violence of Representation: Literature and the History of Violence* (London and New York: Routledge, 1989). The exhibition *Beautiful Suffering: Photography and the Traffic in Pain* (Williamstown, MA: Williams College Museum of Art, 2007) generated a catalogue attending to this problematic of how to represent suffering ethically, or, indeed, if it can be done. Reinhardt et al., *Beautiful Suffering: Photography and the Traffic in Pain* (Chicago: University of Chicago Press, 2007).

take the risk that the gesture of representation will re-inscribe the ontology of the victim by which the victim is oppressed. This specific risk of representation faces, of course, even those photographers and writers who object to the original act of violence that they re-present.[70]

Beautiful Suffering: Photography and the Traffic in Pain, a 2007 catalogue of photographs and criticism, makes an effort to come to terms with representations of suffering, and the effects of injustice, by theorizing the place of audience as privileged culturally, and protected physically. Representing the work of a diverse group of theorists and critics, the book is unified in its implicit assertion that the audience is safe from threat of war, murder, homelessness, death by starvation or AIDS, fates represented in the photographs that make up the exhibition.[71] *Beautiful Suffering* largely assumes that the audience for photography of suffering is wealthy, Western, straight, and white.

Beautiful Suffering positions its theory of gazing in postmodern terms—rehearsing Sontag's paradigmatic assertion that as a culture we have become saturated with images of violence and have lost, therefore, our capacity to respond meaningfully to such images. But the question of the suffering of the distant other (and a representation is a gesture of distancing) is both older and newer than postmodern theory. Even a photograph taken seconds earlier and placed on a screen emplaces a distance between the audience and the subject of the photograph.

The suffering of the distant other is an ethical question that arises through the fulcrum of representation as such. On the suffering of the distant other, here is Adam Smith writing in 1759:

> Let us suppose that the great empire of China, with all its myriads of inhabitants, was suddenly swallowed up by an earthquake, and let us consider how a man of humanity in Europe, who had no sort of connexion with that part of the world, would be affected upon receiving intelligence of this dreadful calamity. He would … first of all, express very strongly his sorrow for the misfortune of that unhappy people, he would make many melancholy reflections upon the precariousness of human life, and the vanity of all the labours of man, which could thus be annihilated in a moment. … And when all this fine philosophy was over, when all these humane sentiments had been once fairly expressed, he would pursue his business or his pleasure, take his repose or his diversion, with the same ease and tranquillity, as if no such accident had happened. The most frivolous disaster which could befall himself would occasion a more real disturbance.[72]

---

[70] Susan Sontag makes very nearly this argument in the essays contained in *On Photography*, where she famously asserts that photography numbs us into anti-ethical postures.

[71] Reinhardt et al., *Beautiful Suffering: Photography and the Traffic in Pain*.

[72] Adam Smith, *The Theory of Moral Sentiments* (1759; repr., Indianapolis: Liberty Fund, 1984), 233–4; on this topic, please also see Carlo Ginzburg, "Killing a Chinese Mandarin: The Moral Implications of Distance," *Critical Inquiry* 21 (1994): 46–60.

This idea that representation both co-occurs with and also effects distance applies to photographic reportage as well as verbal. Through photographs, as from a distance we see war, famine, and disaster. In response to such visions we may not be personally inconvenienced. We may be affected by representations of violence in very much the way that Smith's representative citizen responds in knee-jerk fashion to hearing of the suffering other. Just as Smith describes the response of a European hearing reportage of mass death in China, we can imagine an American in our time who might look upon a photographic representation of a death by starvation in the Sudan, or mutilation in the Congo, and respond with fine humanitarian sentiments, and then go out and buy a steak and enjoy it, and sleep well that night.[73] Smith suggests that any representation achieves distancing and skews the ethical field.

My argument for the similarity of representation in written text and in photographs draws from Walter Benjamin's theory of the photograph as inhabiting an "optical unconscious," in which photographs work not like physically seeing someone else suffer (literally standing beside a suffering person), but like remembrance distilled, rather like a powerful piece of writing.[74] The minutiae of vision that the camera records, capturing what we see but do not know that we see, makes of the photograph an unconscious space, analogous to Freud's notion of the linguistics of memory in the mystic writing pad, insofar as it gives representation to that which we habitually elide.[75] Indeed, Richard Mosse's project of photographing atrocities in the Democratic Republic of Congo with infrared detecting aerochrome film, achieving a bubble-gum pink quality in the images, plays eerily on the dream-like force of the aesthetic.[76]

The ethical questions photography of suffering poses for its audience are not fundamentally different than those posed by the writing of violence and suffering,

---

[73] Modes of representation by which we learn of the other's suffering predispose the possibilities of our ethical response to that suffering, but do not conclusively write the script of our response. Sontag argued vehemently that photographs were both produced by definitively different inspiration—willed as opposed to passive inspiration—than written pieces, and as well that photographs do not explain the world, only reflect the world, while written text, she argues, is inherently meditative. While the idea of photographs as categorically different forms of signs than written text could be compelling, my point in this chapter is to note that ethically the audience is not in a different relationship to the victim whose suffering is described in a photograph than to the victim whose suffering is described in written text.

[74] Walter Benjamin, "A Small History of Photography," in *One Way Street and Other Writings*, trans. Edmund Jephcott and Kingsley Shorter (London: New Left Books, 1979).

[75] *Sigmund Freud,* "A Note upon the 'Mystic Writing Pad.'" 1925. Trans. James Strachey. *General Psychological Theory*. Ed. Philip Rieff. New York: Touchstone-Simon & Schuster, 1963, 1997. 207–12.

[76] Please see, Marina Galperina, "The War Horrors of Congo in Bubblegum Pink," *ANIMALNewYork*, June 3, 2013, http://animalnewyork.com/2013/the-war-horrors-of-congo-in-bubblegum-pink-richard-mosses-film/ (accessed June 21, 2013).

though there may be a different level of instantiation of the image. A photograph can, in theory, be made more quickly than a written text. And yet for photography and literature of violence, the issues of how one does respond versus how one should respond run parallel. My ethical obligation to the man whose suffering is reported in written text is like my obligation to the photographic subject whose suffering is shown. As Kant's *Metaphysics of Morals* makes clear, emotive response and ethical obligation are not only different things, they are *categorically opposed.*[77] I may, possibly, feel more gut-level emotion looking at Richard Mosse's hot pink images of brutality than reading a news article about the war in the Congo, but the ethical obligation of the audience to both forms of reportage is the same.

A representation wrests its imagery from the world in which it was created: that is representation. A representation also molds its audience's interaction with the image, written or photographed. The impetus to take a photograph, sometimes, is to capture the real.[78] Certainly, the photograph mimics the real with eerie verisimilitude. And yet the photograph does not, once it makes its way to its audience, represent something that is happening *right now in this very instant in the space of the image*. The photograph is not the real, except as representation; it is real only as a representation.

The faux immediacy of the photograph's representation is not that of temporal immediacy in its performance for audiences. For example, if I now look at the horrific image of a starving person taken by photographer James Nachtwey in the Sudan in 1993, featured in *Beautiful Suffering*, the immediacy of the image would be illusory—in purely ethical terms that is, in terms of what I could do to actually help the starving person. Behind the instantaneous look of the photograph is the stopped past that the photograph demarcates rather than replicates. Although the Nachtwey image seems immediate, when I, as audience living far from famine and at a vantage of two decades later, see this image of a fellow human being's starvation, the moment of the photograph is far away and long past. The photograph turns on the illusion of immediacy but its ontology tends towards history.[79]

---

77 Immanuel Kant, *Fundamental Principles of the Metaphysics of Morals*, trans. Thomas Kingsmill Abbott (Raleigh, NC: Alex Catalogue, 1999).

78 Barthes, "The World of Wrestling."

79 Of course, the audience can do something to save others from suffering a similar fate—the entire point of Nachtwey's career, as he claims in the documentary *War Photographer*. Christian Frei et al., *War Photographer* (Brooklyn, NY: First Run Features, 2003). Here, I mean very specifically the audience who sees the photograph. The photographer him or herself is obviously in a different relationship to the victim, and that relationship may be torturously complicated. It would seem clear that when the photographer could help the victim, s/he should do that, but it is unfortunately equally clear that many life or death situations—famine, war, mob violence—do not very easily permit a single photographer to make a difference. Regardless, the audience is always looking at the image after it has been taken, published. Even if published shortly after the image was taken, the image, like journalistic text that reports, almost but never quite instantaneously, reaches the audience as aftermath.

The quickness with which a photograph is shot belies the temporal distance between the instant of its shooting and the photograph's long-term fate as an object that performs for an audience, an object that reaches its audience as aftermath. Even if the photograph is published minutes or seconds after the moment it captures has passed, the immediacy is already gone, because representation, re-presentation, itself belies immediacy; moreover, the usual time difference between the making and the showing of a photograph of violence means the chance to reverse the victim's fate is gone or greatly diminished by the time the audience watches, even if that watching happens only minutes later. In ethical terms, the *feeling of immediacy* that a photograph evokes is not of the essence to the ethical position of the audience.

This feeling of immediacy that accrues around the image in the photograph of a victim may spur the illusion that the audience is somehow more connected to the victim than Smith's hypothetical hearer of the news of mass death on another continent is connected to those hypothetical victims. But despite the visceral tug of, say, Nachtwey's famine victim, the audience is no more or less ethically bound, merely by dint of being an audience, to the starving man whose photograph is seen as to, say, Ellen West, descriptions of whose lengthy death from self-starvation have survived in the work of Ludwig Binswanger. Compared with written text, a photograph gives the audience a greater illusion of proximity to its subject. Carrie Mae Weems's series *From Here I Saw What Happened and I Cried* works brilliantly precisely because Weems's work plays on the conceit of this illusion, using this illusion of immediacy to spur her audience into contemplation of ethics. Weems profoundly understands her medium, the photograph, and deploys its spectral force for contemporary activist purpose.

Fig. 2.1 *From Here I Saw What Happened and I Cried*, Carrie Mae Weems (American, born 1953) 1995. Chromogenic color prints with sandblasted text on glass. "From Here I Saw What Happened." Courtesy of the artist, Carrie Mae Weems, and the Jack Shainman Gallery, NY.

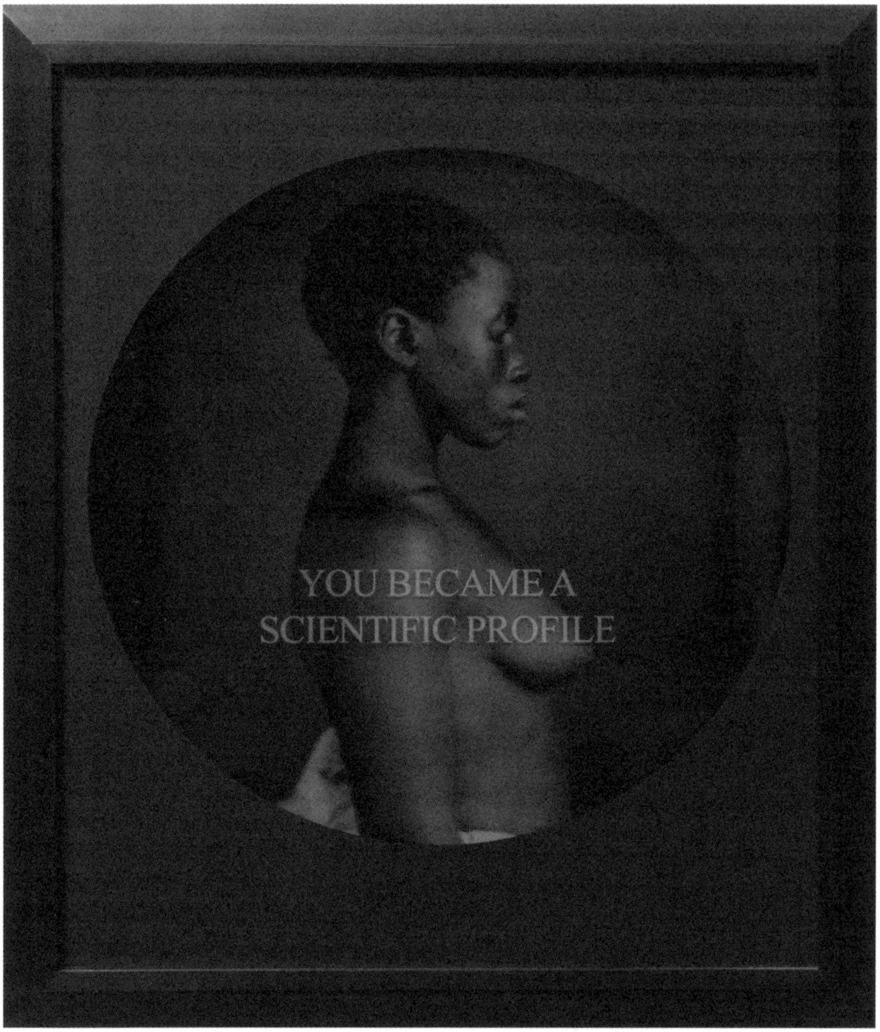

Fig. 2.2 *From Here I Saw What Happened and I Cried*, Carrie Mae Weems (American, born 1953) 1995. Chromogenic color prints with sand-blasted text on glass. "You Became A Scientific Profile." Courtesy of the artist, Carrie Mae Weems, and the Jack Shainman Gallery, NY.

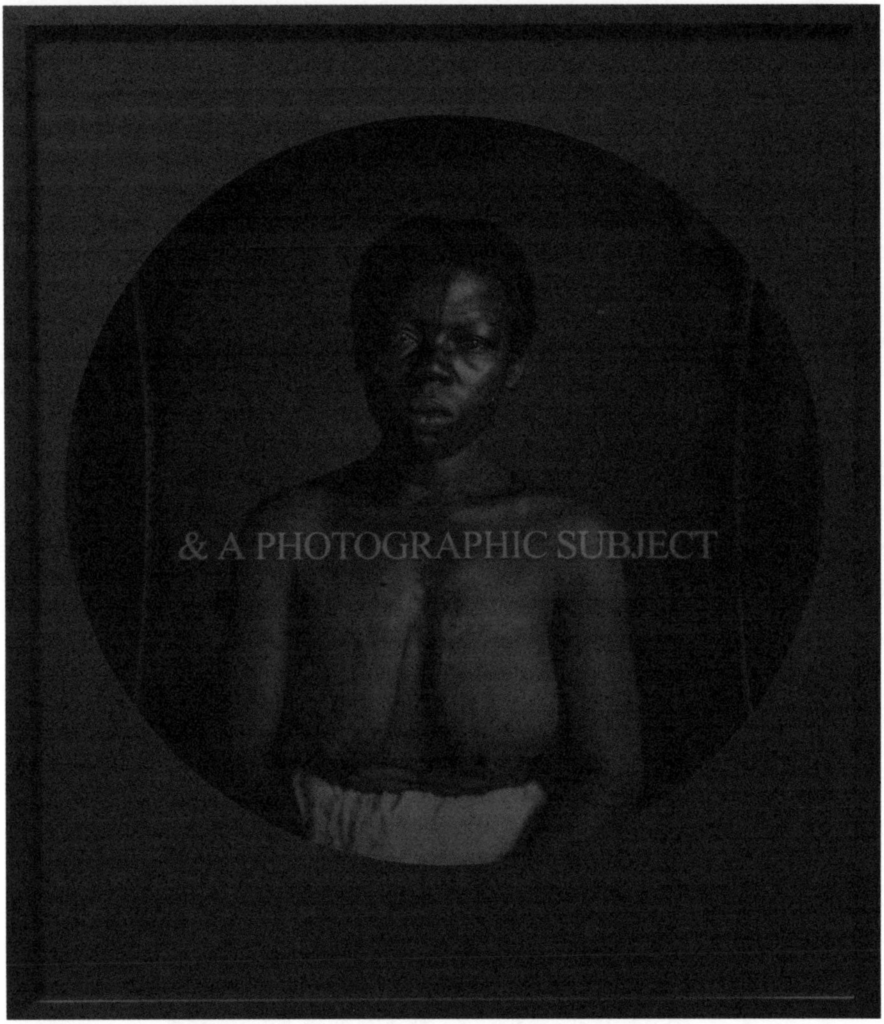

Fig. 2.3 *From Here I Saw What Happened and I Cried*, Carrie Mae Weems (American, born 1953) 1995. Chromogenic color prints with sand-blasted text on glass. "& A Photographic Subject." Courtesy of the artist, Carrie Mae Weems, and the Jack Shainman Gallery, NY.

Fig. 2.4 *From Here I Saw What Happened and I Cried*, Carrie Mae Weems (American, born 1953) 1995. Chromogenic color prints with sand-blasted text on glass. "And I Cried." Courtesy of the artist, Carrie Mae Weems, and the Jack Shainman Gallery, NY.

Chapter 3
Sacrificed Daughters and the Grammar of Enslavement in Toni Morrison's *Beloved*, Flannery O'Connor's "A View of the Woods," and Dorothy Allison's *Bastard Out of Carolina*

Toni Morrison's *Beloved* is positioned, by its powerful dedication to the "Sixty Million and More" who died during America's enslavement of Africans, as a novel written to mourn the unnamed dead.[1] The violence depicted in *Beloved* by this dedication is positioned as violence explicitly offered for the purpose of catharsis and grieving. In this chapter, I look at two other works written during the twentieth century and placed in the South that, like *Beloved*, depict an extraordinary level of violence against daughters. I make this move to query the terms by which we read these representations of violence, focusing my inquiry on the figure of the sacrificial daughter that ties together these texts. The daughters are sacrificed with flagrant violence. Flannery O'Connor's story "A View of the Woods" describes in graphic detail a grandfather beating his granddaughter's head against a rock until she dies. Dorothy Allison's *Bastard Out of Carolina* represents a no-holds-barred depiction of incestuous rape. *Beloved* frames the horrifying tableau of a mother slitting her baby daughter's throat to save the little girl from enslavement.

Bastard Out of Carolina is positioned, by its status as memoir, as heroic self-revelation, its author laying bare cultural truths of gender and violence that shaped her life. *Beloved* forges its link to the historical real in the novel's foreword, where Morrison states that the novel is based on the figure of Margaret Garner, the enslaved woman who killed her infant daughter in 1856 rather than see her returned to slavery.[2] *Beloved*, "A View of the Woods," and *Bastard Out of Carolina* contain scenes of intense violence, culminating, respectively, in the slaughter of an infant, the brutal murder of a young girl, and a young girl's graphically rendered rape.

1 In a 1989 *Time Magazine* interview, Morrison was asked about this dedication. Asked the question, "*Beloved* is dedicated to the 60 million who died as a result of slavery. A staggering number—is this proved historically?" Toni Morrison answers, "Some historians told me 200 million died. The smallest number I got from anybody was 60 million. A lot of people died. Half of them died in those ships." See Bonnie Angelo, "The Pain of Being Black: An Interview with Toni Morrison," *Time Magazine* 133, no. 21 (May 22, 1989): 120–23.

2 Morrison, *Beloved*, xvii.

The scene of the beaten child, Freud describes as the iconic form of masochism.[3] In this chapter focusing on the representation of the beating, murder, and rape of daughters, I ask: what if the beaten child wants to connect *not* with the sadistic father who beats her but instead with the surrounding others—mothers, aunts, and other womanly watchers of violence—who watch the scene of the abused child? For I believe that Morrison, O'Connor, and Allison address just these people, the hoped-for redeemers, the womanly watchers. And in Morrison, O'Connor, and Allison, the watchers are mothers, or motherly. The problem of the witness who watches the sadistic violation of a young girl and either does not respond or responds in ways that do not save the sacrificed daughter is a central concern raised by *Beloved*, "A View of the Woods," and *Bastard Out of Carolina*.

Despite the different reception histories of these works—Morrison's and Allison's representations of violence are often read as activist works, O'Connor's often read as grotesque—Morrison's depictions of torture in *Beloved* are similar in intensity to O'Connor's evocations of a child's murder in "A View of the Woods," and while Allison's *Bastard* does not contain literal child sacrifice, the raping of the young daughter is described in terms that evoke the sacrifice of the child, the phallus described as a weapon-like object gouging the child's interior. Each of these twentieth-century texts, then, circulates the representation of the image of the sacrificed child who is a girl. In drawing parallels and looking at connections between these works I do not intend to elide that problematic of race that should and must be considered in reading texts written about the South.[4] And yet the similarity of these depictions of violence bears comparison not despite but because of the differences of race perspective that the works engage. That is, Morrison explicitly wrote *Beloved* to commemorate sacrificed, enslaved women, while Allison explicitly positioned *Bastard Out of Carolina* as a text that she wrote to heal from violent, childhood, sexual abuse, and O'Connor wrote "A View of the Woods" as a form of religious practice, to expose the violence needed to open religious belief.[5] And all three writers converge on the figure of the sacrificed daughter.

The question I raise in this chapter is how does the representation of the sacrifice of the daughter function as that revelation which lays bare the fabric

---

[3] Freud, "A Child Is Being Beaten," 405–6.

[4] See Flannery O'Connor, *The Habit of Being: Letters*, ed. Sally Fitzgerald (New York: Farrar, Straus, Giroux, 1979) for O'Connor's collected letters. See also Toni Morrison, *Playing in the Dark: Whiteness and the Literary Imagination* (Cambridge, MA: Harvard University Press, 1992).

[5] See Kelly Gerald, "Flannery O'Connor and the Habit of Art," *Paris Review Daily*, April 30, 2012, http://www.theparisreview.org/blog/2012/04/30/flannery-o%E2%80%99connor-and-the-habit-of-art/ (accessed August 4, 2012); see also Carolyn E. Megan, "Moving Toward Truth: An Interview with Dorothy Allison," *The Kenyon Review* 16 (Autumn 1994): 71–83; Susanna Rustin, "Predicting the Past," *The Guardian*, October 31, 2008, http://www.guardian.co.uk/books/2008/nov/01/toni-morrison (accessed August 4, 2012).

of a culture, in particular the culture in common between Morrison's *Beloved*, Allison's *Bastard*, and O'Connor's "A View of the Woods," the traditional slave-holding or Jim Crow South: the racist South. Morrison's *Beloved* is a repository of represented violations—rapes, beatings, death by fire, hanging, and a baby's throat slit in graphic clarity of red—and the sheer range of violations described has led to the charge that Morrison, in her most acclaimed novel, writes melodrama.[6] Melodrama is a charge that has also been leveled at O'Connor, placing her in the "Southern grotesque" rather than realist tradition.[7] Likewise, Dorothy Allison's *Bastard Out of Carolina* has been both lauded as a kind of purifying testimony, a truth told with religious reverence, and also condemned as too similar to Allison's earlier work as a porn writer.[8] These ambivalences in reception are my point of entrance into these texts insofar as I believe reception history reflects the way that we read the image of the sacrificed girl child, this image that I will argue underlies the traditional South.

What differentiates Morrison's *Beloved*, O'Connor's "A View of the Woods," and Allison's *Bastard Out of Carolina* from melodrama is the coolness of their tactics of witnessing, a stricture of narrative distancing, an effect of placing boundaries on emotion, as they present events that qualify as melodrama, a kind of operatic quality attending them. But I will argue that Morrison's novel, O'Connor's story, and Allison's novel, are not melodrama. They dramatize a sacrifice underlying a culture, and in this sense function as a kind of expiation of a collective representation.

Grammar of Enslavement

The writing of violence is not always melodrama insofar as melodrama means that which is both exaggerated and stereotypical. In the hands of Morrison, O'Connor, and Allison, representations of violence are decidedly not stereotypical. More to the point, the killing of Mary Fortune Pitts, in "A View of the Woods," the killing of Beloved in *Beloved*, and the rape of Bone in *Bastard Out of Carolina*, are not necessarily exaggerations of what is done to female children in the patriarchy of the slave-holding and Jim Crow South. Indeed, Morrison's novel, as noted, is based on Margaret Garner, who killed her daughter to save her from returning to slavery. In this sense, Morrison, O'Connor, and Allison are not exaggerating the risk to a young girl's body in this culture, but instead are laying bare the way that the representational force of this sacrificial girl's body structures the culture as a

---

6 See Stanley Crouch, "Aunt Medea," in *Notes of a Hanging Judge: Essays and Reviews, 1979–1989* (New York: Oxford University Press, 1990).

7 Please see Patricia Yaeger, *Dirt and Desire: Reconstructing Southern Women's Writing, 1930–1990* (Chicago: University of Chicago Press, 2000).

8 Dorothy Allison's response is the book *The Women Who Hate Me* (Hanover, NH: Smith and Kraus, 2006).

whole.[9] That Morrison depicts the sacrifice of the enslaved child while O'Connor and Allison depict the sacrifice of the impoverished white child is not central to my argument. That does not mean that I think slavery was equivalent to other forms of violence in the traditional South; rather my argument will be that the practice of enslavement—the grammar of enslavement—shaped the treatment of the female body *tout court*. My concern is with the phenomenon of the representation of violence as an entity. The representation of violence against girls, in the texts considered in this chapter, pivots around the painful and differently resolved problem of the female witness to that violence.

The centrality of witnessing in Morrison's novel is established by the creation of the extraordinary character, Beloved, a character Teresa de Lauretis memorably calls a figure for the abyss of subjectivity, the "inexpressible chasm in the self that Toni Morrison named Beloved."[10] Daughter, lover, antagonist, ghost, the character Beloved exists structurally in the novel *Beloved* to elicit tales of the gesture of Sethe's witnessing violence; *all* the violence Sethe has witnessed and experienced is the violence of slavery. The impetus for the ghost's appearance, structurally, is to cause Sethe to tell the tales of horror that shape the novel's arc and also to give Sethe her audience, figured in the novel as Beloved. The ghost arrives to hear the tales of violence that Sethe has to tell and, structurally, this character Beloved is the device by which Morrison's novel generates the telling of Sethe's tales of violence.

Sethe's baby girl is not a benign ghost, and the ghost's capacity for violence reflects that the arguably most violent act of the novel—the murder of a baby girl by her mother—is enacted against this very character Beloved who performs as both victim and interlocutor in the novel. Morrison characterizes Sethe, the witness, through her stories of violence and testimony in memory of her own prolicide, by a chilling stillness. Beloved is hungry for Sethe's narrative of horror: and Beloved's murder at her mother's hands is at the very center, the very heart, of Sethe's story of violence. The story of her own death is the one Beloved longs insatiably to hear.

Yet unlike insatiable Beloved, Sethe is able to survive during and after her act of prolicide because she is an "iron-eyed" witness, a character capable of watching

---

9 One could not possibly list all the texts, histories, and studies that investigate violence against African American women and violence against all girls as cultural realities. However, here are a few: George Levesque and Nikola Baumgarten, "A Monstrous Inconsistency: Slavery, Ideology and Politics in the Age of the American Revolution," *Contributions in Black Studies* 8 (1986): 20–34; Maxine D. Jones, "The Rosewood Massacre and the Women Who Survived It," *Florida Historical Quarterly* 76 (1997): 193–208; Ervin L. Jordan, Jr., "Sleeping with the Enemy: Sex, Black Women, and the Civil War," *Western Journal of Black Studies* 18 (1994): 55–63; Jennifer Freyd, *Betrayal Trauma: The Logic of Forgetting Childhood Abuse* (Cambridge, MA: Harvard University Press, 1996); Judith Lewis Herman *Father Daughter Incest* (Cambridge, MA: Harvard University Press, 1981).

10 Teresa de Lauretis, *Figures of Resistance: Essays in Feminist Theory*, ed. Patricia White (Urbana: University of Illinois Press, 2007), 256.

extreme violence, including that which she enacts, and never turning away by succumbing to madness.[11] Sethe's status as an iron-eyed witness is essential to the novel's narrative momentum. Iron as a substance becomes not just repeating metaphor but functional integument for the novel. The word *iron* occurs frequently in the first chapter in conjunction with Sethe. Sethe is introduced as "iron-eyed," as the narrative clarifies that even as a young girl Sethe was marked as a witness figure: "Sethe was thirteen when she came to Sweet Home and already iron-eyed."[12] Sethe is further described as "Halle's girl—the one with iron eyes and backbone to match."[13] Her near-destruction by schoolteacher is described as punching the iron out of her eyes: "But what he did broke three more Sweet Home men and punched the glittering iron out of Sethe's eyes, leaving two open wells that did not reflect firelight."[14] Indeed, her iron eyes appear to prevent the enslaved men of Sweet Home from raping her: "They let the iron-eyed girl be, so she could choose in spite of the fact that each one would have beaten the others to mush to have her."[15] The iron eyes embody the dignified ethos of the enslaved in the face of the master's barbarity. Sethe's scar, the choke cherry tree, is described as iron work: "when the top of her dress was around her hips and he saw the sculpture her back had become [it looked] like the decorative work of an ironsmith too passionate for display."[16] A woman whose gaze is iron and whose very flesh becomes imbued with the properties of iron, Sethe is the paradigmatic witness figure, the figure who sees and is marked by, and therefore remembers in her body, every violation: a witness who does not succumb to madness despite the extremes of torture she must witness—her imperviousness tested by the appearance of her murdered revenant daughter.

Sethe regrets this gift of the ability to always remember lucidly violence that drives others to blindness or madness—she asks pointedly why her mind won't refuse the knowledge of her husband's having watched while she was raped, the boys taking her milk, since her husband lost his sanity as a result of this watching. By Sethe's tenacious grip on sanity and on memory she becomes a paradigmatic witness figure in a novel of apocalyptic violations. And yet Sethe's implicit double, the daughter she murdered to save her from slavery, is equally stalwart insofar

---

[11] Iron is clearly a leitmotif in *Beloved*. What I wish to point out is that iron is also used as a substance that fuses the gaze with the gazed upon. Eyes are iron and also ruined flesh is iron, in *Beloved*. In other words, the metal is invoked in Morrison's novel to forge, if you will, the way that the act of looking shapes the gazed-upon body. Images of madness also percolate through the novel—Paul D. "saw a witless colored woman jailed and hanged for stealing ducks she believed were her own babies" and also watched Halle's descent into madness, "Last time I saw him he was sitting by the churn. He had butter all over his face" (78, 80).

[12] Morrison, *Beloved*, 10.

[13] Morrison, *Beloved*, 8.

[14] Morrison, *Beloved*, 9.

[15] Morrison, *Beloved*, 10.

[16] Morrison, *Beloved*, 17. Please also see Morrison, *Beloved*, 12, 14.

as she returns from the dead to claim her place in Sethe's house.[17] Beloved's function in the novel is this return to listen to, and thereby conjure, Sethe's story of violation.[18] Beloved also is a witness, or, as Avery Gordon puts it, Beloved the ghost is herself haunted.[19]

The "work of an ironsmith too passionate for display," the metaphor Morrison uses to describe the scar on Sethe's back, the scar that records her vicious beating, while pregnant, at Sweet Home, indicates the kind of witnessing that Sethe performs.[20] She does not rest on the surface, watching the victim and telling the story of violation like a film. Instead, she enters the space of violation, and is marked by her multiple acts of witnessing to such a degree that her own innocence is compromised (she is jailed for her daughter's killing, maybe jailed justifiably). Witnessing compromises Sethe's innocence specifically in the sense that her innate nature of being a witness—a character type that Morrison develops thoroughly with Sethe—also drives her to kill the child whose degradation she cannot bear to see. "Too passionate for display" indicates the graphic and murderous terms of witnessing that Morrison's novel explores in its effort to trace one strand in the history of enslavement in the American South.[21] Sethe is too passionate to show her emotions, a pattern that the other women of her community read as pride.

Sethe's iron-eyed gaze ultimately turns her body to iron. Sethe's iron-eyed witnessing is a phenomenon the import of which partly inheres in the way in which the witness's depicted action of watching implicates us, the audience. The novel's rejection of sentimentality asserts a mode of witnessing in which the witness is inscribed in text even as the text calls for witnessing from its audience. The centrality of the daughter sacrifice, re-envisioned as representation, presents a healing-violence-by-representing-violence paradox. *Beloved* centers on the act of sacrificially murdering a daughter figure, the killing allowing the family to move forward into the post-slavery nation. The text is obsessed with the problematic of the sacrificial body eviscerated by the brutal effects of slavery and racism as systems of unlimited domination, and also haunted by the female body harmed and mutilated by slavery, racism, and misogyny, the memory of which is suppressed as time moves forward into the world of aftermath—postmodern, post-feminist, post-racial. The novel leverages depictions of extreme violence and sadistic voyeurism

---

17 Sethe says of Beloved, the sacrifice, "You came right on back like a good girl, a daughter." Morrison, *Beloved*, 238.

18 This need to explain to the killed girl why she was killed is compulsive: "I'll explain to her even though I don't have to … Now I can look at things again because she's here to see them too." Telling becomes relief to one who already knows, in the sense that the murdered revenant can bear everything. Morrison, *Beloved*, 183.

19 Avery Gordon, *Ghostly Matters: Haunting and the Sociological Imagination* (Minneapolis: University of Minnesota Press, 2008), 175.

20 Morrison, *Beloved*, 17.

21 Caroline Rody, "Toni Morrison's *Beloved*: History, 'Rememory,' and a 'Clamor for a Kiss,'" *American Literary History* 7 (Spring 1995): 92–119.

to argue for some residual persistence of the effect of violation—to argue that those who are violated, even if they're killed, don't disappear.

Beloved asks its audience to refuse to accept the disappearance of the sacrificed other. And yet it simultaneously presents the moment of the murdered young girl as that moment in which is engineered the survival of the rest of the family. This act of killing the daughter implicates us, the audience who occupy the space of survivors, in the questionable ethical position of benefitting from the sacrificial murder of the young daughter.[22] Although we as audience may benefit only in the sense of experiencing the aesthetic power of the presentation of violence, in reading these texts our position is profoundly problematic in the sense that we, like the witness figure embedded in the text, cannot act to appease or deter the violence enacted on the body of the young girl.[23] *Beloved* presents the sacrifice of the daughter's body in depressingly nihilistic terms, suggesting that in our culture this is the oblation. Denver drinking her killed sister's blood, as in medieval imagery of Christ's blood as milk, strongly suggests the sacrificial terms of Morrison's novel's symbolic landscape.[24]

Morrison is concerned intensely with the violence of racism in *Beloved*. The implicit treatment of race that O'Connor brings to the symbolic tale, "A View of the Woods," a tale that lays bare the violence of the one-drop rule, is also a powerful revelation of the intractability of racism, a tragic vision.[25] In "A View of the Woods" that paradigm of evil exposed is the fusion of racism and sexism that leads the grandfather Mark Fortune to murder his granddaughter Mary Fortune because he sees her as a product of miscegenation—not *all* Fortune, not all his flesh and blood, but mixed with the blood of the Pittses.[26] It expresses O'Connor's

---

[22] Travis, "Beyond Empathy," 231–50.

[23] If it is naïve to assume that an audience for a scholarly book, a book of criticism, could not possibly enjoy the sadistic gaze analyzed in these pages, it is worth considering whether this conceit of the innocence of the reader is in line with Morrison's authorial project, or indeed with Allison's, or O'Connor's.

[24] Sharon Patricia Holland suggests that if we read the novel drawing on West African religious tropes, the sacrifice and revenance of Beloved also becomes a scene of rebirth. See, Holland, *Raising the Dead: Readings of Death and (Black) Subjectivity* (Durham: Duke University Press, 2000), 24.

[25] In terms of reading Morrison, Allison, and O'Connor side by side, considerations of representations of race could be informed by the authors' personal testimony. O'Connor lived most of her adult life in a refurbished, family plantation home, a house built by slave labor, an ethically compromised position. See Alice Walker, *In Search of Our Mothers' Gardens: Womanist Prose* (San Diego: Harcourt Brace Jovanovich, 1983). And yet in my readings of O'Connor's stories, I am hewing more toward consideration of the work from within rather than as refracted through the authors' letters and interviews. This focus is in keeping with my emphasis on *the act of representation* of violence as the object to analyze.

[26] Here I mean that O'Connor represents the Southern obsession with "blood" transposing that obsession from race, since both Pitts and Fortune seem to be Caucasian, to simply *blood* as such. What she reveals is the nightmare incestuous logic of the "one-

emphasis on the depth of the structure of racism that forms the cognitive frame for patriarchy in the South. Given the racist views O'Connor espouses in her letters, we can only guess what enables her to write short fiction that critiques the structure of racism. Maybe that is a mystery of faith.

While in "A View of the Woods" Mark Fortune's son-in-law Pitts is also white, the story takes up the conceptual frame of Southern fears of miscegenation, this obsessive fear that white might contain black, or vice versa, a perpetual anxiety in the Reconstruction and Jim Crow South. O'Connor mines this madness and writes this story of fear by using the hierarchically coded names Fortune and Pitts, white and black in the hierarchical codes of the Jim Crow South. A writer steeped in the racial codes of the South has written a story violently and depressingly expositive of the brutal torque of miscegenation paranoia; obviously that does not mean that O'Connor was victimized by these codes, only that she saw them firsthand and wrote about what she saw. This point is not to say that it doesn't matter that O'Connor sometimes sounds racist in her personal letters. Rather it is to say that O'Connor's sense of the intractability of racism makes "A View of the Woods" depressing but also curiously, given that O'Connor wrote it, *anti*-racist. The story argues implicitly that racism merges with misogyny in an apocalyptic violence that must be fought against.

Like *Beloved*, "A View of the Woods" is Nietzschean—both stories explore the notion of human nature as ill-fated, violent, pleasured by bloodshed. Is *Beloved* a redemptive novel? Some have argued that it is. In *Beloved* sadism is ascribed to whites, who are called bad luck, and are associated with supernatural evil, while in O'Connor's oeuvre, sadistic, post-lapsarian human nature is ascribed to all characters. "A View of the Woods" offers no redemption within the story but, possibly, redemption may come through the response of its readers, if the reader is encouraged by the story to disagree with the one-drop rule and the ideology that spawned that system of racism.

The positioning of images of violence raises other questions in response to *Beloved*, *Bastard Out of Carolina*, and "A View of the Woods." Allison stages the effect of representation by setting up her central character Bone as a teller of violent tales, giving Bone an audience that parallels Allison's audience. O'Connor raises the question of spectacle by invoking the gaze of the murdered girl in her title, "A *View* of the Woods." Morrison risks everything, narratively, by writing a main character who performs extreme violence so that it shall be seen. When Sethe murders her daughter, she does so not only to spare her daughter the unending humiliation of being enslaved to schoolteacher but also to mirror

drop rule." On this question, please see Nicholas Crawford, "An Africanist Impasse: Race, Return, and Revelation in the Short Fiction of Flannery O'Connor," *South Atlantic Review* 68 (Spring 2003): 1–25; also, Sura P. Rath and Mary Neff Shaw, eds., *Flannery O'Connor: New Perspectives* (Athens: University of Georgia Press, 1996); for a concise exploration of race laws, please see Robert Westley "First-Time Encounters: 'Passing' Revisited and Demystification as a Critical Practice," *Yale Law and Policy Review* 18 (2000): 297–349.

back to schoolteacher, the sadistic master, his own sadism. The violence of killing the infant daughter is performed because seeing the sacrificed infant frightens schoolteacher enough to stop him from taking Sethe and her remaining children back into slavery. She hopes to "out-hurt the hurter," to stop schoolteacher's sadism by reflecting it back to him.[27] This proscenium effect in common between the three works indicates their investment in the claims of representation.

Even as in the story of the historical Margaret Garner, by whom *Beloved* was inspired, the tactic of murdering her daughter accomplished little—Garner and her surviving children were returned to slavery—in Morrison's novel the performed sacrifice does save the other daughter, Denver, and even the mother, Sethe.[28] In other words, it is Morrison's virtuosity in framing questions of the means and meaning of representation that makes of the scene of sadism a readable pivot for her novel even as its outcome, of redemption, does not reflect the known historical reality.

What Teresa de Lauretis terms the "Violence of Rhetoric," the capacity of the act of representation to repeat the sadism it describes, functions powerfully in *Beloved*. De Lauretis's idea, of rhetoric as inherently linked to violence, is relevant to Sethe's later narrations of her story. Sethe compulsively tells her story of violence. The act of killing her infant firstly was itself conceived as an act of representation: she performed for schoolteacher the logical extension of his sadism to show him the meaning of this sadistic system of enslavement.[29] The success of Sethe's tactic of performing sadism, firstly by killing her daughter for the audience of schoolteacher and then by repeating for Paul D. the story of this killing of her daughter, determines the structure of the novel—her success in "out-hurt[ing] the hurter" by opening her daughter's throat with a saw works insofar as schoolteacher, who has come to reclaim his so-called property (according to the notorious Fugitive Act) turns back and goes south without his quarry.[30] But

---

27 Morrison, *Beloved*, 234.

28 Gordon's *Ghostly Matters* pays tribute to Morrison's *Beloved* in both the introduction and in a long central chapter, "not only the footprints but the water too and what is down there." Gordon's book gives a good history of the real Margaret Garner. Please see Avery Gordon, *Ghostly Matters*, 137–93. Margaret Garner was very likely a child born of master/slave rape and was as well raped by her uncle, the white man who owned her, he from whom she sought to save her infant daughter, with a logic that is very hard to deny. She was trying to protect her child from incest. Like Sethe, Margaret Garner was married and gave birth to children who were her husband's progeny. Unlike Sethe, Margaret Garner was both a product and victim of racist rape. To be clear, the historical Margaret Garner would have had overwhelmingly compelling reasons to believe that her daughter, should she be re-enslaved, would be raped, humiliated, and debased by white men to whom she was biologically related. Morrison's novel is less horrific than the real story.

29 As opposed to other systems of slavery that did not necessarily depend on the belief in the subhuman status of the enslaved. Please see Orlando Patterson, *Slavery and Social Death: A Comparative Study* (Cambridge, MA: Harvard University Press, 1982).

30 Morrison, *Beloved*, 234.

the tactic also works in that the repetition of the description of violence is staged in the novel so that the audience comes to occupy a place analogous either to schoolteacher's or Paul D.'s. Reading the violence, the audience is challenged, as Paul D. is challenged, to give ourselves wholly to the project of recuperation.

Morrison couches schoolteacher's terrified response to Sethe's violence in both practical and psychological language. Schoolteacher pragmatically decides that his "property," Sethe, has shown herself too damaged to be worth the retrieval. The quality of this damage inheres in Sethe's response to watching her own act of killing her child. As the scene plays out, schoolteacher sees that Sethe has cut open the throat of the baby girl whom she holds in her arms and he, schoolteacher, steps back terrified—the scene of violence is extreme enough to find the limit of schoolteacher's sadism, the visual mark he can no longer bear to watch.[31] And yet even this limit does not challenge the paradigm of sadism that has inculcated in schoolteacher a desire to prove that enslaved African Americans are bestial in essence. On the contrary, schoolteacher analogizes Sethe to a damaged horse, a brute creature. Sethe's act of violence defeats schoolteacher's goal of remanding her and her children into slavery; despite that, she does not change his cognitive structure of pleasure in sadism. Indeed, she succeeds *because* she operates within this system, beating him at his own game.[32]

Authoring (the Body as) Text

In killing her small and treasured daughter, her "best thing," Sethe violently grabs the reins of the linked symbolic performances that govern enslavement.[33] I do not mean here that enslavement is only a symbolic system: needless to say it produced massive, real, bodily effects.[34] Rather, the engine of enslavement, as the effect of Sethe's killing of her daughter makes clear, is the way that the enslaver (schoolteacher) authors the script, creating and parsing meaning across the bodies of those he has captured. The grammar of enslavement in the scene of

31 Morrison, *Beloved*, 174.

32 Schoolteacher repeats twice his claim that Sethe is a "creature"; to say Sethe beats schoolteacher at his own game is to take for granted that the system of slavery has twisted the ethics of the novel, making ethical luminosity impossible for anyone, winning impossible for anyone in this Nietzschean scenario. And I mention Nietzsche not to invoke the Überman but rather the bitter sadistic impossibility that clarifies Nietzsche's analysis of power.

33 Morrison, *Beloved*, 262.

34 To think through this question of physicality in Morrison's novel, please see Jean Wyatt, "Giving Body to the Word: The Maternal Symbolic in Toni Morrison's *Beloved*," *PMLA* 108, no. 3 (1993): 474–88. On slavery and the social symbolic, see Orlando Patterson's *Slavery and Social Death*, in which Patterson makes the incredibly influential argument that enslavement works by symbolically killing the enslaved who then occupy the realm of the socially dead.

the daughter's killing is revealed as the grammar of humiliation. Sethe refuses that grammar insofar as her refusal to have her children measured as bestial manifests as a universal and absolute refusal: she refuses schoolteacher's terms of dehumanization even though she cannot refuse his terms of sadism. It may be humiliating—among other things—to Sethe to have no recourse under the system of slavery other than to kill her child, and yet in degrading herself by performing this act that prompts Paul D. to compare her to an animal, Sethe protects her child from a lifetime of humiliation.[35]

Sethe becomes the author of the story in this act of violence. Her authority is created by an act (killing her child) that places Sethe on a foundation of such radical loss that the novel's culminating in Sethe's symbolic of death and rebirth is the only possible logic of survival. The rhetoric of violence is Sethe's claim and yet Sethe, like "crawling already? baby girl" must crawl by the end of the novel. Sethe's act of killing her daughter gradually erases Sethe, and yet it stands as an act of authority, *the* act of authority in the novel. That is, the act that Sethe chooses she *authors* in the sense of writing on her daughter's body this act. And this act of her killing her daughter is the reiterated fact—the authority—that guides the narrative.

The return of the dead girl, the revenant, cannot give back to Sethe what she lost, but this figure of the revenant does indicate the way that the story shows the grammar of enslavement: for the ghost-as-revenant stands as that marker *par excellence* of the symbolic of loss, and shows the way that language can reveal the terms of enslavement, even though, as schoolteacher's notebooks make clear, language, the violence of rhetoric, also sets the terms of enslavement. What I mean is that Morrison writes, in her novel, the grammar of enslavement, insofar as she writes violence to expiate violence. Her language is the expiation of the language of slavery, a catharsis; Morrison's grammar is the expiation of the grammar of enslavement.

Sethe becomes an *author—one who takes authority through inscription*—in the scene in which she, by killing her beloved daughter, refuses not only her submissive position in schoolteacher's code but as well refuses her place in the semiotic chain, her place as a mother who replicates herself as a sexually violated daughter (and who under the terms of enslavement for women creates the renewable victim of white-on-black, master-on-slave rape).[36] Sethe refuses schoolteacher's grammar and the terms she asserts for her dignity, her status as an end and not a means, have nothing to do with survival. In effect, she refuses survival and by chance is spared to tell the story of that refusal in her own terms. The terms of the grammar of

---

[35] Paul D., horrified by the story she tells, comments "You got two feet Sethe, not four." Morrison, *Beloved*, 194.

[36] As Roland Barthes indicates in "The Death of the Author," the struggle between author and reader is one of fatality, mortality. Barthes writes in structuralist metaphors, arguing that the death of our false concept of authority is necessary for proper reading, but Morrison's novel exemplifies Barthes's argument.

enslavement are *not* Sethe's own and yet the novel so violently breaks these terms as to leave space for Morrison, writing in memoriam to the historical Margaret Garner, to write outside and against the egregious grammar of racism.

But Sethe can tell this story of forging, as in iron, in her own grammar only when the embodied ghost, the revenant, arrives at her doorstep to *ask* her for the story. Only Beloved can function as the proper witness to Sethe because only Beloved is the sacrificed girl. Here is the function of the sacrificial girl: as a zero sign Beloved absorbs the violence of one system of signification in order to allow others to forge a new one. She persists as the evocation of erased footprints that foreclose the novel's ending and yet are not completely erased in that they persist yet in the novel as representation. The violence of rhetoric masters, in Morrison's novel of the grammar of enslavement, the violence of rhetoric: only the devil can eat the devil out.[37] "Not only the footprints but the water too and all that is down there" works as an explicit *coda* to make the novel endless, a circle to which we must return for the sake of the sacrificed for whom there was and is no reprieve.[38] The sacrificed remain sacrificed even as survivors gain a new language that erases the terms by which the sacrificed were (almost) completely erased. The impossibility of escape from the effects of violence is structured into the coda of Morrison's novel (though Denver escapes, Beloved never can). And this structure asks, demands of the audience, what kind of witnessing do we perform?

Watching with Iron-Eyes

Beyond the surface and virulent racism that guides schoolteacher's actions, he ironically is able, fleetingly, to see Sethe's humanity when he recognizes that what has been broken in her connects to what is broken in him.[39] They have both witnessed the violation of the sacrificial daughter's body, and they have both been broken by the visual manifestation of this sacrificial body. In other words, schoolteacher and Sethe share the moment of spectating sadism.[40] Schoolteacher describes Sethe, after her violent act, as if she had disappeared—"nothing left to claim"—and this erasure indicates that for him, her substance was coterminous

37 Sylvia Plath, "Witch Burning," in *The Collected Poems* (New York: Harper Perennial, 1980), 135.

38 Morrison, *Beloved*, 322.

39 Note that this moment of seeing does not *change* schoolteacher's racist trajectory. Instead, he disappears from the novel, indicating his almost satanic identity as purely racist. On the riddle of *Beloved*'s ending, please see Mary Paniccia Carden, "Models of Memory and Romance: The Dual Endings of Toni Morrison's *Beloved*," *Twentieth Century Literature* 45, no. 4 (Winter 1999): 401–27.

40 Here I again define my use of the term sadism to emphasize that in this book I do not by the term sadism mean Freudian sexual sadism. For a consideration of ethics that is not primarily concerned with sadism in *Beloved*, see Yung-Hsing Wu, "Doing Things with Ethics: Beloved, Sula and the Reading of Judgment," *Modern Fiction Studies* 49, no. 4 (2003): 780–805.

with passive acceptance of suffering. And yet Sethe survives in Morrison's novel, a character not entirely coterminous with suffering.[41]

Sethe is closest to schoolteacher's subjectivity in the moment that she performs the logical extension of his sadistic program—the voyeuristically offered sacrifice of her own daughter's body. It is an act that ingeniously expands to its logical conclusion schoolteacher's erotics of submission: that is, schoolteacher's desire for the absolute sacrifice as erotic fulfillment. It reveals the sadistic visual underpinnings of racism—the notion that only the violation of the enslaved female body can continue the programmatic of racism—the desire to mark and fragment the sacrificial victim whose marked and fragmented body underwrites the power of the slave owner.[42] Ultimately, Sethe herself participates in this contestation of power: she has had no choice. The witnessing position of iron-eyed Sethe—who never looks away, who sees everything without diverting her mind to madness—manifests as a crisis of witnessing in *Beloved.* It is precisely Sethe's ability to see everything and never turn away that is necessary for testimony, and yet it precludes any response to violence but *rememory*. Only because Sethe's capacity for recording events of violence and humiliation is extraordinary do we hear her story. Sethe cannot circumvent the sadism of slavery. But by telling the story, Sethe opens an ethically ambiguous space. Sethe's mother slaps the young girl Sethe when she sees her mother's brand and begs, "Mark me too"; by contrast, Sethe the storyteller of horrors marks her audience—her daughters Denver and Beloved—exactly where her own mother, kidnapped from West Africa, hanged in America, refused to mark Sethe.[43]

Morrison's novel thus calls for an interpretation of language as physical mark and space. Morrison's neologism "rememory" inscribes in the novel the idea of memory that is physical—not inside the body of the one who remembers but in the landscape that is remembered—an intensely, provocatively, architectonic definition of memory. Words, thoughts, and actions are written into place; for example, Sethe remembers the truth of her mother's love for her only when she fleetingly recalls the West African language her mother spoke. Language here becomes a physical container, a house, like 124.[44] Language is a physical inscription, a mark,

---

41 Aisha Damali Lockride, "Toni Morrison's *Beloved*: Origins," *Callaloo* 33 (Summer 2010): 892–4; Justine Tally, *Toni Morrison's* Beloved*: Origins* (New York: Routledge, 2009).

42 Sharon Patricia Holland draws on Hortense Spillers's term "vestibular" to describe the singular position of the African American female body as quintessentially performed by Beloved, a body that Holland argues functions culturally as a scene for both violation and passage through, passage for *others*. See Holland, *Raising the Dead*, 43.

43 Morrison, *Beloved*, 71.

44 The magical properties of the number 124 are notable (see, Stephen Hart, "Magical Realism in the Americas"); it is also notable that the number references Paul D.'s exclamation to Sethe, "You have two legs … not four," an exclamation which itself summarizes the novel's painful unpacking of the terms of dehumanization, debasement, suffered by the enslaved.

with which Sethe inscribes her daughters, a kind of violence that the novel itself interrogates, offering a witness whose societally enforced inability to intercede on behalf of herself or a helpless other forces her into actions of great violence.[45] The ethical puzzle of Sethe's killing of her daughter to save her from a worse fate of debasing enslavement is not only the core of Morrison's novel but also forms the structure, in a sense, of any consideration of the puzzle of representing sadism: how can representations of sadism not replicate the very terms they might hope to correct? If we follow Barthes's argument that the reader is born from the author's death, then the reader of violence is responsible for ethical action in response to this authorial sacrifice.

Watchers and Readers

Representations of course re-present, and in the representations of violence in Morrison, Allison, and O'Connor, acts of violence are reported in ways that focus on the character that witnesses the violence, structuring a third level of reportage, or an already-witnessed quality to the violence represented. Sethe, Mark Fortune, and Annie Boatwright are introduced to the reading audience as characters compelled to watch the violation of others. Annie listens through the door to Daddy Glenn beating Bone in the bathroom, Mark Fortune watches Mary Fortune being beaten in the woods, and Sethe is forced to watch multiple violations of other slaves, as well as perform in *Beloved* as witness to her own violation through the trope of "rememory."[46] *Bastard Out of Carolina*, "A View of the Woods," and *Beloved* present the witness to violence as the first entrance to violence and then circularly work through the terms of violation via the witness figure.

And the witness figure in these texts is *not* benign. Mark Fortune goes from witnessing his granddaughter's whippings to enacting a whipping that kills her; Sethe shifts from witnessing the suffering and murder of enslaved people to murdering her daughter; Annie Boatwright responds to her daughter's horrific incestuous rape by *comforting* the rapist and abandoning her daughter, his victim. The witness figure that is not heroic haunts these configurations of representing violence. One might say that the non-heroic witness figure, in text, figures

---

45 Morrison, *Beloved*, 12. The terrifying and grotesque specter of those who enslave African women seeing these women as animalistic leaks through most of Morrison's novel, a kind of background leitmotif like heat lightning behind the novel's landscape. For example, Paul D. accuses Sethe of behaving as if she has four legs while Sethe's mother wears the bit, and strikingly, Beloved herself appears the day "Here Boy," the family dog, vanishes, as if Beloved and Here Boy each fulfilled the same role in the family. Morrison notably shows how the degrading tendency of white men to act violently against black women corrupts also black men and black women's vision of black women, creating especially scapegoated black women: Beloved, in this sense, is a true daughter of Pecola Breedlove.

46 "Mama would stand right outside the bathroom." Allison, *Bastard Out of Carolina*, 110.

forth the deeper problematic of the representation of violence, querying when such representation is ever useful and good. And yet, for Morrison and Allison, representing violence is pitched to audience as catharsis. And the audience response to *Beloved* and *Bastard Out of Carolina* is overwhelmingly appreciative of the catharsis performed by these texts. Even the less acclaimed short story "A View of the Woods," despite its nihilism, asks its readers to see the powerless position of the daughter of Fortune and Pitts in a way that inscribes her killing as sacrificial; a sacrifice killing that possibly allows the sins of the South expiation.

Ethics of Sacrifice in *Beloved*

Despite the similarities between *Bastard Out of Carolina*, "A View of the Woods," and *Beloved*, Morrison's novel works differently in some key ways from the other texts. For Morrison's novel explicitly develops the idea that the revenant Beloved is a sacrificial figure, a girl whose erasure bestows on survivors the chance to survive.[47] Is it possible that, as is suggested by the symbolism of Denver's drinking Beloved's blood when she is nursed by her mother immediately following the killing, Morrison intends to represent sacrifice as a way of refusing an oppressive system, suggesting that sacrifice actually does (though at horrific cost) enable cultural progression?[48] If so, then this process raises problems about witnessing—if sacrifice of the daughter is instrumental to progress for others, to wit Denver's success as a college-educated woman, to wit Sethe's possible happiness with Paul D., then what are the implications for the writing of sacrifice? Does the writing of sacrifice participate in the problematic of sacrificing the daughter's body to save others? To approach this question, I draw on Jacques Derrida's *The Gift of Death*.

Derrida posits the sacrificial work of Abraham (in the Old Testament)—his willingness to sacrifice his son for Yahweh—as central to a system of ethics that might overturn Kant's theory of *a priori* ethical laws.[49] I look more thoroughly at Kant's ethics later in this book, but for now it is important to note that Kant's concept of a *categorical imperative* is the assertion that only those actions that do not *necessarily* bring the actor pleasure and that also if extrapolated and repeated by all actors would benefit all are truly ethical. Kant's *categorical imperative* has been interpreted by Jacques Lacan as a blueprint for sadism, as I consider more fully in my closing chapter, which looks in depth at Lacan's essay "Kant avec Sade." Suffice it to say that Lacan may misinterpret Kant's injunction that pleasure cannot be the guide for right behavior to mean that pleasure must not be the guide for right behavior. Unlike Lacan, Derrida does not argue that Kantian ethics are

---

[47] And I think Morrison has long meditated on this notion of the sacrificial daughter, for she wrote in *The Bluest Eye* of Pecola Breedlove, "we were so clean when we wiped ourselves on her." Morrison, *The Bluest Eye* (New York: Plume, 1994), 208.

[48] Morrison, *Beloved*, 152, the living infant is nursed after the murder along with the dead baby.

[49] Jacques Derrida, *The Gift of Death* (Chicago: University of Chicago Press, 1995).

the framework of sadism; however, he does argue that the messianic structure of early Judaism may correct flaws in Enlightenment ideology. Derrida suggests that the fault of Kant's ultra-rational theory of ethics is its willful ignorance of the sacrificial economy of the sacred.

Regarding the sacrifice of Isaac (which almost but does not occur), Kant would specifically argue that Abraham, sacrificing Isaac, had to withdraw fatherly feeling in favor of rational devotion to God, performing an action for universal good that still pains him personally. And yet Derrida's suggestion is that it is precisely fatherly feeling that enables the scene of Abraham's sacrifice to function as a foundational scene of ethics. For Abraham, knife ready to open his son's body, hesitates above his son's body, and in this hesitation *hears* the voice of the deity, hears God. Derrida considers in *The Gift of Death* the sacrificial economy that might preempt Enlightenment ideology of the rational actor: the sacrificial as that moment in which, from love, one pauses and hears God. The sacrifice of the male child, pivotal to Old Testament ethics, ethics that take into account emotion, incommensurable love, as Derrida would have it, is the proper pivot of ethics. Needless to say, Girard's notion of the sacrifice refracts this terrain through the rubric of Christian sacrifice of the deity's son, transposing sacrifice to the realm of the symbolic. But Girard and Derrida retain in common a focus on the meaning of the sacrifice of the male child.[50]

In *Beloved*, human benevolence is precisely what Morrison's novel encourages its readers not to trust: human benevolence, from white people, is impossible in *Beloved*. Sweet Home is portrayed as a destructive and debasing place for its enslaved workers even when the kindly Mr. Garner owns it. Just because schoolteacher behaves sadistically does not mean that the system of slavery wasn't already functioning in a *structure* that was sadistic even when practiced by Mr. Garner. *Beloved* points out that certain structures of domination are evil no matter whether some who benefit from those structures of domination behave in a kindly way to those whom they do not hesitate to dominate. Kant's metaphysics, with their emphasis on the difference between dignity and price, and on defining each human being as an end in herself rather than a means for others' use, aligns with this chilling aspect of Morrison's implicit moral philosophy: that the mother must create for her child a world in which her child is not a means to an end for others, in which her child is a "dignity" not a "price." Here is the Kantian impetus of Morrison's re-writing of the sacrifice.[51]

The sacrifice of the child underwrites a crisis of ethics, underwrites the movement by which the parent figure moves into a society that has permanence.

---

[50] René Girard, *Sacrifice*, trans. Matthew Pattilo and David Dawson. (East Lansing: Michigan State University Press, 2011).

[51] I take up these Kantian terms in my closing chapter, but briefly, for Kant a "dignity" means that each human being must first and foremost be sustained in a state of dignity, whereas a price is the corruption of ethics, a system in which a person is merely a means to an end. Enslavement obviously turns a person into a price.

In ways that I hope to unpack later in this chapter, I believe that *Beloved* very painfully asks this question: how does the daughter's dead body allow the family to progress? In this book, I look at multiple instances of the sacrificed daughter because I believe that those who can help us understand why our culture sacrifices its girls to rape, incest, battery, and child murder, are the writers and photographers, like Toni Morrison, Carrie Mae Weems, Flannery O'Connor, Dorothy Allison, and Emily Dickinson. They may not formulate explicit theory but their representations of daughter-sacrifice clarify this problematic image of the sacrificed daughter's body as the central underlying motif of Southern culture.

"A View of the Woods," like *Beloved*, is concerned with the progress of the family and its sacrificial cost. In "A View of the Woods," Mark Fortune's land, it seems, will furnish the basis for a new economy, the sunny post-Depression South. Indeed, he is willing to kill the little girl who tries to stop this economic progress. It is for her view of the woods that the little girl dies: her desire for the bucolic agrarian South is fatal. Likewise, Sethe, who will send a daughter almost born into slavery to Oberlin College (this daughter is Denver), is willing to kill another daughter in order that she not be returned to debasing enslavement. Denver flourishes, arguably, because Beloved died and because she drank Beloved's blood, absorbing the life sacrificed for her. The sacrifice of the child precariously stands beneath culture in these texts, the child's small body, in sacrificial erasure, supporting the family's movement into the dominant culture, in "A View of the Woods" and in *Beloved*.[52]

Beloved interrogates the specular, mirroring economy of the sacrifice. Morrison's Sethe and Beloved the revenant converge in a space in which mother and child seem one, or rather, their roles interchangeable, as Denver watches horrified the penultimate movements of the novel. Denver notes, shortly before she sets out to save her mother, that "the change was complete, now Sethe was the child and Beloved the parent."[53] Beloved's pregnancy prepares the novel's coda, establishing Beloved, the revenant, as the sacrificial body who mothers survival for others.[54]

---

52 Derrida in *The Gift of Death* maintains the position of Abraham in his musings on sacrificial ethics. That is, he writes from the position of Abraham: "I offer a gift of death, I betray, I don't need to raise a knife over my son on Mount Moriah for that. Day and night, at every instant on all the Mount Moriahs of this world, I am doing that, raising my knife over what I love and must love" (*Gift of Death*, 68). But my concern is with the very elision of the perspective of the sacrificed child, and this perspective, oddly, is one that Kant's ethics is capacious of considering. For Kant does not position himself as fixed victimizer or victim in the ethical schema he proposes. Instead he seeks schemata that are sufficiently supple to undo this dichotomy of domination.

53 Morrison, *Beloved*, 297.

54 But if Girard argues that the sacrifice as image in representation stands behind culture, I'm also still uncertain as to how the statistical prevalence of violence against girls fails to enter Girard's theory of the sacrifice. In truth, girls are oftener the sacrificed bodies of our culture, although Girard elides this fact by confessing its prevalence—arguing that

Like Derrida's *Gift of Death*, Morrison's *Beloved* frames the limits of Enlightenment ethics, showing the sadism of schoolteacher's Enlightenment-based Darwinian theory of the bestial slave. As Derrida writes: "I offer a gift of death, I betray, I don't need to raise a knife over my son on Mount Moriah for that. Day and night, at every instant on all the Mount Moriahs of this world, I am doing that, raising my knife over what I love and must love."[55] Sethe not only raises up but also brings down the saw, draws the saw across the infant's throat and cuts it open. Sethe's motivation for this violence is not cruelty but love. For in *Beloved*, Sethe's harshest trauma is not physical violation but the moment she overhears schoolteacher telling the nephews to make a chart listing Sethe's "human" characteristics on one side and her "animal" characteristics on another side.[56] The refusal to allow her daughter to be made into an animal is the pivot of Sethe's love.

When Sethe first hears schoolteacher instructing his pupils to list her animal and human characteristics in separate columns, she is so traumatized that she walks into a tree. Immediately, she begins to see the animal world all around her, as if animal-nature were closing in on her—she sees in lucid, terrifying detail the farm animals and even the flies as suddenly threatening to her in their role as exemplars of animal nature.[57] Sethe's trauma on hearing schoolteacher instruct his pupils in her lack of humanity is the central trauma of the novel: it is this trauma that forces her to run, forces her to kill her daughter—"No notebook for my babies, and no measuring string either"—Sethe states in allusion to schoolteacher's so-called scientific program of analysis of enslaved people.[58] Morrison posits some aspects of Enlightenment ideology as specially treacherous and sadistic: Morrison exposes the way that schoolteacher's pleasure in humiliating other human beings allies with scientific racist discourse of the nineteenth century, discourse that becomes if

girls cannot be sacrifices since they are so often violated. My book looks at some of the ways we read representations of this compulsive sacrifice. Please see Carole Pateman, *The Sexual Contract* (Stanford, CA: Stanford University Press, 1988). Pateman argues that the female body is the sacrifice behind the creation of the social contract.

55 Derrida, *The Gift of Death*, 68.

56 This moment of trauma connects powerfully with Weems's invocation of enslaved "scientific specimens" in *From Here I Saw What Happened and I Cried* discussed in Jason R. Young, *Rituals of Resistance: African Atlantic Region in Kongo and the Lowcountry South in the Era of Slavery* (Baton Rouge: Louisiana State University Press, 2007). Young makes clear that the color red, in African theology of the nineteenth century, was a color signifying the space between life and death, a space that connected the living and the dead. Weems's red-tinted "scientific specimens" literally are positioned by the artist as translating figures, mediating between the living and the dead.

57 I am grateful to a student, Adwoa Owusu, for pointing out in class discussion way that Sethe's thoughts, after hearing schoolteacher categorize her as an animal, turn to a traumatic and shocked hyper-awareness of the animals around her—flies, pigs, and so on. Adwoa Owusu, personal communication, February 2011.

58 Morrison, *Beloved*, 228.

not his engine of sadism, certainly its form. Imperialism as anthropology Morrison exposes as a privileged trope of the sadist.

Here, it is interesting to note that Morrison's creation of schoolteacher's list categorizing the so-called animal and human characteristics of Sethe seems to allude to Thomas Jefferson's elaborate charting of how the so-called animal characteristics of mixed race children are "diluted" over generations. Of course, Jefferson's chart, so uncannily like schoolteacher's lists, is rendered all the more invidious insofar as it is extremely likely that Jefferson was the father of Sally Hemings's children, all of whom were of mixed African and European parentage.[59]

Strikingly, when Derrida proposes an alternative to Kant's categorical imperative, he reaches for the very scene of the sacrifice of the beloved child that Morrison also inscribes. In Genesis, the sacrifice of Isaac is averted: "He bound his son Isaac, and laid him on the altar, on top of the wood. Then Abraham reached out his hand and took the knife to kill his son. But the angel of the Lord called to him from heaven and said 'Abraham, Abraham!' and he said, 'Here I am.' He said 'Do not lay your hand on the boy or do anything to him; for now I know that you fear God, since you have not withheld your son, your only son, from me.'"[60]

But in *Beloved*, neither Yahweh, nor fate, nor angels intervene to save the child who is female, and black. The specular dimensions of the sacrifice are clear: the fearsome spectacle of the child's body laid out for sacrifice. *Beloved* pivots on the emblematic sacrifice of the Beloved child and specifically contends with its visual register—the very problematic of bringing pleasure to the audience by representing the sacrifice. Importantly, in the chapter before Isaac's near death, Abraham's actual firstborn son, Ishmael, also almost dies as another kind of child sacrifice, insofar as it is his father, Abraham, who has banished him and his mother, Hagar, to the wilderness. Hagar cannot bear to sacrifice her son, but she has no way to save him. Instead she chooses *not to watch* her son die—"Do not let me look on the death of the child"[61]—and in this refusal to watch her child's death, Hagar recuses herself from the ethical nodus of watching violence. Sethe is positioned more as Abraham than as Hagar. Sethe watches and acts, willing forward the violence that alone will spare her sacred and treasured daughter the horror of rape and debasement in slavery.

Girard's theory of the sacrifice is important to my book but also inadequate for my consideration of the sacrifice of the girl child because of Girard's somewhat skewed vision of the cultural structure and force of gender. I take the

---

[59] Please see Werner Sollors, "Presidents, Race, and Sex," in *Sally Hemings & Thomas Jefferson: History, Memory, and Civic Culture*, ed. Jan Ellen Lewis and Peter S. Onuf (Charlottesville: UP of Virginia, 1999). See also. Werner Sollors, ed., *Interracialism: Black White Intermarriage in American History, Literature, and Law* (Cambridge, MA: Harvard University Press, 2000).

[60] Genesis 22:9–12; please also see Jeremiah 11:15.

[61] Genesis 21:16.

fundamental structure of Girard's theory of the role of the sacrifice, and violence, in representation, and turn this structure to accommodate an interpretation of the sacrifice of girls, also a performative sacrifice, a mode of sacrifice performed for the inscribed audience of female characters who are themselves vulnerable to violence but uncannily protected when they inhabit the role of the witness, in the texts under consideration in my study. That I am reading this configuration of witness and sacrifice in photography and literature melds with Girard's theory of mimesis and violence insofar as Girard argues that only through the gesture of representation is the physical violence of the sacrifice symbolically displaced.[62] And yet there is an unsolved remainder, a way in which gender is left un-theorized, if we pull Girard's theory of the sacrifice to help us unpack the sacrificial daughter. For the daughter, it would seem, is sacrificed also for the sake of those who watch her being violated. This unstable iteration of the violence of representation is different from Girard's notion that the act of representation (using symbols in art and literature, for example) defuses real violence. Unlike the sacrifice of the son, the sacrifice of the daughter seems to compel further violence.

I agree with Girard's thesis that violence and mimicry are deeply structurally entwined in the act of representation.[63] And yet, I note that in the stories and photographs investigated in this book, the violated girl functions as a double figure. Even within the work in which she is represented, the sacrificed is already a representation. A prolepsis of representation attends this gendered sacrifice. The clearest way to explain what I mean by this trope of double representation is to look again at Carrie Mae Weems's *From Here I Saw What Happened and I Cried*, insofar as Weems's series forefronts the act of representation as a violent act. Weems re-photographs images, as noted, of daguerreotypes from the mid-nineteenth century. The images were themselves violations when they were created of the enslaved "country born" daughters of fathers who had been kidnapped in Africa and brought to the low country (South Carolina) and enslaved. The nineteenth-century anthropologist's concept for their study was to take images of father-daughter pairs, fathers born in Africa, daughters born in the United States of America.[64] These "country born" daughters, daughters born enslaved in the United States, were forcibly made to sit for daguerreotypes in order to provide evidence for racist science. Weems takes the offensive mid-nineteenth-century photographs, images that were in their very making violations—not merely representations of violations but in their creation acts of violation—and re-photographs the images. She then re-presents the images of the violated American daughters in her series *From Here I Saw What Happened and I Cried*, and in this deployment of re-photographing Weems forefronts the fact that these daughters already performed

---

[62] René Girard, *Violence and the Sacred* (Baltimore: Johns Hopkins University Press, 1977), 143–69.

[63] Girard, *Violence and the Sacred*, 53–68.

[64] Brian Wallis, "Black Bodies, White Science: Louis Agassiz's Slave Daguerreotypes," *American Art* 9, no. 2 (Summer 1995): 38–61.

as representations from the beginning. Their absolute elision as actors in their culture forced them to live as representations. This elision of power holds true for the photographed daughters more completely than for the photographed fathers, in Weems's series, insofar as it is the young women whose frontal nudity articulates a gendered humiliation in ways that the exposure of the series' fathers does not. In Weems's *From Here I Saw What Happened and I Cried* sacrificed daughters are double representations, violated young women who originally (in the nineteenth century) were violated for the sake of others' being allowed to see, being granted audience, to their violation. Weems's series articulates the scandal of this originary violation.

The Sacrificed Girl Child: "A View of the Woods"

What makes the sacrifice of a girl child different? That is one of the questions linking *Beloved* and "A View of the Woods" with *Bastard Out of Carolina.* I consider this question by drawing parallels to and finding places of difference with *Beloved.* How does the sacrifice work in the economy of these stories, a historical novel, an autobiographical novel, a fictional commentary on the shifting economy and static politics of the South? This image of the sacrificed child who is female and who is not saved plays through O'Connor's "A View of the Woods," a story in which young Mary Fortune is murdered by her grandfather. Unlike Morrison's *Beloved*, in which the killed daughter returns as a revenant, there is no afterimage of Mary Fortune: she is completely used-up, discarded. My argument is that her murder *is* a sacrifice. And yet the killing of Mary Fortune is *not* intended to serve some salvific purpose, at least not by the grandfather who kills her.

However, O'Connor presents the image of the killed daughter in sacrificial terms. O'Connor's text, unlike the grandfather's actions within the story, uses the pivot of sacrifice in the sense that we read the representation of the daughter's violated destroyed body as a sign to indicate problems that need to be addressed going forward in Southern culture (problems such as racist violence, and also the loss of agrarian economies). Like Morrison, O'Connor troubles the relationship between audience and text by providing a connection between the witness figure and the figure who murders/sacrifices. For Sethe and Mark Fortune are both firstly presented in their respective narratives as witnesses of others' suffering. Sethe is the iron-eyed girl who never turns away from watching, while Mark Fortune is the grief-stricken and frozen grandfather who powerlessly watches his son-in-law whipping Mary Fortune.[65] This witness figure is necessary for the sacrifice to have its transformative power and yet it is also necessary, for the sacrifice to go forward, that the witness not stop the violence. This essential paradigm is unbearable. I do not suggest that one should bear it. Rather I present it here for consideration. Sethe watches others be violated until she herself is compelled to perform an absolute

---

[65] O'Connor, "A View of the Woods," 530.

violation: cutting open her daughter's throat. Similarly, Mark Fortune watches his little granddaughter being beaten by her father until he, Mark Fortune, feels compelled to beat his granddaughter to death. I do not assume, here, that Sethe and Mark Fortune have similar motivations for the violence they commit, clearly not. But it is uncanny that these very different characters move in a similar arc from watching to committing violence, their choices skewed by the field of violence that is Southern culture.

When Mark Fortune follows Pitts and the captive Mary into the woods and watches the little girl's father beat her, the grandfather is pained and grieved by what he sees, and is feminized by his position as a watcher of violence that he feels powerless to stop.[66] In witnessing the beating, the grandfather acts as a guarantor of reality, insofar as Mary Fortune, in typical post-traumatic fashion, *cannot remember* that her father beats her.[67]

Frozen in traumatic disassociation, Mary Fortune claims she has never been beaten. The grandfather's role in silently watching the beating is important as a tactic that O'Connor uses to show her reader that the little girl is indeed being beaten, even though Mary Fortune cannot remember her beatings. The grandfather's act of watching sadism is not only functional but also emotive. While it is not correct to say the grandfather enjoys the vision of watching his beloved granddaughter being beaten, the scene evokes strong emotion in him. And yet he does not act to stop the beating. He is feminized as he watches the beating, aligned with his daughter, the girl's mother, whom he calls "no kind of mother" because she permits the beating.[68] But the grandfather permits the beatings, as his daughter permits the beatings. Both mother and grandfather witness and do not intervene in Mary Fortune's frequent whippings at the hands of her father.

Watching the child Mary Fortune being beaten by her father Pitts, the grandfather Mark Fortune who owns the property that Pitts farms, is radically disempowered and feminized in his status as a man whose body is too old to fight his son-in-law. The feminization of the grandfather begins with description of physical decrepitude and draws traditional lines of gender as powerful (masculine) and powerless (feminine), articulating the feminine as that which watches the masculine perform sadism. At first, the grandfather powerlessly watches, unable to intervene and stop the acts of violence against Mary Fortune Pitts. Later, by mimicking Pitts, Mark Fortune becomes the violator who kills the little girl.

In *Violence and the Sacred*, Girard maps his seminal thesis of mimetic acts as displacements of violence, arguing that the principle of substitution at the heart of sacrificial violence also is the engine of symbolic representation. "The principle of human substitution of one victim for another appears in its most savage form"

---

66 Compare to Barbara Shapiro's argument about *Beloved* in "The Bonds of Love and Boundaries of Self in Toni Morrison's *Beloved*," *Contemporary Literature* 32, no. 2 (Summer 1991): 194–210.

67 O'Connor, "A View of the Woods," 530.

68 O'Connor, "A View of the Woods," 534.

in human sacrifice, argues Girard, insofar as the "victim is a substitute for all members of the community."[69] And yet this *pharmakos*, Girard argues, is male: male because maleness ensures mysteriously the purity appropriate to the sacrifice.

Morrison, Allison, and O'Connor mobilize this cultural problematic of gender: to whom does suffering accord purity? My suggestion is that O'Connor, Allison, and Morrison display and deconstruct the notion of female suffering as a form of powerlessness—the characters of Mary Fortune, Bone, and Beloved, innocent and powerless, are also victims who queer femininity in their transgressive representation as powerful sacrificial figures.

Mary Fortune fights against her grandfather, mauling him and partially blinding him before he ultimately kills her, while Beloved returns not as a ghost but as an embodied revenant who is supernaturally strong, as Paul D. notes.[70] I don't think the idea that female suffering is a form of power is what Morrison, Allison, and O'Connor are hoping to convey in *Beloved*, *Bastard Out of Carolina*, and "A View of the Woods." Instead, they question the erasure of the sacrificial daughter, the way that the story of her embodied suffering is not preserved and retained as cultural artifact but rather erased, written out of the economy of symbolic discourse as sacrificially based that Girard limns. Certainly I do not mean here to imply that Morrison, Allison, and O' Connor are writing intentionally to refute Girard. Rather, I indicate the power of Girard's thesis by suggesting that in writing about the sacrificial figure, Morrison, Allison, and O'Connor write in conversation with what is Girard's consideration of this figure of the sacrifice, indicating both the correctness of Girard's thesis and its gendered limitations.

In discussing the concept of the *pharmako*s, who is "a substitute for all members of the community," René Girard points to the unappeased vulnerability of the sacrifice: "between these victims and the community a crucial social link is missing so they can be exposed to violence without fear of reprisal."[71] Although Girard pointedly excludes female children and women from the category of the sacrifice, it seems clear that Mary Fortune, Beloved, and Bone are sacrificed precisely because their role as daughters, in the cultural/political situations in which they are placed, occupies a broken link that the community *should have* with a small child, the premise and promise of developing the child's potential to become an adult. Instead, these daughters are erasable marks, goods not so much for exchange as for absorption without trace. Moreover, the sacrifice of each child in fact, in the structure of these fictions, ensures the survival of others in the story.

In "A View of the Woods" O'Connor presents a distinctly martyred, murdered body, a girl smashed against a rock by her grandfather in the woods, that bears comparison with *Beloved*'s equally horrific scene of the Ohio cold house and the mother's hand on the saw and the baby's throat, which in turn bears comparison with the splayed, raped body of Bone in the violent closing scene of *Bastard Out*

---

69 Girard, *Violence and the Sacred*, 106.

70 Morrison, *Beloved*, 274.

71 Girard, *Violence and the Sacred*, 13.

of Carolina. Unlike Beloved, the un-named, eponymous infant of Morrison's novel, Mary Fortune is over-determined by her name, her fate written in it, and the sacrificed daughter here is ten years old, old enough to speak and to argue, old enough to call her feminized grandfather the "Whore of Babylon."[72] (Of course, in *Beloved*, when the revenant returns and is named Beloved, at that point the un-named baby girl sacrificed gathers full force as a name—Beloved—that indicates not fate to come but retroactive fate that carries through time.)

O'Connor's Mary Fortune is aggressive and powerful except in her role as her father's favorite object to whip. But the separation of male and female is also crucial to these stories' plots. Mary Fortune expresses masculine tropes of aggression and power, but when she is beaten and when she is murdered, O'Connor is careful to describe her as wearing a dress. Indeed, the grandfather, who ultimately murders her, crudely jokes with the little girl that she is a "barefoot woman," connoting the phrase "barefoot and pregnant" (hardly an appropriate jest with a pre-pubescent child), as well as the traditional Southern slur that a barefoot woman has loose morals.[73] The story highlights the strictures of gender as they are placed on the body of the young Mary Fortune (as the grandfather kills her, he sees her as Mary Pitts, killing her because she insists that she is pure *Pitts*).[74] These strictures of gender also are placed on the body of Sethe's baby girl, whose beauty and sexual allure, as a teenage revenant, her affair with Paul D. and the pregnancy it produces, are central features of the character.

Both Mary Fortune, ten-year-old granddaughter, and *Beloved*'s unnamed "crawling already? baby girl" are killed gruesomely. The image of the martyred female body, then, centers the texts of "A View of the Woods" and *Beloved*. Morrison's ethical code is inscribed in her dedication: she writes to honor the dead. O'Connor's explicit allegiance is to a Catholic understanding of theology through the contemplation of the suffering Christ. Morrison focuses the image of the female martyr to signify the deaths of 60 million men, women and children. How do Morrison and O'Connor suggest this redemptive quality rather than only the victimization? In what way are Beloved and Mary scapegoats, rather than only victims? O'Connor's story undoubtedly risks a pornography of violence, and yet my argument is that the very grotesque rendering she gives the violence she represents is an activist gesture, much like Morrison's representation of many acts of violence condensed in the one intolerable act of sacrifice.[75] By refusing to make

---

72 O'Connor, "A View of the Woods," 533.

73 O'Connor, "A View of the Woods," 539.

74 O'Connor, "A View of the Woods," 545.

75 I take this concept of pornography of violent imagery not from Catharine MacKinnon's work on pornography, *Only Words* (Cambridge, MA: Harvard University Press, 1993), which often is itself violent (that's another story), but rather from Allan Sekula's *Photography Against the Grain: Essays and Photo Works 1973–1983* (Halifax, N.S., Canada: Press of the Nova Scotia College of Art and Design, 1984) and Sontag's *On Photography*.

these violent scenes sexy, by making them real—as O'Connor famously quipped, reality is grotesque—O'Connor's "A View of the Woods" and Morrison's *Beloved* press the reader to consider not how the daughter's actual murder allows the culture to progress, since that murder is presented as apocalyptic horror, but rather how the *representation* of these murders engenders their sacrificial function.

Morrison's novel is Christian in its allusive framing, *Beloved* beginning with a quote from Saint Paul's letter to the Romans—"I will call them my people, which were not my people; and her beloved, which was not beloved"—and interpolating the scene of the murder of the baby girl with iconography of the four horsemen of the Apocalypse. The apocalyptic reach of both "A View of the Woods" and *Beloved* suggests Southern culture's compulsive sacrifice of the daughter. And yet in the paradox that is the violence of rhetoric, the very representation of the violence makes it sacrificial rather than pornographic. Mary Fortune is described as a mirror image of Mark Fortune, this identity of repetition at first securing his love for her and then securing his desire to kill her: after he kills her he gazes at "his own conquered image."[76] When Mark Fortune kills Mary Fortune, he kills himself; when Sethe kills Beloved, she kills herself. Likewise, we may consider the rape of Bone as a sacrificial scene in that it removes Bone from her mother and generates a kind of rebirth, when Annie, in abandoning Bone, gives her daughter a new birth certificate.[77] The sacrifice of the daughter, encoded as revelation of sacrifice in representation, is the engine that allows progress beyond actual sacrifice of girls, if we are to read Morrison, O'Connor, and Allison as writers of texts that function as activist works.[78]

As noted in my introduction, the very terms of innocent martyrdom in Christian iconography are heavily gendered.[79] And yet innocence *is* reflected across the field of the female body in O'Connor's radical displacement of Christological iconography, and in Morrison's insistence on the tragic but redemptive force of

---

[76] O'Connor, "A View of the Woods," 545.

[77] Allison, *Bastard Out of Carolina*, 261.

[78] If one thinks of rape as a form of destruction, destroying the subjectivity of the victim at least for the interval of the assault, a few contemporary statistics are relevant: 9 of every 10 rape victims are female; 15 percent of these victims are under the age of 12. Girls between ages 16 and 19 are four times more likely to be victims of rape than the general population. Rape, Abuse & Incest National Network, "Who are the Victims?" http://www.rainn.org/get-information/statistics/sexual-assault-victims (accessed June 20, 2012).

[79] Interpreting Christ as the scapegoat isn't Girard's original insight, to say the least: the pure, male body sacrificed to preserve the community is figured in the Mosaic ritual of the Day of Atonement (Lev. 16), wherein one of two goats was chosen by lot to be sent alive into the wilderness, the sins of the people having been symbolically laid upon it, while the other was appointed to be sacrificed. Thomas Hobbes, for example, connects this sacrifice with Christ, in 1651. In Hobbes's *Leviathan*, he argues "Our Saviour Christ's sufferings seem to be here [sc. in Lev. 16] figured … He was both the sacrificed Goat and the Scape Goat." See A. P. Martinich, *The Two Gods of Leviathan: Thomas Hobbes on Religion and Politics* (Cambridge: Cambridge University Press, 1992), xli.

the infant daughter's blood sacrifice. Mary Fortune's body is explicitly displayed in its martyrdom. This blood in the woods that closes the scene of the murder suggests lynchings, the blood of the innocents. Written into the parable of Mary Fortune, her sadistic father, and her murderous grandfather, is the paradigm of blood sacrifice—subversive, because O'Connor insists on the iconography of holy martyrdom for her female character.

René Girard specifies that symbolic discourse is founded on the murder of the scapegoat: the scapegoat, onto whom the mortality and vulnerability of the community are imaginatively projected, ritually murdered. This ritual murder Girard sees as a foundational move of culture.[80] But symbolic discourse also generates this violence, insofar as only after making the leap to symbolic thought can a culture produce a scapegoat, allowing violence to be displaced onto the symbol—the work of visual art and/or language. Girard's theory of the scapegoat is applicable to Morrison's *Beloved* and O'Connor's "A View of the Woods" against Girard's own terms: O'Connor and Morrison question the guilt of the scapegoat, insofar as they question the concept of the innate guilt of the female body, possibly throwing open spaces of androgyny that place in doubt, that queer, the difference between male and female and between innocence and guilt. But this very explosion of the boundary between the masculine and the feminine, the innocent and the guilty, makes of Mary Fortune and Beloved queer saints: they epitomize, and in death embody, the problematic of the imposition of femininity, the impossible terms of its strictures. Never permitted to fight back while they are whipped and sawed and smashed, Mary Fortune Pitts and Beloved fight back by ultimately trying to kill those who kill them.

To see the proximity of witness and sadist consider the structure of Beloved's murder, Mary Fortune's murder, and Bone's rape. Sethe and schoolteacher face each other and face off over the body of Sethe's murdered daughter. Bone and Daddy Glenn stare at each other eye-to-eye as his member, described like a weapon, assaults the 12-year-old girl.[81] In similar configuration, Mary Fortune and the grandfather face each other as they battle and struggle, a fight culminating in the martyrdom of the daughter. Here I quote Morrison's and O'Connor's descriptions of the daughters' deaths, beginning with "A View of the Woods":

> In the pause she loosened her grip and he got hold of her throat. With a sudden surge of strength, he managed to roll over and reverse their positions so that he was looking down into the face that was his own but had dared to call itself Pitts. With his hands still tight around her neck, he lifted her head and brought it down once hard against the rock that happened to be under it. Then he brought it down twice more. Then looking into the face in which the eyes, slowly rolling back, appeared to pay him not the slightest attention, he said, "There's not an ounce of

---

80 Rebecca Adams and René Girard, "Violence, Difference, Sacrifice: A Conversation with René Girard," *Religion & Literature* 25, no. 2, *Violence, Difference, Sacrifice: Conversations on Myth and Culture in Theology and Literature* (Summer 1993): 9–33.

81 Allison, *Bastard Out of Carolina*, 283.

> Pitts in me." He continued to stare at his conquered image until he perceived that though it was absolutely silent, there was no look of remorse in it.[82]

Because Morrison's novel details a postmodern post-mortem, fracturing the story by circling the story through several tellers, my quote from *Beloved* is a composite from several pages, describing the crisis when schoolteacher, Sethe's so-called owner, arrives with his nephew, a sheriff, and the slave catcher as the four horsemen of the Apocalypse. I begin by quoting Stamp Paid's recollection of the event, which manifests primarily in the text as memory: "… she flew, snatching up her children like a hawk on the wing; how her face beaked, how her hands worked like claws, how she collected them every which way: one on her shoulder, one under her arm …"[83]

And the scene when the slave catcher and schoolteacher enter the shed where Sethe murdered her daughter:

> … two boys bled in the sawdust and dirt at the feet of a nigger woman holding a blood-soaked child to her chest with one hand and an infant by the heels in the other. … little nigger girl eyes staring between the wet fingers that held her face so her head wouldn't fall off. … by the time she faced [schoolteacher], looked him dead in the eye, she had something in her arms that stopped him in his tracks. He took a backward step with each jump of the baby heart until finally there were none.[84]

The kaleidoscopic effect of Morrison's description both magnifies the violence, telling it from several different points of view, and blunts the violence, protecting the reader from the graphic claims of O'Connor's more traditional storytelling mode. O'Connor's character Mark Fortune alludes to the one-drop rule at the crest of the scene of sadistic violence, asserting "there's not an ounce of Pitts in me."[85] Likewise, schoolteacher resists the full implication of the sacrifice before him by asserting a semiotics of difference—schoolteacher's racist iconography manifesting in his vision of "little nigger girl eyes."[86] The sacrificed, violated one, she with her throat opened by a saw, is a "nigger," while schoolteacher sees himself as having "not an ounce" of this vulnerable symbolic blood in his veins.[87]

Beloved and "A View of the Woods" emphasize the momentum of mirroring (or what Girard calls mimicry) between the sadist and his prey.[88] O'Connor describes

---

82 O'Connor, "A View of the Woods," 545.

83 Morrison, *Beloved*, 157.

84 Morrison, *Beloved*, 149.

85 O'Connor, "A View of the Woods," 545.

86 Morrison, *Beloved*, 172.

87 Morrison, *Beloved*, 176.

88 If Girard suggests that "It is hard to know whether one is dealing with a real-life struggle or with ritual mimicry whose cathartic effects are believed to ward off the impending crisis it imitates so faithfully," that the line between violence and representation

as mirror images Mary Fortune and her grandfather fighting to the death, deploying the iconography of the mirror to the hilt. The grandfather and the granddaughter face each other, the granddaughter's face an exact replica of the grandfather's face. But the girl's queerness *and* femininity, her name like her great-grandmother's who died giving birth to Mark Fortune, becomes the fatal mark that holds in place the character's absolute vulnerability to erasure. Mary Fortune Pitts dies, structurally speaking, because she never has her own name but always carries the names of fathers who see her only as an agent to carry their blood. Beloved's death guarantees the structure rebirth that is afforded to virtually every major character in *Beloved* except Beloved herself. Against erasure, Morrison and O'Connor posit a kind of queer martyrdom in which the female body becomes the scapegoat. These moments of facing the enemy instantiate gendered scenes of horrific oppression, a gender as apocalypse; they are also configured as moments in which, to survive, one must take on the characteristics of the enemy, insofar as Mary Fortune's failure to be quite as brutal as her grandfather is fatal, while Beloved's failure to realize that even the women of the community are willing to kill her leaves her vulnerable to the exorcism that finally erases every trace of her. What one notes about "A View of the Woods" and *Beloved* is the texts' assertion of the inevitability of sadism.[89]

The Sacrificial Daughter as Rape Victim: *Bastard Out of Carolina*

Dorothy Allison's autobiographically inspired coming of age novel, *Bastard Out of Carolina*, is connected to Morrison's *Beloved* and O'Connor's "A View of the Woods" in the sense that the three works are centrally focused by the representation of the daughter's violated body. Like O'Connor's story, Allison's novel is set in the Jim Crow South. Like Morrison's historical novel, *Bastard Out of Carolina* draws potency from its avowed and explicit connection to real events. Allison's novel relates to my larger argument about sadism/sacrifice insofar as her autobiographically inspired depiction of a daughter whipped, beaten, molested, and incestuously raped, repeatedly returns to the scene of the opening of the

---

is very thin, O'Connor's story emphasizes the fragility of that division, inscribing onto the sacrificed granddaughter's character the function of mimicry, that is, writing the character as a repetition of the grandfather who murders her. See, Girard, *Violence and the Sacred*, 66.

89 Indeed, Gilman, in "Black Bodies, White Bodies," showed that Nietzsche's theory of the sadism underlying culture was long blamed for actual murders—the theory being that those who read Nietzsche became murderous nihilists. While I certainly do not think that those who read Morrison's *Beloved*, Allison's *Bastard Out of Carolina*, and O'Connor's "A View of the Woods" become murderous nihilists, I do think that representing sadism risks replicating the pleasures of watching violence that are originary to sadism. And there is an apocalyptic bent in these works that show and repeal and revoke the daughter's violation. Please see Sander Gilman, *Difference and Pathology: Stereotypes of Sexuality, Race and Madness* (Ithaca: Cornell University Press, 1985) and Henry Louis Gates, Jr. and Kwame Anthony Appiah, eds., *"Race," Writing, and Difference* (Chicago: University of Chicago Press, 1986).

daughter's body as a scene that must be represented in order for the culture that permitted that violation to be transformed.

Dorothy Allison, in *Bastard Out of Carolina*, appropriating O'Connor's Southern Gothic tradition and directly citing Morrison's *The Bluest Eye* as her inspiration, describes the incest victim, Bone, imagining that people watch her as her stepfather beats her. Bone conjures her audience in a disturbing fashion: she does not specify that this audience watching her stepfather as he beats her would *stop* him from beating her. Instead, she imagines only that they would be unable to remove themselves from the scene, unable to shield themselves from the vision of her violation.

Describing the dangerous performative pleasure of this sacrificial economy, Allison (as Bone) writes: "I imagined people watching while Daddy Glen beat me … Someone had to watch—some girl I admired … sometimes a whole group of them would be trapped into watching … Those who watched me loved me. It was as if I were being beaten for them."[90] This idea that the girl is being beaten "for them," when "them" is a trapped audience, indicates the sacrificial turn of Allison's novel. Bone's desire has gone beyond the desire to be saved from Daddy Glen's violence; she seems to have passed over into a place in which she recognizes that the simple cessation of the violence would not do much, or not do enough, to heal her. Instead, she conjures an utterly performative space in which the dialectic of subjectivity and subjugation is played out as those who have not suffered incestuous abuse, those lucky ones, are forced to watch and experience the reality of abuse forced onto Bone's body.[91]

This notion that only performance, re-iterative performance, performance as a substitute for testimony, can salvage the victim's desecrated spirit places a peculiar pressure on the textual. The text, whether literary or photographic, is not set apart in terms of ethics, and yet it is clearly different from firsthand witnessing. Reading *Bastard Out of Carolina*, the audience is at once punished, with the painful vision of a young girl's violation, and taunted with the accusation that it is *for* their pleasure that she is beaten.

The audience of Bone's fantasy and maybe also of Allison's novel, it seems, is positioned without the possibility of ethical response to Bone's violation. If Daddy Glen violates Bone *for our pleasure* we should put down the book that

---

[90] Allison, *Bastard Out of Carolina*, 112.

[91] Bone comes to enjoy the image of people watching her being beaten. She comes to enjoy herself as an image: not a masochistic fantasy but rather one that violates the premise of redemption on which sentimental narratives turn. Dorothy Allison, like her character Bone, has talked about masturbating to fantasies of being raped and violated. See, Michael *LeMahieu*, "An Interview with Dorothy Allison," *Contemporary Literature* 52, no. 4 (Winter 2010): 650. Here I do not argue that Allison has solved the problem of surviving intact child sexual abuse (personally I find Allison's professed embrace of sado-masochism disturbing). But it is important to note that just as the abused child in the "a child is being beaten" scenario sees herself as visible only when suffering so also the author and her audience align across the image of the suffering body of the beaten/raped child.

enshrines this act as representation. Having taught *Bastard Out of Carolina* in undergraduate college classes, I can attest that some students do make the decision to just put down the book as they cannot bear to finish reading it. I have found myself taking *Bastard Out of Carolina* off a syllabus and then putting it back on, then removing it definitively from the syllabus, deciding it's not worth the pain it causes my students. And yet others, for example, survivors of child sexual abuse, have found Allison's *Bastard Out of Carolina* to be salvific in much the same way that Allison herself claims Morrison's *The Bluest Eye* was a book that saved her. Sharing Allison's pain—and witnessing her process of naming the hurt—may also be an ethical response to *Bastard Out of Carolina*.

To approach the question of whether one may legitimately interpret representation of the daughter's rape as representation of the sacrificial body, I firstly address the fact that *Bastard Out of Carolina* features a middle sequence that culminates with a "burned offering," a literal burned offering, when the young Bone's erstwhile best friend is burned alive at a holiday barbecue, as the girl's gospel-singer mother watches helplessly.

Pearl has befriended Bone mostly as a solidification of the girls' mutual outcast status—Bone is an outcast because she is a "bastard" and little Pearl an outcast because she is albino. If the proximity of love and hatred is beautifully rendered in Allison's description of the girls' friendship, Pearl's death by immolation at first seems gratuitously horrific. Whereas incest crimes, and father-daughter rape, are underreported and under-acknowledged in America, and in a very real sense Dorothy Allison earns her folk title as patron saint of abused women by authoring a book in which patriarchal abuse against little girls is laid bare, the death by fire of Pearl is positioned in the novel solely to force the reading audience to accept greater and greater measures of descriptive violence. In this way, *Bastard Out of Carolina* asserts its own violative force on its reader.

The reader must accept the representation of the burning alive of a little girl while her mother watches in order to continue reading the book. Here I mean simply that either the reader decides, upon reading the hideous immolation scene, that the violence the book offers is too much and puts the book away, or the reader accepts the level of violence the book offers and continues to read. In a performative sense, the reader of *Bastard Out of Carolina* is trained towards the almost unbearable scene of Daddy Glenn's brutal beating and rape of Bone, trained by being shown greater levels of violence as the novel progresses.

If the reader stops reading in the middle section, that is, if at the burning alive of Pearl the reader turns away and puts away the book, not finishing the novel, then the bargain struck at the novel's beginning between author and audience is broken and the author's performance is done, her reader gone. Here I do not necessarily mean to imply that one can only read about violence because one relishes it; rather I make a structural argument. To get through Allison's novel's apocalyptic rape scene at her novel's ending, one has to accept the narrator's representing multiple acts of violence that increase in intensity. The terms of reading, offered by Allison, are important for the novel *Bastard Out of Carolina* because in parallel fashion the bargain of mother and child is broken by Bone's mother: not necessarily because she is a powerless woman who cannot stop her husband's violence, but also possibly because she enjoys watching her daughter being raped and beaten, acts that increase in intensity of violence as the child grows. Pearl's mother—who wants to save her daughter but cannot—is contrasted to Bone's mother who refuses to stop what Daddy Glenn does to her daughter. The evidence of the text fully allows this second interpretation: that Annie lives for the spectacle of Bone's humiliation. Annie is Bone's first and best and most beloved audience.

The live burning, immolation, of Pearl functions as a kind of diegetic bargaining tool in *Bastard Out of Carolina*. If the audience accepts—and here I suggest that continuing to read is a form of acceptance—this scene of graphic and senseless violence, the burning of Pearl, we will read on towards the culmination of the novel in which Bone is horrifically raped before she reaches puberty. Allison in interviews has stated that she toned down rather than ramped up the violence in her novel as she drew from her real-life trauma this testimony. And I do not doubt that she did minimize the violence of her abusive childhood. Nevertheless, here I point out that the tactic Bone deploys in the novel, of forcing children to listen to progressively more hideously violent stories, is precisely the approach that Dorothy Allison as author takes: she trains her audience to accept scenes of progressively worsening violence, throwing us Pearl's immolation to prepare us for the sacrifice of Bone, in which Daddy Glenn's member acts as the knife, opening the innocent child victim. The little girl burned alive in a barbecue accident, a pure scorched sacrifice, comparable to the Genesis description of the burned sacrifice Abraham is to make of Isaac, functions to test and show Bone's sacrificial role in Allison's novel.

What then is the significance of Allison's strategy? Firstly, she juxtaposes the "innocent" child, Pearl, who has never been sexualized, with the "guilty" child, Bone, who is violently sexualized, I believe to suggest that these terms of comprehending girls need to be altered. Little girls should not be molested and raped and those who are molested and raped must be seen as just as innocent as any other child. I believe this point is what Allison is driving home by juxtaposing the representation of the "burnt sacrifice" of Pearl with the scene of the rape of Bone with the phallus as knife. Allison's novel forces its reader to approach the pain of the victim and it accomplishes this formidable task through structural devices that I have described above.

The three texts—*Beloved*, "A View of the Woods," and *Bastard Out of Carolina*—forge an almost illicit bond with readers in which we witness the representation of the violation of the female child's body in comprehension of and/or collusion with the cultural terms that depend upon the simultaneous immanence (and suppression) of that image.[92] That the image of the martyred body of the young

[92] Please see, for example, Peggy Phelan, *Unmarked: The Politics of Performance* (London and New York: Routledge, 1993) and Andrea Dworkin *Pornography* (New York: Perigee Books, 1981). Phelan and Dworkin approach, from very different perspectives, this question of how the image of the feminine, the violated feminine, functions in culture.

daughter haunts culturally legible images of the cherished and putatively protected heteronormative daughter is the central argument of this chapter. We could consider not only *Beloved*, which is obviously about haunting, but also "A View of the Woods," and even *Bastard Out of Carolina*, to be a stories about haunting, haunting as that which represents the residue of unresolved sadistic violence.

Toni Morrison's implicit theory of haunting, conveyed in multiple and complicated ways in *Beloved*, relates to "A View of the Woods" and *Bastard Out of Carolina* in a few key ways. The first two fictions concern the Reconstruction and Jim Crow, and the third the poverty of the South, depicting not only the oppression of African Americans but also the pejorative term "white trash" to separate the middle class from the poor whites.[93] These works display representation of abuse that is not remediated.[94] They make the implicit claim that some forms of violence and violation, however many years ago they occurred, remain vivid in the social world of the present, possibly because the social world of the present hasn't changed enough from that of the past.[95]

"A View of the Woods," *Beloved*, and *Bastard Out of Carolina* do not offer suggestions as to what one ought to do about the problems (racism, sexism, child sexual abuse, child abuse) exposed in the texts. Representation in these texts instead takes on a kind of mytho-poetic power. The ghost in *Beloved* exemplifies the problem of un-expiated, and impossible to expiate, residue after sadistic violence. That is, the sacrificed baby daughter cannot be appeased because her suffering was so extreme that nothing really appeases it. She doesn't have a focused goal of vengeance because what possible vengeance would satisfy the depth of her radical loss of self? This residue of the insolvable appears in these stories like a ghost-function, that is, as a breakdown in language, a fall into muteness or fractured language. O'Connor ends her short story abruptly, leaving the reader in a place of abyss, while the mother in *Bastard Out of Carolina* remains an uncanny and disturbing residue figure. She exposes the depth of the problem of womanly pleasure in watching the body of the feminine other, the daughter, violated and sacrificed. *Beloved*, by its coda, circles back to the pivotal sacrifice of the un-named daughter. Even as the novel represents the possibility of departing from the place of enslavement, the daughter's sacrificed image returns to haunt the survivors.

93 "A View of the Woods" deals with the shift from agrarian Georgia to the new South of super-aggressive capitalism: problematically, that mourning of the loss of the agrarian South is usually linked politically with States Rights, or racism. But I think O'Connor's story evokes the multiple losses of Georgia, the land lost to the Muskogee, for example. The land lost is her body, metonymically. Her sacrificial body transcends codes of racism that impel her death.

94 I note here that both *Beloved* and *Bastard Out of Carolina*, as historical fiction and autobiographical novel, have a liminal relationship to the term "fiction."

95 Important to "A View of the Woods" is the story's exposition of the sacrificial nature of eradicating the rural landscape in favor of economic "progress" represented and manifested in the form of gas stations. The Native American claim of the land, erased by whites, is re-erased as whites use their ownership of land to destroy the land, in this story.

Chapter 4
"The Adequate of Hell," or, How to Watch the Other Suffer: Dickinson, Ransom, and Tate

In this chapter, I take a small detour from works evoking the geographical South in order to consider how the cultural South influences paradigms of reading women's writing in American literature through the pivotal figure of Emily Dickinson. Dickinson's use, in some of her poems, of imagery that seems to reflect the problematic of the subjectivity of enslavement coheres with my book's central question of staging the representation of watching violence. Although Dickinson, of course, was no Southerner, and does not explicitly invoke the South, I will make the case that some of her most violent poems are distinctly in conversation with the violence of slavery and the Civil War that shaped American discourse in the latter half of the nineteenth-century.[1] In particular, I pay attention to the reception history of Dickinson's work, following the uncanny way that the New England poet came to national attention when her poetry was championed by Southern critics John Crowe Ransom and Allan Tate. If one could make the claim that a reading of Emily Dickinson's poetry does not belong in a book on witnessing violence in the South, I would counter that precisely Dickinson's transformation from virtually unknown poet to national icon follows the contours of Southern culture, playing on tropes of hyper-femininity, tropes that allow femininity to function as a medium for the scene of representing sadistic violence.

A scalped soul, "stapled feet," eyes "put out" and "took away": these startling images of bodily violence in Emily Dickinson's lyrics have been read as engagements with tropes of feminine suffering.[2] Notable examples are Marianne Noble's *The Masochistic Pleasures of Sentimental Literature*, Robert McClure Smith's "Dickinson and the Masochist Aesthetic," and Cynthia J. MacKenzie's "'Heavenly Hurt': Dickinson's Wounded Text."[3] These readings typically interpret

---

1 And continues to shape intellectual conversation. Consider Ta-Nehisi Coates's blog, http://www.theatlantic.com/national/archive/2012/01/civil-war-counterfactuals/251325/ (accessed June 25, 2013). Coates writes in response to recent inflammatory claims that the Civil War never need have been fought.

2 All references to Dickinson's poetry indicate *The Poems of Emily Dickinson: Reading Edition*, ed. R. W. Franklin (Cambridge: Belknap Press of Harvard University Press, 1998). Following standard practice, I refer to the poems by the numbers Franklin has assigned them. Here I allude to poems Fr 477, Fr 709, and Fr 336.

3 Noble, *The Masochistic Pleasures*. See also her article, "The Revenge of Cato's Daughter: Dickinson's Masochism," *Emily Dickinson Journal* 7, no. 2 (1998): 22–47;

Dickinson's portrayals of violence as manifestations of femininity as a site of damage, suffering, and, most pointedly, masochism. In this chapter, however, I diverge from the psychoanalytic tradition that links masochism with femininity. Instead, developing my approach from Michael Snediker's intriguing reading of Dickinson's lyrical ethics, I will explore the borderlands (within and between text and critique) where embodiments of violence chart a space that is ethically fraught: my concern is with relations of social power, rather than interior psychodynamics, and I hope to take account of a dimension in these poems that is bio-political in addition to psycho-personal, ethical rather than just erotic.[4]

A narrow but important strain can be seen in Dickinson's poetry that dramatizes the witnessing of physical harm done to an unprotected other. A few, but a key few, of Dickinson's poems speak of a victim of violence, characterized, I will argue, by coded depictions of the suffering body as feminized (at times "queer") and often racially marked. This attention to the problematic intersection of the figure of the witness and the figure of the victim as a transaction within gender—a feminine watcher watching a feminine victim—I read in conjunction with the way that Dickinson's poems bring race into this configuration, a coded intervention into the poetics of erasure and abjection. Whether Dickinson's handling of this coded racial and gendered terrain works to release the racialized, gendered subject from the space of abjection is certainly a complex question. My argument will be that we have reached a terminus in the literature on Dickinson's poetic "masochism," for up to this point, the end of a good portion of the work invested in psychodynamic interpretations has tended to perform rather than to illuminate the politics of gendered poetics recoverable in her texts. As I will stress, interpreting her depictions of violence along ethical lines (that point outside of interior psychodrama) offers a way to interpret Dickinson's sometimes very "queer" poetics. It is in the space of the queer, if anywhere, that Dickinson asserts her ethics.

In reading Dickinson's articulations of violence, I want to draw on the terms and indices of a critical moment in our thinking about trauma and its aftermath, the work of Giorgio Agamben, which is significant to the direction of my thoughts. Attending to these poems' ambiguous intersection of a speaking/witnessing persona and a witnessed victimized other, I see in Dickinson an ethical response to cruelty that coincides with Agamben's theory of ethics in his *Homo Sacer* project, especially as he presents the question of a "bare life" in the *Remnants of Auschwitz* text.[5] Crucial to Agamben's reconfiguration of ethics for what remains of the

---

Robert McClure Smith, "Dickinson and the Masochistic Aesthetic," *Emily Dickinson Journal* 7, no. 2 (1998): 1–21; Cynthia J. MacKenzie, "'Heavenly Hurt': Dickinson's Wounded Text," *Emily Dickinson Journal* 9, no. 2 (2000): 55–63.

4 Michael D. Snediker, *Queer Optimism: Lyric Personhood and Other Felicitous Persuasions* (Minneapolis: University of Minnesota Press, 2009).

5 Giorgio Agamben, *Remnants of Auschwitz: The Witness and the Archive* (Brooklyn, NY: Zone Books, 1999). For a useful assessment of Agamben and ethics, see Catherine

human after the Holocaust is the necessary separation, the "non-coincidence," of the speaking subject and the living human, a split that makes testimony possible when one must respond to the unspeakable. The remnants of extreme abjection epitomized by the Holocaust present life, according to Agamben, reduced to a state barely human, beyond the terms of gender and far from the work of psychological motivations. Agamben's remodeling of the claims of ethics, with its focus on the singularity of the traumatized response, his structuring of an ethical response within language, is based on a fracture between subjectivity and abjection that opens a way to read Dickinson's slant poetics of testimony.

Dickinson, in poems such as "Split the Lark" (Fr 905) and "Rearrange a 'Wife's' Affection" (Fr 267), produces a slant testimony that instates slippage between subject and object, male and female, human and animal. The violence to which the poems attest tarries with the abject, but also abjures abjection. Notably, there is a tendency in the poems for the speaker to veer towards the subjectivity of the victim and then pull away repeatedly. "Split the Lark," for example, features the suggestion that by reading the work of the poet addressing us we are destroying her gift—splitting open the source of the private and privative music. The speaker seems to be testifying to her own victimization, and yet she is also testifying to the impossibility of testimony. It is the testimony itself that causes the victimization; therefore an impossible testimony is the ruse of this poem. Similarly, "Rearrange a 'Wife's' Affection" produces a victim who is neither male nor female, and who is mute, suggesting that the core trope of violence is muteness, a nodus against which the poem composed of words strives even as its effort is to reveal the mute core of violated subjectivity.

Benjamin Friedlander's essay "Intention in Extremity: Reading Dickinson after the Holocaust" is framed as a response to the way that Dickinson poses impossible testimony, for the editors of the special issue of the journal *Poetics Today* in which Friedlander's essay appeared make the case that responses (like Dickinson's) to the American Civil War properly belong to a modern ethics and aesthetics of testimony, for which the Holocaust "figures as the generic paradigm."[6] With that problem of the impossible testimony in mind, one might ask whether we should now perhaps be "moving away from the discourse on trauma," as Lauren Berlant contends in *Cruel Optimism*.[7] Although much can be learned from Berlant's timely consideration of our affective attachments to love objects as "clusters of promises" that suspend hope in the face of cruelty and despair, I take special interest in her claim, which she makes in a note on abjection, that "subjectifying" and "desubjectifying" are "inassimilable."[8] For Dickinson's poetics *is precisely*

Mills, "An Ethics of Bare Life: Agamben on Witnessing," Review Essay, *Borderlands e-journal* 2, no. 1 (2003), http://www.borderlands.net.au/vol2no1_2003/mills-agamben.html (accessed January 4, 2013).

6 "How Testimony Communicates," *Poetics Today* 26, no. 2 (Summer 2005): 171.

7 Laurent Berlant, *Cruel Optimism* (Durham: Duke University Press, 2011), 9.

8 Berlant, *Cruel Optimism*, 287.

about the inassimilable language of the abject. In other words, Dickinson shapes witnessing sadism as that which denudes the watcher of love and this core trauma cannot be moved away from. Dickinson, like Agamben, brings into question the cultural mark and meaning of trauma, not to elide the fact of violence (that produces trauma) but instead to remark the sublimity of the effect of violence, specifically the way that violence haunts subjectivity. Although Berlant's and Snediker's works belong broadly to the same project, *Cruel Optimism*'s gesture towards leaving behind the discourse of loss may not come to terms fully with the latent power of the place of violence still within language, a potentiality that Snediker seems much more comfortable in articulating.[9]

Snediker, in *Queer Optimism*, reads "queer" optimism as a modality that enables the speaker to inhabit fluid subject positions, indeed to infuse trauma with melancholy and inhabit melancholy with hope, as opposed to leaving behind the effort to articulate trauma. Like Snediker, I rely on a definition of "queer" as a subjectivity of the borderlands. Queer is that which eludes heteronormative injunctions to be stably and singly masculine or feminine; queer eludes the capitalist injunction to earn one's keep at the expense of the other. Judith Halberstam's notion of queer as "subcultural" chimes with my usage, and specifies an inhabitation of the borderland territory not only between genders but also outside of heteronormative time: "queers use space and time in ways that challenge conventional logics of development, maturity, adulthood and responsibility."[10] The optimism of resistance pulses through Dickinson's most bleak work in large part because Dickinson represents the negative sublime of violence as a limit-state that, while inassimilable, haunts.

The Pleasures of the Reader

But what are the contours of this haunting? How does violence generate Dickinson's poetics of subjectivity? Marianne Noble's *The Masochistic Pleasures of Sentimental Literature* interprets Dickinson's metaphors of bodily violence as self-styled bodily punishments, going so far as to diagnose Dickinson as a masochist, at least in fantasy. Noble surely hopes to refute Camille Paglia's notorious typification of Dickinson as a sadist.[11] Noble's classification of Dickinson as a masochist, like Paglia's argument that Dickinson was a sadist and therefore not feminine, depends heavily on a cliché of gender. Noble groups Dickinson's poetry—largely considered un-publishable in the nineteenth-century—with popular sentimental women's fiction of the nineteenth century, pinning her reading of Dickinson on deterministic notions of gender, and following an assumption

---

9 See Berlant's discussion of Snediker, *Cruel Optimism*, 12–13.

10 Judith Halberstam, *In a Queer Time and Place: Transgender Bodies, Subcultural Lives* (New York: New York University Press, 2005), 13.

11 Camille Paglia, *Sexual Personae: Art and Decadence from Nefertiti to Emily Dickinson* (New Haven, CT: Yale University Press, 1990).

that to be masochistic is to be feminine, an assumption that is striking given that Dickinson's poetry, however well regarded now, was not popular, not published, during her lifetime.[12]

Noble insists that because Dickinson was a woman—that is, is properly placed in the company of other women writers—she should be interpreted as a masochist. If she writes scenes of violence she must be *fantasizing* violence done against her. Thus Noble, like Paglia in *Sexual Personae*, tautologically aligns masculinity with sadism, and matches femininity with masochism—tautological definitions that, ironically, given the core disagreement between Noble and Paglia, reinforce each other. Dickinson presented her poetry in a fashion that was construed as feminine, tilting her elliptical expressions towards an appearance of extreme verbal delicacy. And yet, as Snediker's *Queer Optimism* argues, within Dickinson's couched performances of femininity in poems, there is ample textual space to question the very gendered alignment of masochism and sadism on which Noble and Paglia alike insist. As Martha Nell Smith and Ellen Louise Hart have long suggested, Dickinson's apparent femininity, her reclusive bent, can be interpreted as a refusal of the terms of traditional womanhood.[13] Dickinson's depictions of violence in her poems may be read not as steeped in feminine masochism but rather deconstructing or laying bare the very problematic of enforcing a correlation between femininity and masochism. A queer definition of gender as social interpretation, or code, then, focuses my investigation into Dickinson's linguistic evocations of violence. My aim being not to deny the force of gendered clichés but to show how Dickinson uses them poetically, abstracting them from herself, to dramatize the split between speaking subject and victimized (de-subjectified) object, both of which have always only a slant relationship with the living, autobiographical self.

My aim is to interrogate the way Dickinson's poetic descriptions of bodily violence infer a speaker whose most salient characteristic is the ability to watch violence calmly. This persona seems neither to fit the feminine cliché of the masochist, as it is *not* the speaker who is violated in most of Dickinson's violent lyrics; rather, she recounts another's violation. Nor is the subject who gives voice to cruelty the masculine cliché of the sadist, for the speaker is rarely performing the violence she recounts. This speaking identity is developed in Dickinson's poems' reportage of the violence that her speaker sees while not flinching or responding emotively to the violence described. Should this witness-as-speaker be gendered at all? Dickinson, in the poems driven by violent imagery, develops a testifying persona that complicates clichés of gender by evoking key gendered *topoi* in ways that have to bend gender clichés. In other words, the witness who

---

12 Helen Malson, in *The Thin Woman: Feminism, Post-Structuralism, and the Social Psychology of Anorexia Nervosa* (New York: Routledge, 1998), beautifully glosses the false genealogical link between femininity and masochism.

13 Ellen Louise Hart and Martha Nell Smith, eds., *Open Me Carefully: Emily Dickinson's Intimate Letters to Susan Huntington Dickinson* (Ashfield, MA: Paris Press, 1998), xiv.

utters violence done upon the body of the other in Dickinson's poems is at once drawn as a paradigmatically feminine subject, a witness who cannot intervene and stop violence, and also as what we might conceive of as a masculine voice, insofar as the interlocutor does not respond emotionally to the violence she describes but maintains an extraordinarily stoic disposition.

To slide a little from Dickinson's poems to the poet's self-presentation, I believe it is worth noting that by her peers Emily Dickinson was interpreted as manifesting traits considered hyper-feminine, a supremely delicate creature described by her beloved sister-in-law as too fine for human interaction.[14] Dickinson's life-long performance as a woman too delicate for social intercourse proved to be unforgettable: as a performance artist offering nineteenth-century feminine delicacy, Dickinson became literally untouchable. I mention Dickinson's performance of gender because her personal deployment of femininity as a strategy may suggest Dickinson's sensitive ear for the feminine line. Critics have correctly argued that the gender and sexual orientation of Dickinson's speakers in general shift from poem to poem, but I would argue further that the speaker who calmly performs the role of witnessing and reporting violence in Dickinson's poetry is marked by key gestures both as a feminized speaker and as a masculinized observer, gestures that ultimately throw into question the gendering of speaking and watching.[15] This performance of witnessing transgresses the typology of the female-masochist/male-sadist paradigm followed by Paglia and Noble. The speaker who watches and reports violence in Dickinson's poetry is at once hyper-feminine, utterly powerless, and stringently masculine, without emotion or empathy.

The violent poems on which I will focus, then, articulate a speaker-position solely characterized by a superbly and problematically capacious gaze—a gaze that can watch and encompass horrific violence, even as the speaker possessing this gaze either cannot or will not respond to alter the conditions generating the violence s/he watches. Dickinson's speakers in violent poems are radically disempowered and yet also powerful in their insistence on their singular gaze as a source of truth that may surpass empathy.

The sadism of which Paglia and Noble speak invokes psychoanalytic concepts of erotic desire. But as I have noted, in my work, "sadism" denotes cruelty and violence enacted against a victim who cannot meaningfully defend herself and who also is "on view" to others. I argue for this different definition of sadism to use in reading Dickinson because in considering the very complicated intersections of ethics and aesthetics that occur in Dickinson's violent poems, one needs, I think,

---

[14] Please see Susan Dickinson's moving obituary for Emily, in which Susan admiringly describes her late sister-in-law as having "too fine a mesh" for human interaction. Susan Huntington Dickinson, "Obituary of Emily Dickinson," *Digital Amherst*, Item #904, http://www.digitalamherst.org/items/show/904 (accessed August 5, 2012).

[15] Sylvia Hennenberg, "Neither Lesbian nor Straight: Multiple Eroticisms in Emily Dickinson's Love Poetry," *The Emily Dickinson Journal* 4, no. 2 (1995): 1–19.

to dislodge the heteronormative assumptions that engender Paglia's and Noble's arguments that Dickinson's writing of violence is erotic fantasy.

Ignoring the cultural effects of power, Paglia and Noble both write as if Dickinson's handling of violence in text could only be understood sexually, that is, as erotic fantasy—an assumption with which I disagree. That is not to say that cruelty and spectacle do not have an erotic component, but rather to argue that sadistic violence in Dickinson's poetry is not primarily erotic. Instead, it is described in moments of grief and insolvable mourning—and this mourning is not so much for the suffering other as for the witness to insolvable violence. Following the direction of Snediker's *Queer Optimism*, which opens the door to a reading of Dickinson as engaged in the project of developing ethics, or "grace," outside heteronormative parameters, I suggest against the grain that Dickinson's poetry of violence can fruitfully be interpreted as her engagement with the key cultural *topoi* of her era—that is, the sadism expressed in racism and patriarchy, antebellum style.[16]

The violence described in some of Dickinson's work is intense. To reflect this intensity, I will place Dickinson's descriptions of violence in the context of Civil War poetry—not a new move but one that I hope provides a framework for conceptualizing Dickinson's depictions of violence in an era that was steeped and suffused in violence.[17] Betsy Erkkila beautifully makes the argument that Dickinson writes not from isolation but from community: however reclusive she eventually became, in the 1860s Dickinson long followed the news, and the news of the early 1860s was the war. Developing from Erkkila, I would suggest that even as the reclusive Dickinson bowed out from political engagement, she retained a sensitive awareness to events unfolding nationally in the early 1860s.[18] If we understand Dickinson as, despite her hermitage, a watcher of the broader American community experiencing the Civil War, we must assume that the connections between Dickinson and war bear scrutiny. The war was violent and also responded to the violence of enslavement.

I would approach Dickinson's evocations of violence, then, with this question: whose erotics do we read in Dickinson's violent poetry? Dickinson's verbal evocations of violence may not reflect her own erotic fantasies, but rather may function as a mirror that Dickinson places before constructs of gender and race and

---

16 To point out, as I do, that Dickinson was not a well-known poet during her lifetime does *not* mean that Dickinson was not aware of cultural trends and events occurring around her. Dickinson's capacity to watch the culture around her, her national culture, is not necessarily connected to the ability of that culture to watch her.

17 Notably, Faith Barrett and Cristanne Miller edited a book of Civil War poetry which included Dickinson and indicated the appropriateness of reading Dickinson not as a masochist fantasizing harm, but as a realist recording wartime suffering. Please see Faith Barrett and Cristanne Miller, eds., *"Words for the Hour": A New Anthology of American Civil War Poetry* (Amherst: University of Massachusetts Press, 2005).

18 Betsy Erkkila, *The Wicked Sisters: Women Poets, Literary History, and Discord* (New York: Oxford University Press, 1992), esp. 19–24.

the violence that holds in place these constructs. In other words, we must recognize as Foucault long ago made clear that gender constructs are themselves generated by hierarchical, sadistic paradigms.[19] The hierarchical, sadistic paradigms exposed in her violent poems are not necessarily part of Dickinson's own eroticism.

Indeed, I object to the heteronormative paradigm that insists on reading Dickinson through erotic motifs. This paradigm should be refined, expanded, and challenged, because implicit in such readings is the idea that Dickinson's descriptions of violence must be personal fantasies because she is a woman. Noble, for example, effectively assumes that because Emily Dickinson was a woman she could not represent violent reality—rather, she must be fantasizing suffering. I hope to argue for the importance of Dickinson's invocation of the role of the witness, one who sees and reports the traumatic real, as a way to open up and reexamine this critical alignment of femininity and fantasy.

For, far from playing through fantasies, Dickinson's approach to violence uses language as a performative tool that teaches and indeed trains the speaker-as-reader to face violence. The violent poems of Dickinson's flood years face and apparently expect no possibility of changing violence. Dickinson's poems delineate tragic systems of sadism, driven not by the speaker's erotic pleasure, in the pleasure of exposing a system of sadism that seems invulnerable except in this paradoxical vulnerability to exposure by representation.

Southern Belle, Posthumously

Dickinson's early twentieth-century rise into canonicity is bound up with Southern Agrarian critics John Crowe Ransom and Allen Tate.[20] Ideologically steeped in Civil War angst, the Southern Agrarians rescued Emily-as-belle from critical trivialization. Rather than seeing Dickinson's twentieth-century canonization as a misreading forced upon the delicate recluse, I suggest that links to the Southern Agrarians were already present in her poems—not only the class-based ideological

---

19 Michel Foucault, *The History of Sexuality: Volume 1* (New York: Random House, 1978), 75–115.

20 See John Crowe Ransom, "Reconstructed but Unregenerate," in *I'll Take My Stand: The South and the Agrarian Tradition*, ed. Lewis P. Simpson (Baton Rouge: Louisiana State University Press, 1977), 1–27. See also his essay, "Emily Dickinson: A Poet Restored," in *Emily Dickinson: A Collection of Critical Essays*, ed. Richard B. Sewell (Upper Saddle River, NJ: Prentice Hall, 1963), 88–100. These writings provide Ransom's interpretation and rationale of Dickinson's superiority to other late nineteenth-century woman poets. Ransom's "Emily Dickinson: A Poet Restored" enacts the gesture of Ransom "restoring" Dickinson, focusing on presenting the feminine, retiring nature of the poet that caused her to be in need of restoration. For example, he writes that "Emily Dickinson was a little, home-keeping person" who was "by nature gentle but indecisive" (89, 97). Ransom goes on to describe Dickinson as "a kind of Cinderella," bringing into the open the gender dynamics of the poet's restoration (98).

links that Erkkila so persuasively elucidates, but also topical links: a sustained consideration of sadism, the violence of racism that presses behind the Civil War. Ransom and Tate were hardly *freedom riders* but their knowledge of the contours of racism finds uncanny coded echoes in Dickinson's violent poetry. Dickinson's violent poetry mirrors, witnesses, and faces Southern antebellum and Civil War sadism. The Southern Agrarians found in Dickinson the witness they wanted: a poet who revealed and yet did not agitate against violence.

Admittedly, the difference between these terms—witness, agitate—the difference between seeing and acting against violence, might indicate the difficulty of interpreting the ethics of Dickinson's reportage of violence. Interpreting Dickinson's verbal acts of mirroring, facing, and witnessing violence leads us to a place of vertigo, for her ethics of watching violence are embedded in what can be read as a privative personal discourse. But, if we decide not to subscribe to the belief that women fantasize violence for their erotic pleasure—a belief that long ago was discarded in the realm of feminist law reforms—then we are compelled to interpret Dickinson's representations of violence as scenarios that may bear witness to sadism, rather than scenarios that take pleasure in sadism.[21] Dickinson's deployment of a steely-eyed watcher of violence, a watcher who does not respond directly to the violence she describes herself seeing, may also function as a partial answer to this question of belated canonicity that defines her posthumous career.

The imagery of violence in Dickinson's poetry of the 1860s is so thick that I believe a partial list will suffice. I will focus on Dickinson's poems 267, 309, and 656 alongside two Civil War poems popular in their day: Mary H. C. Booth's "While God He Leaves Me Reason, God He Will Leave Me Jim," and Caroline A. Ball's "The Jacket of Gray."[22] I want to read the representation of violence that so impressed Ransom in his critical recuperation of Dickinson, but interpret this representation of violence in the context of Booth's and Ball's Civil War poems—pointing out that Booth's and Ball's poetry also describe violence. I will read for the differences in describing and representing violence that inflect canonicity, Dickinson's production of canonical literature, and Ball's and Booth's production of popular literature.

One question I hope to make central to this chapter is that of the wisdom of choosing to ignore the real violence—of racism, misogyny, and homophobia—in whose terms Dickinson's poems' performative world is caught when we read her poems as personal, private fantasies. For the discourse in which tropes of misogynistic and racialized sadism were tragically prevalent, as Hazel Carby's landmark 1987 work makes clear, was the coin of the realm when Dickinson was

---

21 Please see Linda Gordon, *Heroes of Their Own Lives* (New York: Viking, 1988; Champaign-Urbana: University of Illinois Press, 2002).

22 As noted earlier all references to Dickinson's poetry indicate *The Poems of Emily Dickinson: Reading Edition*, ed. R. W. Franklin. The poems of Booth and Ball are found in Barrett and Miller, *"Words for the Hour."*

writing.[23] Far from performatively fantasizing masochistic or, for that matter, sadistic eroticism, Dickinson's speaker compulsively creates a scene reflective of real violence from which she distances herself. Dickinson's gesture of writing to represent violence creates a hypothetical other—a body not the speaker's body, a body observed by the speaker in the performative space of the poem. Importantly, the speaker is not the force that enacts violence; rather, the speaker is positioned as a witness, and possibly as an interlocutor. This suffering described in the poem's other may be intimately bound to the "I" of the speaker, the witness, but the body described as suffering in Dickinson's violent poems functions as an other, even as a body-double, for the speaker. Here, then, is the "I" that Dickinson brilliantly glosses as a "single screw of flesh" (Fr 293, line 1).

Dickinson's violent poems describe sadistic systems from which the speaker cannot extricate herself, and this depiction mirrors sadistic paradigms of violence that were not experienced as fantasy, but as reality by, for example, enslaved African American women during Dickinson's life.[24] Why would Dickinson be concerned with enslaved women when she lived in New England? Important work has been done on Dickinson's relationship to the servants of her household,[25] and some of the servants in the Dickinson household were African American. But more to the point, Dickinson's use of the metaphor of slavery has been remarked on by Galway Kinnell, and it is in homage to Kinnell's poetic encounter with Dickinson as a writer who fully conceived of and witnesses, in her writing, the horror of slavery that I write this chapter.[26] We need not look to the realm of fantasy to read Dickinson's violent lyrics. Dickinson's poems of violence reveal sadistic pleasures driving the systems of racism and patriarchy in the latter half of the nineteenth century, and this revelation functions not as Dickinson's fantasy, but as her skillful reporting and recording of sadism. Whether Dickinson's witness-as-poet is satisfactory as a political gesture is not a question I take up in this chapter. Instead, I am simply arguing that she is acting as a witness to violence in her role as poet.

In Dickinson's violent poems, the speaker describes violence without engaging the reader as an active agent who should or could stop the violence the poems describe. Instead, the precise threat of the sadism she describes is to render all possibility of stopping violence impossible. The claims of sentimental prose with which Noble identifies Dickinson are defined by just the opposite gesture: the sentimental gesture would be that of engendering the reader's response against violence. But Dickinson apparently resists the evocations of such a response.

---

23 Hazel V. Carby, *Reconstructing Womanhood: The Emergence of the Afro-American Woman Novelist* (New York: Oxford University Press, 1987).

24 Carby, *Reconstructing Womanhood*, esp. 20–40.

25 Aife Murray, *Maid As Muse: How Servants Changed Emily Dickinson's Life and Language* (Durham: University of New Hampshire Press; Hanover, NH: University Press of New England, 2009).

26 Galway Kinnell, "The Deconstruction of Emily Dickinson," *The Poetry Ireland Review* 43/44 (Autumn–Winter 1994): 177–8.

"The truth is bald and cold, but that will hold," she writes (Fr 281). In other words, steel yourself.

In reading representations of violence in Dickinson's poetry I want to shift my approach to the concept of constructs of subjectivity, suggesting against the grain that Dickinson's poetry is not necessarily a vivarium of self-regard but instead a forum for performing the watching of others through the poetic voice.[27] It is not that constructs of subjectivity are not of concern but rather that, given the extraordinary emphasis in Dickinson's poetry on performing witnessing, in the sense of writing a speaker who functions as a witness to violence, to read her work as interior discourse would seem to miss the point of her performance. In her poems describing violence, Dickinson is concerned with publicity and the exterior push and thwart and tragedy of violence. These poems are performances before a tribunal of some kind: an audience.

The speaker of Dickinson's poems depicting violence is learning to bear seeing violence that it seems the speaker cannot stop.[28] Dickinson's violent poems construct a bridge, however disturbing, between the aesthetic and ethical registers.[29] What Dickinson asks of her violent poems is that they freeze the reader. This stillness that Dickinson problematically calls forth from her audience contrasts with the responsive reading engaged by sentimental literature. Dickinson's evocation of awe not un-problematically allocates to aesthetic power a force of stillness.[30]

In the context of American racism and misogyny in the nineteenth century, this aesthetic of stillness is possibly unethical because such a freezing of the viewer precludes active response to the violence described in the poems. And yet this lack of sentimentality, lack of calling for active audience response, is central to the task of Dickinson's poetry. By not invoking abolitionists or feminists, Dickinson retains a private ground—an ironically privative *topos*—for her exploration of the poetics of abjection in public discourse.

---

[27] Joanne Feit Diehl "Selfish Desires: Dickinson's Poetic Ego and the Rites of Subjectivity," *The Emily Dickinson Journal* 5, no. 2 (Fall 1996): 100–106.

[28] See Joanne Feit Diehl, "The Poetics of Loss: Erotic Melancholia in Agamben and Dickinson," *American Imago* 66, no. 3 (2009): 369–81. Diehl is here relying on Agamben's writings on melancholy and image, his Benjaminian work on aesthetics which can be seen to set the foundation for his later writings on ethics and trauma.

[29] Looking to current work on intersections between ethics and aesthetics, I explore ways that aesthetics and ethics cross in Dickinson's violent poetry. In other words, Dickinson presents moments of empathic crisis, asking the audience to enter deeper into the space of the victim until suddenly the speaker withdraws empathy, leaving the audience to, in effect, make its move: will we retain empathy for the victim? It is important in this consideration to separate empathy and sympathy. Dickinson's poetics rarely ask for sympathy. For a discussion of empathy, see Mitchell Green, "Empathy, Expression, and What Artworks Have to Teach," in *Art and Ethical Criticism*, ed. Garry L. Hagberg (Oxford: Blackwell, 2008), 95–122.

[30] This function of the aesthetic as that which stills the viewer is central to Schopenhauer's theory of looking. See Arthur Schopenhauer, *The World as Will and Representation*, trans. E. F. G. Payne (New York: Dover Publications, 1969).

For example, in the tormented love poem "Rearrange a 'Wife's' Affection" the trope of the "secret" sequesters violence, as the poem points to a space beyond salvage (Fr 267, line 17).

> Rearrange a "Wife's" Affection!
> When they dislocate my Brain!
> Amputate my freckled Bosom!
> Make me bearded like a man!
>
> Blush, my spirit, in thy Fastness—
> Blush, my unacknowledged clay—
> Seven years of troth have taught thee
> More than Wifehood ever may!
>
> Love that never leaped it's socket—
> Trust intrenched in narrow pain—
> Constancy thro' fire—awarded—
> Anguish—bare of anodyne!
>
> Burden—borne so far triumphant—
> None suspect me of the crown,
> For I wear the "Thorns" till *Sunset*—
> Then—my Diadem put on.
>
> Big my Secret but it's *bandaged*—
> It will never get away
> Till the Day it's Weary Keeper
> Leads it through the Grave to thee.
> (Fr 267)

The poem begins dramatically with the invocation of sadistic and unexplained violence: the speaker invites her own brutal mutilation. In response to the threat of violence, the poem then moves by sequential sequestering into privacy, beginning with a traumatically threatened speaker and culminating in a vision of privacy for the traumatized body-double of the speaker. Importantly, by the poem's end, the "secret" and the "keeper" are not the same.

Instead, the "secret" is rhetorically positioned to perform as the implied body-double for the "keeper," while the secret's keeper is the speaker. The poem, to be sure, centers on the problem of keeping a secret and, when the secret being kept is the suppressed speaking of violence, the impressment of the secret becomes itself a form of violence. The poem juxtaposes the power of keeping a secret with the violence of the need to keep a secret. The speaker seeks privacy, for her love, her condition as a more than "wife" because only privacy will save her from the sadistic mutilation of an un-named "they" who seek to mutilate the speaker. The speaker who defines herself as feminine seeks privacy for her love because that love is bound tightly with the punitive acts of an unspecified but powerful "they," a force that can, and apparently would like to, mutilate both the speaker and her beloved.

But to return to the "secret": the speaker's capacity to speak is secured by the rhetorical construct of the "secret" as a personified figure. The body-double of the speaker is "the secret" and the "secret" gains for the speaker security from audience invasion, this seal posited as balm. For the speaker asserts a chilling identity between the audience and the "they" who seek to mutilate the speaker. As the speaker works deeper into the problematic of speaking for an audience that seeks to mutilate her, the embodied "secret" is developed and comes to occupy a space of enslavement by the poem's close, enchained by the secret's "keeper" (line 18). The "keeper" is none other than the poem's speaker. The "keeper" speaks the poem despite the threat of violence that hangs over her decision to speak. The keeper implicitly is able to speak the poem because that violence ultimately falls on the embodied secret that the speaker splits off from the capacity to speak.

In poem 267, the dramatic final lines produce a "big" and "bandaged" "secret" (line 17). Here is a figure produced entirely by textually unexplained violence. Healing is only permitted for the "secret," after this violence, in the excessively private space of death: "through the grave" (line 20). When I argue, above, that this "bandaged," "big" "secret" is posed as a body-double to the speaker, the secret's "keeper," I mean also that the abject double (the "secret") takes on aspects of the enslaved body—a body forced to be mute, a body violently led by its "keeper." The "secret" is mute embodiment that the poem generates as a bandaged other, while the speaker who calls herself a "keeper" retains her capacity to speak precisely by the act of constructing this double. A "kept" thrall, this secret wears the wound and "bandage" of embodiment, while the speaker/keeper leads the "secret," which has been demoted to the status of an "it." The speaker sheds her horrifically threatened body (threatened with amputation) only by creating through rhetoric a body-double that cannot refuse to wear "bandages" because this "secret" is mute. I would not press so hard on the racialized dimensions of this poem's construction of bandaged enslaved embodiment—this embodied "it" might be read as Dickinson's representation of the female body—were it not for the poem's composition in the thick of America's battle over the terms of racism *in extremis*. The bandaged secret, like the enslaved body that haunted the national imagination in the 1860s, Dickinson terrifyingly tells the audience "will never get away" (line 18).

The audience is implicated in the violence the poem describes insofar as the audience is the implicit "thee" addressed in the poem's final stanza. In the poem's rhetoric, Dickinson's audience is structurally responsible for the brutalized, bandaged, and silenced body that the poem imagistically traces, insofar as the poem leads the image of suffering embodiment to the *reader*, presenting the figure of the bandaged secret to the reader. Indeed, the audience is the "thee" of the poem's final line, towards which the violent acts described in the poem have all the while been led.

In unpacking what I argue is the racialized dimension of Dickinson's poem above, Jacques Derrida's notion of "trace" is useful.[31] Insofar as Dickinson's poem

---

[31] Jacques Derrida, *Of Grammatology*, trans. Gayatri Chakravorty Spivak (Baltimore and London: Johns Hopkins University Press, 1976).

invokes the terms of enslavement without mentioning race, one may yet contend that these terms of enslavement, in the context of America in the 1860s, were obviously culturally legible as having to do with race. Just as Derrida argues that the meaning of a given word contains not only its defined meaning but also traces of other meanings dragged along with the word as historical residue, we may see that in the immediate history just before, during, and just after the Civil War, in the United States, *virtually any reference to slavery would invoke race*.[32] The terms of bondage and submission, in the context of the American Civil War, the historical context in which Dickinson wrote, are laden with the weight of racism and the racial imaginary. Dickinson's poem, although it does not explicitly mention race, I argue, evokes the climate of racism and, with this evocation, the traumatic terms by which the erasure of the subjectivity of the racial other is enforced: the racial other becomes, in the climate of racism, a "bandaged secret" forcibly made mute.

Poem 267 does not begin with the invocation of enslavement, but asserts its concern with the gendered violence done to a "wife" (line 1) who apparently loves too ardently. And yet even this easy gender identification is queered as the poem opens. For the word "wife" appears in quotes, suggesting that the speaker may not in fact *be* a wife, but in some unspecified sense *like* a wife. The speaker desires to be like a wife but is denied, for unexplained reasons, the full status of wife. A possible reason for the speaker's being deprived of cultural status as a fully acknowledged wife is given by the speaker's invocation of "unacknowledged clay" (line 6). Mentioning "unacknowledged clay," the body she possesses and suppresses, shifts the discourse from matrimonial love (the wife) to suffering a trope of enslavement (being rendered "clay," mere body)—a shift that is not erotic fantasy but that brilliantly, if depressingly, links gender violence to racial violence, connoting racist misogyny in America in the 1860s. This suffering embodiment does not represent a space of erotic fantasy but, on the contrary, a space of foreclosed erotic fantasy whose only hope for recuperation, in the structure of the poem, is the afterlife. This suffering body with a "brain" (line 2) rather than a mind is vulnerable to devastating dislocation: a body of "unacknowledged clay" in its abject status at risk of violence.

In favor of a reading that places Dickinson writing in response to the symbolics of race, rather than only gender, that reads her work in response to the culturally inscribed vulnerability of race as well as that of gender, one notes that gender is dramatically unstable in Dickinson's poem. If the feminine "bosom" in poem 267 is vulnerable to "amputation" (line 3), this violence makes the speaker masculine, "like a man" (line 4). If the vulnerable body begins feminine, the effect of the violent amputation and lobotomization described in the poem also is to make the speaker "like a man."

---

32 Please see, for example, Elizabeth Barrett Browning's poem "Hiram Powers Greek Slave." Based on Powers's statue, The Greek Slave, nevertheless the poem is rightly read as Browning's abolitionist argument. Elizabeth Barrett Browning, *Selected Poems*, ed. Marjorie Stone and Beverly Taylor (Peterborough, Ontario: Broadview, 2009).

The conflation of femininity with suffering that is proffered by Noble's vision of sentimental masochism in this poem, it seems to me, is in fact subverted by the terms of the poem itself. Yes, the body conjured for suffering in poem 267 is feminine, but the effect of the violence described would be to make the "wife" "like a man." That is, the suffering body *in extremis* becomes an un-gendered body, a body forced to move beyond gender. Evacuated subjectivity holds the place of this tortured body—and torture, here, apparently causes one to lose one's womanly subjectivity. This loss of "subjectivity" in the face of witnessing extreme sadistic violence (amputating a woman's bosom and brain because she loves someone whom "they" deem she ought not love) is the key move in Dickinson's rhetorical development of the figure of the witness who is not sentimental.

Without question, suffering is the poem's core concern: "anguish—bare of anodyne" (line 12). And yet, the poem does not follow the gender designation of sentimental masochism, and it hollows out subjectivity. The poem does not follow the contours of fantasizing sadism delineated by Noble and Paglia. Instead, the speaker is masculine when tortured, a Christological figure wearing a crown of thorns (line 15), and feminine specifically when released from torture, a princess or queen in a "diadem" (line 16). Dickinson's deployment of gender instability revokes the possibility of easily categorizing her along the lines of nineteenth-century sentimentality. Sadism, here, is no erotic fantasy but the force that curtails Eros, and the gendering of those who inflict and those who suffer sadistic violence is radically unstable in the poem.

As interesting, however, as questions of gender instability, is to query the link between punishing and watching in the extraordinary violence described in the poem—the amputation, the crucifixion, the crown of thorns. At first, the audience will stand by and watch as "they" dislocate the speaker's brain, but then the audience becomes the "thee" for whom the violence is performed and perhaps the audience is indicated as the originator of that violence, of amputation and lobotomization of the speaker, and enslavement of the secret. The speaker punished for her love suffers pain, torment of fire and crucifixion (lines 10, 11, and 14)—violence culminating in the "secret's" forced enslavement to a "keeper" (line 19). The poem's first audience, the speaker suggests, is a feminine other: a feminine beloved "thee" whose femininity initially is secured by her difference from a violently masculine "they." A presumptively feminine audience that will not stop the violence is evoked for this scene of torture. For it is to this audience that the poem's violence is all along directed and presented; this audience permits the violence of the poem, in the representational register. We "watch" the amputations. We accept the mutilations of the "secret."[33]

And yet, a third term, a queenly and disturbingly dissociated watcher of violence, supervises a textual revelation of sadism. The dissociated watcher, the

[33] Here, I refer the reader to Spelman's controversial interpretation of "sympathy" and gender, compassion and womanliness as tools of racial oppression. Elizabeth Spelman, *Fruits of Sorrow: Framing Our Attention to Suffering* (Boston: Beacon, 1997).

diadem-wearing figure, is trained in the performative space of the poem to face suffering and do nothing about it, to powerfully witness while exposing the ethical problematic of the act of witnessing. The diadem functions as a kind of troubling prize marking a chill, feminine gaze, not a feminine figure who enacts sadism but one who reports in stillness.

But is the dissociated third element in Dickinson's poem—the posited watcher of sadistic violence—the audience, or is it the speaker herself, fragmenting from the bodily torture she receives? Or is the speaker her own first and worst audience? Jeffrey Hammond's work on the Puritan self-elegy helps us interpret Dickinson's poetics of violence as a staging of audience and identity.[34] As Hammond unpacks the rhetoric of the self-elegy, the speaker in the self-elegy is split into a dissociated watcher by envisioning his own death. In poem 267, Dickinson evokes just such a split in her depiction of a faithful, suffering "wife." The "wife" observes her own dismemberment as she splits into a debased "it" and a "keeper" (lines 18, 19).

Dickinson's dissociated speaker, I suggest, is twice split, twice fragmented. I mentioned in my initial reading of the poem that the "secret" towards which the poem moves becomes a personified "it" that is both mutilated ("bandaged") and powerless, a figure that, reading by Derrida's notion of "trace," we can interpret as enslaved. Yet in that enslavement precisely arises a second critical split, for at the poem's close the speaker leads a damaged "it"—a "big," "bandaged" "secret," a manifestation of a debased self that has completely fragmented and become personified as an abject other. The poem performs self-splitting twice, not just along the lines of gender, but also along the lines of racist, nineteenth-century typology, in which the enslaved body is mute.

In this performance of the doubly split gaze Dickinson represents a complex sadism. The speaker who divides herself from a suffering body that she implies is enslaved not only reprises Puritan ideology of the sinful flesh, but also potently re-inscribes racist ideology of the enslaved body as damaged object. In other words, the poem at once lays bare the sadism of enslavement as a sadism inextricably bound with terms of patriarchy and yet dangerously reprises the image of the feminine and the raced subject as mutilated (amputated) and mute (entrapped).

The speaker's pleasure in poem 267, as in the self-elegy, is the pleasure of rhetorically separating a vulnerable, embodied self from a diadem-wearing, speaking self. As in self-elegy, when the speaker performatively survives the body's death through speech, in poem 267 the speaker supervises the body's suffering by splitting voice from body. The pleasure is neither that of giving nor receiving pain, so much as that of learning to bear the witnessing of pain—in the

---

[34] Jeffrey A. Hammond, *The American Puritan Elegy: A Literary and Cultural Study* (Cambridge: Cambridge University Press, 2000), esp. 92–7. Of course, Dickinson also constructs herself as her own audience, here as elsewhere. Regarding Dickinson's inheritance from Puritan poetics, see H. Jordan Landry, "The Touched, The Tasted, and The Tempted: Lesbianizing the Triangles of Puritan Conversion Narratives in Emily Dickinson," *Women's Studies: An Interdisciplinary Journal* 33, no. 7 (2004): 875–906.

scopic register, training oneself to see unbearable torture and lead that vision into text (see line 20).

This paradigmatic pleasure of the aesthetic moment, what Schopenhauer in *The World as Will and Representation* defines as the freeze or stopped time of aesthetic pleasure, in Dickinson's poem 267 is troublingly crossed with ethical concerns because of the poem's subtle citation of Civil War-era racial injustice and violence. Around Dickinson's description of amputation and enslavement lingers an inescapable unease, for one cannot help but read the violence of dismemberment, amputation, and enslavement, upon which the speaker trains herself to cast a cold eye in not only aesthetic but also ethical terms. Dickinson's powerful evocation of witnessing violence would seem paradoxically to derive its power from the accomplishment of aesthetic stillness as opposed to sentimental ability and activity, and yet such stillness may be read as less than noble when sadism was a key element of nineteenth-century racism, a cultural force that, maybe, should not be aestheticized.

Reflecting the sadism inherent in racism, the speaker of Dickinson's poem faces sadism not as fantasy, but primarily as performative memory. For in poem 267, the poem's structure reflects a rigorous system of violence in which all spoken ideas and/or commands of a victim are rendered void and mute. No matter how brilliant the speech of the big, bandaged secret might have been, no one will listen to this debased "it," and so the speaker's witnessing of the sadistic amputations from which she splits is as close as we come to the aesthetic prize of the possibility of justice—freeing the "bandaged" "secret." The secret remains mute, and yet the secret is also the speaker's possession.

The threat of muteness, of having one's speech rendered un-hearable, forms the core drama of Dickinson's poem 267. The poem at last stages the failure of the attempt to gain speech for the suffering body. This dislocated, amputated body is ultimately only witnessed by a speaker whose speaking re-inscribes a paradigm in which a split occurs so that a body without voice—an "it"—absorbs the suffering, leaving a speaking "I" free to lead the poem to a fully legible and articulate exposition of a system controlled by a denoted, sadistic "they." This narrative of the sadistic system that has "amputated" the speaker is breathtaking, but the residue of the abject other, an other so violated as to have been rendered mute, makes the poem uncomfortably an-ethical, a poem that reveals violence but literally cannot figure a way to stop that sadism.

Civil War Era Poetry

The ethical parameters of Dickinson's descriptive violence may be illuminated further by setting her work in contrast to that of other Civil War era poets. Barrett and Miller's placement of Dickinson's work alongside other Civil War poets suggests the plausibility of such comparison.[35] If poem 267 turns on a revelation of racism as sadism, "sadistic" here would be a descriptive term mapped and defined within nineteenth-century American slavery, a theme of course also connected to the Civil War. In turning to another violent Dickinson poem, I would like to consider Dickinson's work in conjunction with Caroline Ball's immensely popular, at the time of its publication, Civil War poem, "The Jacket of Gray," once considered a poetic staple, but no longer part of the canon of American poetry.[36] Like Dickinson's poem 309, "Kill your Balm," Ball's poem about the uniform of the Confederacy deals in a sacrificial aesthetic. Dickinson's and Ball's poems both foreground imagery of blood and gore, and connect shedding of blood, through figurative description, with aesthetic pleasure. Ball's poem was well received in its day.[37]

Ball's "The Jacket of Gray" focuses on a physical emblem, the soldier's uniform, as an iconic marker whose aesthetic presence rewards the bereaved with a surpassing melancholy pleasure. The melancholy economy in Ball's poem surpasses the pleasure of a non-violent alternative to the poem's narrative (i.e., Confederate surrender) precisely by constructing the jacket of gray as aesthetic reward for shedding blood. The jacket of gray is posited or figured by Ball as an aestheticized object—a keepsake, a memento, yes, but more than that, an emblem whose worth, the poem ultimately argues, is greater than the worth of the living son who might have surrendered.

The aesthetic register in Ball's poem is stealthily valorized in the poem's exceedingly sentimental parlance. Ball does not stint on gruesome details as she describes "life-blood" oozing onto the jacket of gray, and describes the jacket "stained … with gore" (line 29). Dickinson's roughly contemporaneous poem 309 also describes, gruesomely, blood bubbling up into the throat, although here the ravaged throat is that of a stabbed, dying songbird—the bird's song imbricated by the sound of blood rising into the throat on the bird's "last refrain" (line 6).

Kill your Balm—and it's Odors bless you—
Bare your Jessamine—to the storm—
And she will fling her maddest perfume—
Haply—your Summer night to Charm—

Stab the Bird—that built in your bosom—
Oh, could you catch her last Refrain—
Bubble! "forgive"—"Some better"—Bubble!
"Carol for Him—when I am gone"!
(Fr 309)

---

35 Barrett and Miller, *"Words for the Hour."*

36 See Barrett and Miller, *"Words for the Hour."*

37 Please see Appendix for the poem's full text.

This performance of violence in language, punctuated by gruesome, onomatopoeic evocation of the fluent sound of blood rising into a stabbing victim's throat, locates Dickinson's aesthetic in proximity to Ball's similarly bloody writing. Dickinson's "bird" is feminized. Importantly, both Ball and Dickinson describe in their poetry a sadistic economy in which the thing one most treasures—a songbird or a son—gives the greatest yield of pleasure when it is stabbed and bleeds to death.

Ball describes the soldier boy as literally worth more, for the poem's aesthetic repertoire, after his treasured blood stains the gray jacket. In a similar equation, Dickinson states that if you "kill your balm," it will "bless you" (line 1). The soldier boy and the balm both must be killed in order to dispense their aesthetic blessing in the sadistic economy reflected by Dickinson and Ball. Ball and Dickinson draw heavily on the dramatic description of shed blood to anchor the aesthetic of their poems. Dickinson's "bird—that built in your bosom" is, of course, an easy metaphor for a child (line 5), and the son described in Ball's sentimental poem is also marked as a child.

The excess of Dickinson's poem 309, reminding one of horror films in which the dying speak while blood bubbles into their throats, diverges from Ball's imagery insofar as Dickinson locates the place of violence as the throat and the mouth—the sites of speech. Dickinson performs in her poem an investigation into the way that writing of violence is a performative act, sharply differentiated from experiencing violence. This distinction or clarification offered by Dickinson's poetics of violence stands in contrast to Ball's sentimental depictions of violence, depictions that do not theorize within the text problematics of the articulation of violence; that is, Ball's poem does not frame or confess its mediated quality. By contrast, Dickinson's bird, in poem 309, is a theoretical object, an injured speaker that supervises the poetics of violence that govern the poem's performance of speech. This injured speaker calls attention to the poem's own effort to speak of violence and to the questions this effort raises.

Dickinson and Ball are writing during a time (the Civil War) when violence, the visual record of war, was traumatically introduced by photography. Civil War photography of the dead was often staged tableau, belated and indeed staged reportage of violence that could be traced but not mended by the time you saw the photograph.[38] Dickinson asks her audience to see, while acknowledging the impossibility of mending what has been seen: she asks us to imagine dismemberment in specific, graphic terms without the possibility of healing the fleshly wreckage. While Ball writes to incite mothers to offer up their sons to fight, Dickinson has no explicit agenda. She does not directly tell us to do anything; she describes violence calmly, as if already instilled with photography's elegiac distance, possibly reflecting the influence of Civil War photographs. The chill configurations of a watcher of violence who cannot stop the violence s/he sees may reflect a photographic aesthetic, emerging at the time Dickinson writes.

---

[38] For examples of Civil War photography, see Naomi Rosenblum, *A World History of Photography*, 4th ed. (New York: Abbeville Press, 1984), esp. 184–91.

Dickinson's poem 309 concerns itself with staging the problematics of representation and audience, exploring this configuration signally through violence. Poem 309 interprets its own effort to represent violence as itself a source of pain inflicted on the speaker. The feminized subject—the Jessamine-like bird clearly defined as "she"—must be killed to release aesthetic pleasure, blessing, and ominously transfers onto the poem's speaker the imprimatur that she please the sadistic audience: "Carol for him—when I am gone," sings the bleeding bird (line 8). But the gender designation of suffering "she" and torturing "he" are less transparent than Noble's paradigm of feminine masochism suggests.

The feminized songbird in poem 309 calls the poem's speaker to stand in for her after masculine sadism has completely destroyed her. A sadistic system is revealed not as pleasurable fantasy, but as challenge to the witness, the speaker, to resist: she resists by refusing to be silent. By contrast, Ball describes a feminine speaker, a mother, whose melancholic pleasure comes from meditating on the blood and gore, the life force, on her dead son's uniform. The male body here is sacrificial, represented by the embodied emblem of the soldier's jacket. Like Ball, Dickinson dramatizes the conditions necessary for the violent poem's composition. However, the drama in Dickinson's poem inscribes a radical self-splitting that Ball's sentimental excursus disavows, insofar as the jacket of gray shores up and valorizes gendered customs that separate mother and male child in a discourse of non-recoverable melancholic loss.

Like "The Jacket of Gray," Mary C. Booth's "While God He Leaves Me Reason, God He Will Leave Me Jim" presents the melancholic subversion of the maternal gaze.[39] Here, the poem's description of the mother of fallen Jimmy focuses on the visual register, the act of watching the terrible violence of dying in battle.[40] While Ball's "The Jacket of Gray" displaces violence onto a fetishistic, scopic object (the gray jacket), Booth's poem describes the impossibility of recuperation through the visual register for the melancholic, feminine subject—the mother. In "While God He Leaves Me Reason, God He Will Leave Me Jim," the mother's inability to see the violence of war focuses both the verbal play of the poem, the macabre pun on the meaning of "fallen," and the definition of femininity as blindness. Booth's poem defines a mother's sanity as irrevocably linked to her performance of maternity for a son—for the poem ends with the recognition that the son killed, Jimmy, is the mother's only son. The speaker's gender definition depends on nurturing a male child. In this reductive and patriarchal definition of gender, the definition of womanly is the performative inability to see violence: the mother *cannot* see (i.e., cannot bear to see, but also will not be responsible for seeing) the violent death of her son, which is the poem's imagistic centerpiece, that image of violence which the audience necessarily engages on reading the poem.

This incapacity of the mother to see the violence done to her son is expressed by the poem's verbal play on "fallen," a pun specifying traditional femininity as collapse or extreme delicacy always imminently near collapse. The pun on "fallen"

39 See Barrett and Miller, *"Words for the Hour."*

40 Please see Appendix for this poem's full text.

and the implicit play on themes of blindness are deployed by Booth to hold in place gender positions against the extreme stress of a war that Booth's speaker also perceives as Abraham sacrificing Isaac—a kind of raveling. Booth's poem's extreme effort to sustain representation of traditional gender positions in her poem, by carrying the father's power to the extreme, almost works to deconstruct patriarchy, even as it is clear that Booth, on the surface, intends to convey nothing but a critique of Lincoln. In contrast to Ball's overtly politicized critique of President Lincoln, the rhetoric of Dickinson's poems insists that the speaker can sustain herself despite the ravages of the violence performed as description in the poems. Dickinson's speaker does not need us, or at least she does not claim to need our political alliance.

If Booth produces a femininity that is defined by lacking the ability to see painful realities, and also defined by the gesture of reaching out overtly to persuade the audience of her politics, Dickinson's gendering departs from sentimental structures precisely by the speaker's unwavering gaze at the violence her text contains, and also by her apparent lack of desire to change that violence. Femininity in both Ball's and Booth's sentimental poems is precisely defined by *an inability to sustain the watching of violence*. Booth describes a mother who cannot see that her son has died; Ball describes a uniform whose persistence coverts the deaths it contains. By contrast, in poem 267 Dickinson insists on fidelity to the gaze that sees violence. Dickinson's speaker insists on seeing violence and not turning away.

Turning Away, Turning Toward Sadistic Violence

Dickinson's "wife" character turns not from but *for* viewing violence. Indeed, this speaker, displaced at the outset from normative gender by the placing in quotations of her wifely status, makes the very topic of her poem a discussion of how she will never, ever look away, even though she is tortured. "Love that never leaped it's socket" parses the earlier "affection" (lines 9, 1), which stresses that the "wife's" constancy is oddly ocular—the "wife" in this poem is the one who sees when others do not. In the elliptical, opening displacement of the terms of gender, the making hypothetical of the role of "wife," Dickinson's poem 267 closes the possibility of looking away from violence. Looking away is the main gesture offered by Ball's and Booth's poems. Dickinson closes poem 267 by differentiating her speaker from normative, sentimental femininity, which Ball and Booth make clear is typified by the placing of a screen between oneself and violence. However permeable this screen may be in the practice of Ball's and Booth's violent poems, the ideological insistence upon it is central to their poems' sentimental task.

The speaker of Dickinson's violent poems will not turn away even if she watches torture. This stance is the opposite of the femininity exemplified in Booth's and Ball's—a femininity that performs turning away, even as the audience must suffer the maintenance of some kind of gaze at the images of death on the battlefield intimated by the poems. If not sentimentally feminine, Dickinson's violence in poetry is also not masculine, as Paglia suggested in *Sexual Personae*. Dickinson's feminine speaker describes violence from an anomalous ethical position, neither enjoying the spectacle of violence nor arguing against it. Rather, her poems accept a sadistic reality that, in the world of the poems, cannot change. A circularity takes over, for example, in poem 267, in which the speaker linguistically performs watching violence that is a hypothetical punishment for what might happen if she failed to properly perform her peculiar definition of femininity as the capacity to watch violence without responding—to bear the witnessing of violence "bare of anodyne" (line 12). The poem's urge is to performatively master the act of watching violence. This need for mastery reveals an unchanging sadistic system against which the feminine speaker and her feminine beloved must construct themselves. The placing of "wife" in quotation marks reflects not only an erotic displacement of masculine prerogative, but also a troubling positioning of femininity as that which watches the performance of violence. Despite faithful love for the feminine other, Dickinson's witness-speaker will not explicitly intervene in a sadistic system which constructs the feminine and the racial "other" as victim.

Clearly, part of the stage for watching sadistic violence in the nineteenth-century South was the paradigm of gender: women watching suffering was of course crucial to sentimental literature. And yet Dickinson refuses to hold in place the gendered watcher, the feminine sentimental speaker. Moving away from heteronormative paradigms, one way of interpreting the ethics of watching violence performed in Dickinson's violent poetry is suggested by Snediker in *Queer Optimism*. Snediker's *Queer Optimism* revises earlier interpretations of Dickinson's masochistic/sadistic imagery, what Snediker calls her "queer pain," by looking at the complex performative terms of Dickinson's descriptions of violence.[41] Snediker's emphasis on the un-gendering strangeness of Dickinson's lyrics suggests a way to query the ethical valence of Dickinson's performance of witnessing.

Snediker rightly notes that Suzanne Juhasz's interpretation of Dickinson's sadism is pivotal to later queer readings of Dickinson—Juhasz celebrates what she argues is an emancipatory power in Dickinson's playing with images of erotic suffering.[42] However, Snediker also reminds us that recognition of tropes of suffering in Dickinson's poetry is hardly new with queer theory, but reaches back to Poulet and Gelpi and indeed matches with Dickinson's early valorization by the New Critics.[43] Importantly, Dickinson's act of publicly describing violence in writing is a performance rather than a fantasy. As Snediker suggests, Dickinson deploys text to "insist on its instabilities," for when Dickinson writes about violence she is *performing in text the witnessing of violence*, an act very different

---

41 Snediker, *Queer Optimism*, 79.

42 Snediker, *Queer Optimism*, 81. The reading Snediker is referencing here is found in Suzanne Juhasz, "Amplitude of Queer Desire in Dickinson's Erotic Language," *Emily Dickinson Journal* 14, no. 2 (2005): 24–33.

43 Snediker, *Queer Optimism*, 82.

from S&M fantasizing.[44] The act of such a performance is inherently unstable, for it cedes to audience the power of interpreting and responding to the violence described even as it retains for Dickinson the power of a kind of privative elocution. This, Dickinson's decision to perform, involves ethics; text as performance is inherently unstable, and Dickinson mines this aspect of her medium to create text that shimmers with ethical ambiguity.

Staging the Drowned Female Body

The poems "I can wade Grief—" and, more famously, "I started Early—took my Dog," for instance, depict violence in ways that let the speaker and audience confront and survive confrontation with a system of sadism that is not pleasurable to the one whom it might drown. The violence in these poems is of course the threat of drowning, the threat of sadism metonymically represented as water drowning the speaker, also an image for the threat of discourse overtaking the body. Water is an amorphous and disarticulating power in "I started Early—took my Dog." In suffering death by drowning one would not simply die but instead one would become disarticulated, suggest Dickinson's poems. Retaining the capacity to be articulate is thus both painful and necessary to reverse the sadistic press of the speaker's world.

I started Early—took my Dog—
and visited the Sea—
The Mermaids in the Basement
Came out to look at me—

And Frigates—in the Upper Floor
Extended Hempen Hands—
Presuming Me to be a Mouse—
Aground—opon the Sands—

But no Man moved Me—till the tide
Went past my simple Shoe—
And past my Apron—and my Belt
And past my Bodice—too—

And made as He would eat me up—
As wholly as a Dew
Opon a Dandelion's Sleeve—
And then—I started—too—

And He—He followed—close behind—
I felt his Silver Heel
Opon my Ancle—Then My Shoes
Would overflow with Pearl—

---

44 Snediker, *Queer Optimism*, 85.

Until We met the Solid Town—
No One He seemed to know—
And bowing—with a Mighty look—
At me—the Sea withdrew—
(Fr 656)

Here, Dickinson's verbal rapprochement with sadism is a struggle against being silenced. As Snediker notes, "grace, in this context, has less to do with transformational magic than a kind of anti-melancholic exorcising."[45] The negotiation with sadism for Dickinson is both context and text. Her speakers must navigate the silencing sea for the poem to occur. Is "anti-melancholic exorcising" exorcism of melancholy, and how is exorcism different from transformational magic? In poem 656, the speaker has to outwit the sea or we, the secondary audience, will never gain access to the description of the sea's sadism that the speaker can give us.

While it is true, as Snediker argues, that the speaker of Dickinson's violent poems learns to survive the act of seeing sadism—exemplifying what he calls Dickinson's "aesthetic optimism"—his discussion leaves aside the crucial problematic of Dickinson's de-subjectivization of pain.[46] With Snediker, I agree that the poems have little to do with Dickinson's fantasizing of her erotic desire and much more to do with her recognition of the punitive cultural *response to* lesbian desire. It is crucial, however, to remain focused on the way that reporting pain is a performance for Dickinson, an act placed explicitly and wholly in the aesthetic register.

In poem 656, the mermaids in the basement come out to look at Dickinson's violent language, since identity in the poem becomes synonymous with speaking. Here, I want to look back at these feminine watchers, these mermaids who come out to look at "me," especially tracking how "me" functions as a signifier of identity as opposed to the mermaids' erased subjectivity. Poem 656 indicates that the mermaids' subjectivity is erased: we don't know what they are thinking or how they see. The "mermaids in the basement," looking at the speaker (line 4), epitomize the full deployment of the terms of the feminine gaze on which the poem pivots: images of bodily suffering and the threat of annihilation by drowning—the sea engulfing the speaker—are arrayed for these feminine watchers, the mermaids. And yet the speaker also in turn watches the mermaids. The feminine gaze of the mermaids is called upon to transfigure the threatened speaker's meaningless suffering—her effective rape by the ocean that will swallow and silence her—into a structured and readable aesthetic act, a report of violence to which the mermaids are first witnesses. Whether one reads the ocean in this poem as masculine semen image or as feminine desire for masculine power, the mermaids are the watchers, and they are clearly drawn as feminine watchers.

[45] Snediker, *Queer Optimism*, 119.

[46] Snediker, *Queer Optimism*, 125.

In the world of the poem, the ocean will do what it will do; the ocean as a principle of violence will drown the speaker if she does not escape. The mermaids, the feminine watchers, chillingly observe the violence of the ocean against the speaker and do not intervene. But, equally, there is no indication that the mermaids gain erotic pleasure from watching the possible or threatened rape of the speaker—rape suggested in the figure of the speaker's semen-like scrim, pearl-filled shoes. Instead, the pleasure for the mermaids is hierarchical: that they rise when the speaker, the "me," is threatened. With the figure of such feminine watchers as the mermaids—watchers who witness the sadistic ocean's apparent pleasure in absorbing the helpless speaker—Dickinson posits a paradigmatic feminine watcher who does not intervene to stop the violence. The speaker in "I started Early—took my Dog" functions as a mirror to the mermaids. Dickinson demands our consideration of the tension between aesthetics and ethics in this gendered representation of violence, for here feminine figures are represented watching the violation of other feminized figures, the mermaids watch the "me" who watches the mermaids, all of them drowning in a masculine ocean, a depressingly endless regress.

The speaker's hypothetical violation acts as an impetus to raise the mermaids; indeed, the mermaids' ability to rise from debasement is dependent on their role as watchers of the speaker's symbolic rape by the ocean. In Ball's and Booth's figurations of violence, masculine figures suffer. Even if they are placed in the feminine role of the child, these masculine figures structurally block revelation of the feminine speaker's gendered role as frozen watcher of violence. By contrast, Dickinson is especially concerned with the gender dynamics of sadism: her poems dramatize and subvert these dynamics. While Ball and Booth write poems circling the theme of motherhood as femininity, Dickinson does not ascribe to the feminine witness the socially legitimate control of a masculine body. Dickinson depicts feminine speakers whose role is to reveal, not conceal, gendered abjection: she writes feminine speakers without a screen.

Even so, Dickinson's witness speakers survive. The speaker of "I started Early—took My Dog" escapes intact, escapes into the "solid town" (line 21). This solid space that rejects the ocean's violent advance is the space of the verbal text itself. The speaker can remain feminine and not be raped only because she navigates a way to access a performative space, a textual space, that delineates boundaries and is recognized by the ocean as powerful enough to turn "him" back.

But if the speaker escapes unscathed, the mermaids remain problematic in the poem. For if the "solid town" of verbal skill that saves the feminine speaker from rape seems to allay the violence of the poem, the mermaids are feminine figures who are *not* saved by the solid town of verbal virtuosity, indeed, the mermaids, like the "secret" discussed earlier in this chapter, are mute. But the mermaids are also feminine watchers who do not try to stop the ocean from violating another feminine figure, and who rise up from debasement in the act of watching another feminine figure being violated. If the aesthetic pact of the poem is to remedy the ocean's violence with "solid" language controlled by a threatened speaker, this trope of the solid town of text is also clearly deployed as an exploration of a boundary condition, a limit case. Feit Diehl suggests the possibility of transcendence in Dickinson's violent poems.[47] I believe that poem 656 is better read as a formal interrogation of the difficult ethical terms of feminine witnessing. Because the transcendence that the speaker gains is buttressed by the mermaids' lack of transcendence: the mermaids' apparently only hope for rising is if the speaker, the feminine other, were to sink. And the speaker's capacity to transcend the violent ocean's embrace is also dependent on her willingness to do nothing to aid the debased feminine others that already have been submerged into the violative ocean.

The "mermaids in the basement" (line 3), a hierarchical trope, rise when they look at the speaker who performs as a violated or potentially violated feminine body (depending on whether we read the "pearl"/scrim/semen filling her shoes as rape accomplished or merely threatened). The speaker's femininity is itself dissociative, linked to her costume rather than to any aspect of her described body. This femininity of the costume, however constructed, nevertheless determines the speaker's position as a vulnerable body. And yet, the speaker desires freedom and power, connoted as the desire for the journey that starts early. The ocean's violence tragically curtails the speaker's desire to start early and *take*—that is, behave powerfully (line 1). The sadistic *telos*, the aborting of the journey, is not the speaker's desire, but the reality she confronts: in the feminine position, she will not be able to make good on the active impetus that impels the poem.

The poem's mirror-structure brings up the question of the ethical parameters of the gaze and troublingly complicates strategies for representing gender in text. The mirror-structure of the poem works from the outset to establish that the first witnesses to the feminine speaker's daring attempt to take a journey are the mermaids (line 3). The feminine mermaids watch the speaker and also represent the threatening equation of femininity with abyss: they are debased, inhabiting the basement (line 3). The mermaids perform a limit, the breaching of which the speaker will not risk. In other words, the poem's mirror-structure interrogates the poem's premise for its own existence, asking to what extent feminine agency and articulation are possible in a sadistic system that engulfs vulnerable figures.

In poem 656 from that place of the basement, the abyss of the feminine, the mermaids take the troublingly privileged position of feminine watchers of another feminine figure's assault. The sadistic ocean, whose pleasure is in the assault, contains the feminine watcher, the mermaid, who rises in watching another feminine figure raped.[48] The speaker watches the mermaids' sunken femininity, their presumptive status as earlier victims of the ocean, and also does nothing to help the mermaids. Thus, the mermaids and the speaker are both positioned as

---

[47] Joanne Feit Diehl, *Dickinson and the Romantic Imagination* (Princeton, NJ: Princeton University Press, 1981).

[48] For discussion of gender as performance or inscription, see Judith Butler's landmark work, *Gender Trouble: Feminism and the Subversion of Identity* (New York: Routledge, 1999).

watchers—watching each other. The mermaids come out to look at the speaker of "I started Early—took my Dog" (line 4), but the speaker also significantly looks at the mermaids, insofar as she describes her act of seeing the mermaids' emergence.

Dickinson's poetry gains its balletic grace, its equipoise, from that very taut and singular rhyme and rhythm scheme that reveals the mathematics of sadism, sadism's ineluctable hierarchy. The hierarchical repetitions of the poems rehearse sadism's aesthetic claim, but the poems also bear a grace that develops from the exigency of balancing the ability to see systems of violence clearly and the inability (for reasons of societal constraint or personal proclivity) to act to stop that violence. The poems undercut sadism in their invocation of a feminine speaker's steadfast devotion to speaking; yet the poems also deploy the aesthetic terms of sadism—hierarchy, powerlessness, and relentless power. Indeed, the trauma of seeing so clearly may be the trauma that freezes Dickinson's watchers/speakers in the violent poems.

Snediker refers to Dickinson's grace as metaphysical and ethical, comparing her work to that of Heinrich von Kleist, who argued for a return to innocence through searing knowledge: "Grace itself returns when knowledge has, as it were, gone through infinity."[49] And I am also aware of Dickinson's grace as ethical in another sense—not a proper ending to knowledge (here, knowledge of sadism), but rather a proper beginning. One could argue that although Emily Dickinson eschewed personal engagement in the causes of abolitionism and suffrage, her poems yet engage the urgent and profound need for racial equality and feminism because of their singular capacity to show the core aesthetic function of sadism. The grace of the poems is ethical because the poems reveal rather than conceal, in the violence of power, a razor's edge of pleasure in sadism that the witness must find a way to acknowledge and refuse. Although gifted with the painful ability to see the sadism of patriarchy, which makes up the world of Dickinson's violent poems, and burdened by an inability to stop the sadistic violence which she is singularly well able to see, the speaker holds her balance—achieving what Snediker aptly calls "grace."

The ethical turn of Dickinson's poems representing violence is all the greater for their disallowance of easy witnessing. Nothing short of undoing the structures of hierarchy of race, heteronormativity, and gender will appease the violated ghosts in Dickinson's poems that reveal sadism—its pleasure—as the prime motivation for patriarchy, racism, and heteronormativity. But in the tragic world of these poems as well, sadism is presented as human, an ethical problem to be ceaselessly confronted and resisted but, in the poems, never overcome.

---

[49] Heinrich von Kleist, "On the Marionette Theatre," in *Essays on Dolls*, trans. Idris Parry (London: Penguin/Syrens, 1995), 12.

Chapter 5
Queer Southern Belles: The Transgender Object of Desire in O'Connor, McCullers, and Zora Neale Hurston's *Mules and Men*[1]

Flannery O'Connor's position as a writer of violent scenes, in the Modernist Southern canon, is paramount—*The Violent Bear It Away*, the title of her first novel, ushered in her role as proprietress of holy murder and sacred destruction. O'Connor herself explained the apocalyptic bent of her work as a Catholic exposition of the necessity of inflicting violence on the subject to open true belief.[2] Reflective of Jesuit meditations on bodily suffering, O'Connor's Christological thread queers the iconic image of the suffering masculine body—Christ as the centerpiece for traditional Jesuit meditation—insofar as her suffering bodies are often transgender or feminized bodies. She describes not the muscular athlete martyred but often the transgender and/or feminine body martyred, asserting a parity of purity between the athletic masculine body and the feminine, porous body, or the queer or androgynous body. O'Connor's model for writing violence was Jesuit meditation on the suffering of Christ: the figure of the bloodied male body in Jesuit meditations on the suffering Christ encodes a notion of the purity of the virile, decidedly masculine body, a view assumed, for example, as paradigmatic and inarguable by René Girard in *Violence and the Sacred.* Girard understands mimetic desire as central to the structure of the sacrifice and yet he also problematically (or might we say chauvinistically) conceives of mimesis entirely in terms of mimicking a male or masculine "model" whom the penitent admires and strives to emulate.[3]

O'Connor, writing in the 1950s, seems to have predicted Girard's later theory of the sacrificial in her careful depiction of characters whose deaths provide the representational pivot of her narratives, and yet in O'Connor it is the vulnerable,

---

[1] In this chapter, I use the term *transgender* to refer to characters diverging from normative masculinity and, in more complicated ways that I will explain, normative femininity. Transgender identity can be defined in differnt valid and important ways, and in this chapter I use the term to indicate characters markedly between genders.

[2] Flannery O'Connor, *Mystery and Manners: Occasional Prose*, ed. Sally Fitzgerald and Robert Fitzgerald (New York: Farrar, Straus & Giroux, 1969), 112.

[3] Girard, *Sacrifice.*

feminine, or transgender body that is sacrificed through suffering.[4] In this chapter, I look at the way the body represented as between genders, primarily in the work of Flannery O'Connor but also in the fiction of Carson McCullers and the ethnographic work of Zora Neale Hurston, becomes a focal point for violence, an emblem of the most extreme form of witnessing: witnessing up to the point of death. While Hurston's Big Sweet, in *Mules and Men*, McCullers's Miss Amelia in *Ballad of the Sad Café*, and O'Connor's androgynous child figures, in various short stories, appear in texts whose differences are greater than their similarities, my chapter's focus is on the singular figure of the androgynous witness who is martyred.[5]

Witnessing, Testifying

In "A View of the Woods" and "A Good Man is Hard to Find" O'Connor presents murdered, martyred bodies, and the body count includes two small girls. I will argue for a reading of these children as martyrs and note the way their passing androgyny is used, androgyny afforded them in part by dint of their extreme youth. While O'Connor makes clear that Mary Fortune and the granddaughter, in "A View of the Woods" and "A Good Man is Hard to Find," respectively, are nominal girls, her depiction of these characters turns from traditional gender norms. As I've argued, Mary Fortune is aggressive and powerful, except in her role as her father's favorite object to whip. Likewise, the granddaughter in "A Good Man is Hard to Find" is assertive, and rebuffs adults who comment on her feminine cuteness. Even as the young girls are cast as figures in some key ways between genders, the separation of men and women, male and female, is also crucial to these stories' plots, indicating the dangerous cultural no-man's land the girls inhabit. The young girls, in this bifurcated landscape, are drawn as characters at risk. In "A Good Man is Hard to Find," the Misfit separates the family that he murders into the boys—the father and the son—and the girls—the mother and the daughter—and kills them separately according to a darkly comical gentlemanly explanation of maintaining decorum (that the *ladies* not be seen by the men as they are murdered, that the ladies not see the men being murdered, and that the ladies not see the Misfit without his shirt, causing him to don the shirt of the *pater familias*, whom he has just murdered). Likewise, in "A View of the Woods," Mary Fortune evinces masculine behavior, such as her gesture of telling her grandfather

---

4 Interestingly, Girard rules out this possibility of female sacrifice because he argues that women and girls are so commonly violated that the figure of the violated woman/girl would hardly constitute a singular cultural position. I am also aware that both O'Connor and Girard are drawing from a Roman Catholic frame of reference for their notions of the sacrifice. This frame makes O'Connor's depiction of transgender bodies all the more revolutionary.

5 Zora Neale Hurston, *Mules and Men* (1935; repr., New York: Harper Perennial, 1990).

"Take off your glasses"—gestures of aggression and power.[6] But when Mary is beaten and murdered, O'Connor describes her as wearing a dress.

Indeed, in an early scene in the story, O'Connor represents the granddaughter as sitting on the hood of the car with her bare feet on the grandfather's shoulders, an erotically suggestive assemblage. The grandfather in "A View of the Woods" who ultimately murders Mary Fortune Pitts jokingly tells the little girl that she is a "barefoot woman," connoting the traditional slur that a barefoot woman is a slattern.[7] Moreover, Mary Fortune Pitts is claimed in painfully gendering fashion when her father says of her, "She is mine to whip."[8] That is, he claims her body through sadistic eroticism, insofar as a paternal claim to absolute domination of a child implies feminization of the child. Clearly, the story highlights the strictures of gender as they are placed on the body of the young Mary Fortune, forcing the powerful, masculine girl into feminine suffering and ultimately erasure. "A Good Man is Hard to Find" also emphasizes the strictures of gender as they are placed on the body of the young granddaughter, insofar as it is the granddaughter who first attracts the attention of strangers, suggesting the family's vulnerability, a vulnerability ultimately realized when the whole family is murdered by the Misfit.

But the figure set parallel to Mary Fortune is the grandmother whose death is not rendered obscene, off the stage, but described just as Mary Fortune's death is described, fully and frontally, a scene of disrobing precipitated by the girl's saying to the grandfather, "Take off your glasses" and by the grandmother's attempting to claim the Misfit as one of her "own babies." Full and frontal, grandfather and Mary Fortune, grandmother and the Misfit, stare into each others' eyes just before the grandfather and the Misfit murder Mary Fortune and the grandmother, respectively. Both Mary Fortune, ten-year-old granddaughter, and the unnamed woman described only as the grandmother in "A Good Man is Hard to Find" are killed gruesomely, and these deaths are given bold and tactile descriptions in O'Connor's texts. The image of the martyred feminized body, then, centers the texts of "A View of the Woods" and "A Good Man is Hard to Find." Even as O'Connor's explicit allegiance to Catholic, and Jesuit, notions of understanding theology and "faith" through contemplation of the suffering Christ shapes these scenes of extreme violence, what we find in "A Good Man is Hard to Find," and what we view in "A View of the Woods," is the martyred feminine *and* queerly marked body. And this body, it is crucial to note, is not a body killed through slow suffering of disease or asceticism but rather through violent, abrupt, and sexualized penetration by gun and by stone. In effect, the violence done against Mary Fortune Pitts and the grandmother, in "A View of the Woods" and "A Good Man is Hard to Find," feminizes the characters who are, up until the point of being murdered, represented in more androgynous terms.

---

6 O'Connor, "A View of the Woods," 544.

7 O'Connor, "A View of the Woods," 539.

8 O'Connor, "A View of the Woods," 531.

O'Connor wrenches contemplation of the suffering Christ, a meditative act in Jesuit systems, from its masculinist frame and insists on the purifying work of the martyred androgynous turned feminized body. While Elisabeth Bronfen, in *Over Her Dead Body*, among others, comments on the cultural use made of the image of the dead female body, O'Connor's victims differ radically from the marmoreal corpses described in *Over Her Dead Body*.[9] O'Connor's victims are not dead but murdered, and not even so much murdered as martyred, in very Saint Sebastian terms—their bodies opened, their blood flowing, the muscularity of their resistance marked in the violence by which they are overcome. I do not mean, here, to argue that femininity and androgyny are similar at all points; rather, I am interested in the ways that O'Connor's characters travel from powerful positions of female masculinity, queering the diegetic landscape into which they are written, to violently enforced traditional femininity that O'Connor causes to chime with death.

Jesus and Žižek

The grandmother in "A Good Man is Hard to Find" indeed is introduced to the story via a fusion of the specter of dismemberment and gender revelation: as the narrative commences, the grandmother is described as choosing clean underwear to wear on the journey lest an automobile accident leave her exposed on the highway in dirty under-things. This deft coherence of violence, grotesque dismemberment—an accident so violent as to leave the body without consciousness, severing consciousness and flesh—and the anxiety of gender as well as class anxiety, signified by the underwear that covers the grandmother's crotch, predicts the story's close, a denouement that reveals the grandmother's mortally wounded body, a body opened by the wound of a gunshot, a body whose gender is marked precisely by those exposed aforementioned undergarments, and a body whose suffering is deployed like a Jesuit meditation to teach the audience the wages of sin.[10] The Misfit's claim that the grandmother "would have been a

---

9 Elisabeth Bronfen, *Over Her Dead Body: Death, Femininity, and the Aesthetic* (New York: Routledge, 1992).

10 Consider the following excerpt from a spiritual exercise recommended as part of Jesuit practice, urging the practitioner to welcome suffering:

To Follow Jesus Completely:

"My Lord Jesus … I love you so much and so appreciate what you have done for me that I desire to be like you in all things. I desire to live life in your skin—that is, to use your approach in my choices leaving myself open to experience the consequences you experienced. Therefore if it could be done without hurting anyone else or disappointing our Caring God, I desire to be insulted, rejected, and written off as a nobody in order to be more like you my loving Lord and follow more closely in your footsteps. You are the true way that leads us to life. If worldly wisdom can make its adherents greedily love the approval of others, status, riches, pursuit of the illusions of one's 'ego' how much more can you make your followers love integrity, poverty, rejection and the cross!"

good woman if it had been somebody there to shoot her every minit of her life [sic]"[11] is powerfully indicative of the sadistic underpinnings of the story, the very essence of sadism, as Žižek makes clear, being the body that can be repeatedly violated and yet does not die.[12]

Did the grandmother deserve her fate of firstly witnessing the murder of her child and grandchildren, and then being murdered herself? That question is completely outside the concern of the paradigm of sadism. Of course, the difficulty of interpreting O'Connor here lies in the less than transparent nature of the grandmother's sin, and the disparity between what would appear to be her venial sins (that she lies about the location of the house she claims she remembers, that she conceals her cat in the car) and the frightful punishment visited on her: the murder not only of herself but of all her progeny, son and grandchildren, while she awaits her own death.[13] The lesson we learn from meditating on the grandmother's body might be to tell the truth, or, it might be to recognize the violence of the strictures of gender. Or we might learn the lesson of inhabiting the skin of Jesus, to live life in the skin of Jesus, painfully as a woman whose sex/gender designation makes the very intent of inhabiting Jesus's skin a fraught act of imagination. The Misfit's comment that the grandmother would have been a good woman if there had been somebody to "shoot her every minit of her life [sic]" inducts the grandmother perversely into the field of the martyr, the one who, through the act of meditation is "shot every minute of his/her life," that is, is caught up in ceaseless imagination of Jesus's suffering, or, fulfillment of Žižek's notion of sadism.

The grandmother who is never accorded power, privilege, or dignity, who is treated like an annoying child, is depicted as the product of traditional Southern training in femininity—to get what one wants only through duplicity because one will never earn a cultural position sufficiently powerful to ask directly or to demand. On a personal note, as my grandmother, contemporaneous with O'Connor and, like Mary Flannery, also a Georgia girl, once advised me: "We [women] can't go through the front door, but we know how to find the side way in."[14] O'Connor masks the grandmother's structural powerlessness in this story by making the character highly annoying; at the same time, she suggests an implicit, even subterranean sympathy with the old woman. The grandmother is so horribly punished one cannot help but feel, by the story's close, that she is innocent relative to her punishment, with the innocence Girard rightly ascribes to the scapegoat, although he denies the possibility that the sacred, sacrificial figure can be female or between genders. The wildly unjust tally of guilt and punishment is just what obsesses the Misfit, even as he emerges as a genuinely cruel and relatively unpunished man.

---

11 O'Connor, "A Good Man Is Hard to Find," 153.

12 Slavoj Žižek, *Looking Awry: An Introduction to Jacques Lacan through Popular Culture* (Cambridge, MA: MIT Press, 1991), 108.

13 O'Connor, "A Good Man Is Hard to Find," 138.

14 Claire Rogers Peacock, conversation with author, June 1992. Grandmother's elder sister dated Reeves McCullers before he fell for Carson.

And yet I suggest that in this grandmother's relative innocence (her venial sins are so clearly connected to her disempowered gendered position as a woman who is never allowed to directly state her plans or wishes) inheres O'Connor's radical displacement of Christological iconography. How, exactly, does the grandmother's gender displace that iconography, what is the effect of this displacement? The Misfit is obsessed with Jesus Christ, with the question of how one might possibly believe in his resurrection. The Misfit claims that whether this resurrection is true or not changes everything in the world and implies that not knowing whether the resurrection was real or not causes him, the Misfit, to commit murder.[15] The question of faith, he says, causes him to commit violence. As astonishing as such a cause for murder might seem, I believe we should connect the Misfit's bizarre claim that he commits murder because he does not know definitively the answer to the mystery of Christ to the pronounced "misfit" between the grandmother's sin of telling a small lie and her punishment of being slaughtered along with all her progeny. The grandmother, of course, is not a Christological figure, but that is exactly the point. She is a sacrificial witness figure because she witnesses the slaughter of her whole family and, as the last one killed, takes their wounds upon herself. She faces the doubt of the Misfit and sees him as human and saved—one of my own babies she calls him—even though by his actions the Misfit seems inhuman and impossible to save. The radical displacement of faith here is pushed onto the body of the Misfit, the representation of an anti-Christ, but it is the grandmother who subversively performs the position of the witness to the sacrifice to the fullest extent, ultimately becoming herself the sacrifice.

How this carnage in "A Good Man is Hard to Find" may be linked to salvation, O'Connor does not spell out. Her concern is with faith. And yet one may well argue that given the story's emergence from the era of Jim Crow and its virulent racism, we can read it as a story that displays a wish to expiate the sins of the white South, those sins being the enslavement of others, racism, lynchings. Only a violent apotheosis, implies O'Connor's story, cleanses such sins.

Likewise, Mary Fortune's body, in "A View of the Woods," is vividly displayed in its martyrdom, the head crushed, the blood flowing, the eyes staring and then flattening. Written into the parable of Mary Fortune, her sadistic father, and her murderous grandfather, whose murder of his granddaughter may in part be read as self-murder, is the problem of traditional culture being incapable of seeing the feminine at all, its placing the feminine as always already under erasure.[16] O'Connor presents the killing of the girl as martyrdom while her killer, the

---

15 O'Connor, "A Good Man Is Hard to Find," 152.

16 For a brilliant exposition of the problematic ways that femininity is coded as a site of erasure in our culture, please see Teresa de Lauretis, "Sexual (In)difference and Lesbian Representation," in *Figures of Resistance: Essays in Feminist Theory*, ed. Patricia White (Urbana-Champaign: University of Illinois Press, 2007), 48–71; see also Julia Serrano, *Whipping Girl: A Transsexual Woman on Sexism and the Scapegoating of Femininity* (Berkeley, CA: Seal Press, 2007).

grandfather, survives at least for a few minutes the act of killing her. Moreover, my argument would be that this murder of Mary by her grandfather exposes the paradigm of traditional Southern fears of miscegenation—Mary emerges as a racialized subject, her martyrdom strongly if covertly expressive of the abuse and murder of mixed race female bodies and female bodies that produce mixed race children, suppressed martyrdoms that haunt the South. For Mark Fortune kills his granddaughter because he reads her body as marked by the "other" (Pitts signifying the racial other), but he also kills his granddaughter because she verbally valorizes her status as hybrid. The iconography of Southern paranoia that created a term like "miscegenation," a term totally meaningless without the structure of racism, O'Connor reveals in the brutal murder of Mary Fortune.

Underwear

The politics of queerness, and the connection of the queer to the racialized other, Cathy Cohen has exposed in "Punks, Bulldaggers and Welfare Queens," and the queerness of O'Connor and other Modernist Southern writers' martyred feminine characters turns on a definition of difference—different from masculine, privileged bodies, lineated outside the structures of power.[17] The grandmother, on the one hand, is presented as paradigmatically representative of the least appealing aspects of the culture of femininity: she focuses on her appearance in an obsessive and paranoid way, determining to wear special under-garments in case she's in a car accident, envisioning herself as both powerless and female in her extremity. This focus on the under-things, the nether parts, of the feminine, and on making them presentable for the public specifically in the event of violence is both comic in the story and poignant—the grandmother's under-things, in every sense, are ultimately revealed by the violent trajectory of the narrative of "A Good Man is Hard to Find."

The grandmother typifies the violently produced Southern feminine at crucial junctures of the story, and these junctures are also the places of the narrative's apocalyptic bent. For example, the grandmother, as previously mentioned, is defined entirely in terms of her reproductive role. She is simply the grandmother; she exists in the story only as the maternal figure that created the family that will be murdered. The grandmother, in a gesture at once poignant and grotesque, extends this maternal space when she claims at the story's most dramatic moment that the murderer himself is "one of her own babies," a claim that can be read as the grandmother's whole-hearted acceptance of the cultural feminine that limits woman's role to that of mother.[18] In other words, not only is the role of the feminine imposed on the grandmother but she accepts this imposition in ways that destroy both herself and ironically her family. The grandmother is depicted as feminine in

---

[17] Please see E. Patrick Johnson and Mae G. Henderson, eds., *Black Queer Studies* (Durham, NC: Duke University Press, 2004), 1–20.

[18] O'Connor, "A Good Man Is Hard to Find," 152.

her fatal decision to direct the family car to a misremembered house, in particular when she reminisces about her days as a belle, an eligible young woman, and she obsesses on the place of the Southern mansion in which her youthful beauty once was admired.

This gesture that delivers the family to the Misfit is the grandmother's misreading of place via gender. Crucially, it turns on the problematic of the feminine—the problem of the grandmother's refusal to see herself as mattering as anything other than someone who was once a lovely young girl admired, even though what she remembers has disappeared in the sense that she has misremembered it, and also even had she remembered correctly the house itself probably is gone, given the Depression's physically effacing effect on Georgia and the South. The house to which she misdirects her son, in any case, is in another state: not Georgia but Tennessee. This misdirecting of her son makes the family vulnerable to the rough back roads of rural Georgia, resulting in the car crash that then serves them up as fodder for the murderous prison escapee, the Misfit, who typifies the other side, or the true face, of white Southern chivalry. In other words, the entire narrative turns on the gesture of deconstructing, by exposing, the destructive effect of the culture of the (white) feminine in the traditional South.

At the same time, in her very hyper-adherence to femininity, the grandmother of "A Good Man is Hard to Find" asserts a thwarted drive to masculinity. With no grandfather in sight, the grandmother becomes the putative leader of the family, and she leads them straight to gory mass death. The story also functions by constantly crossing the masculine and the feminine: the son is stripped before being murdered and his flesh is revealed as tender and pink; the mother is described not as delicate but as substantial as a cabbage; the younger sister has a smart mouth and refuses to play the role of blond cherub, and the grandmother refuses to obey her son, asserting her power.

If the outcome of the grandmother's assertion of her very limited powers (the power to carry her cat with her on vacation, for example) is disastrous, her disruption of gender designation also ushers in her figuration as martyr. O'Connor's invocation of the grandmother's body as a scene of suffering can be read as queer because she insists on the iconography of holy martyrdom for her female characters in their violent and full frontal (as opposed to decorous fading away) suffering. René Girard argues that the scapegoat and sacrifice onto which the grief and mortality of the community are imaginatively projected is ritually murdered as a foundational move of culture—mimetic drive finds its logical extension in the murder of the scapegoat. And symbolic discourse which itself is a kind of violence also allows violence to be displaced onto the symbol—the work of art, the concept.

The guilt of the scapegoat, argues Girard, is eradicated not only by this shift to the production of art, to figure the scapegoat, but also by the Christian event of Christ Jesus's sacrifice which permits the scapegoat to be innocent.[19] Although one

[19] René Girard, *The Scapegoat* (Baltimore: Johns Hopkins UP, 1989), 117–19.

can take issue with Girard (one may well argue that the Christian frame cannot be translated so neatly across all cultures as Girard would have us translate it), his work is applicable to O'Connor. However, within the shared frame of Western Christianity, the concept of the scapegoat that Girard proffers is applicable to O'Connor's work against Girard's own terms. In Girard, the scapegoat, in the revolution of Christianity, becomes innocent whereas formerly he was not.[20] Does the "also" mean that O'Connor joins Girard in questioning the scapegoat's guilt? Yes. But, O'Connor further suggests that the guilt of being feminine is itself expiated by this structure of mimesis and sacrifice.[21] Precisely because O'Connor *also* questions the imperative of the guilt of the female body, and the guilt of the transgender body, bodies not protected by the culture of masculinity, she goes one further than Girard in terms of questioning the guilt of the scapegoat.[22] In this questioning, O'Connor theorizes spaces of androgyny that throw into doubt, or queer even rudimentary differences between male and female. I will attend more fully to O'Connor's presentations of textual androgyny soon.

When, in "A Good Man is Hard to Find"'s apocalyptic denouement, the grandmother reaches out to touch him and says, "Why, you're one of my babies. You're one of my own children!," she is not only attempting to possibly reclaim the lost role of mother, by making herself mother to the murderer of all her progeny, but also, in a kind of paroxysm, she is asserting maternal power in the face of sadistic masculinity. The grandmother, in her death, embodies the problematic of the imposition of femininity, the impossible terms of its strictures and thereby suggests the need for transgender modality. Her iconically maternal body, at the story's close, is exploded in a gruesome replication of birth—the mother's body opened and bleeding, the "baby" (he whom she calls *one of her own babies*) the Misfit, walking away—precisely makes of the grandmother at once a scandalously female martyr, not a virgin martyr but an opened, porous, maternal martyr, and also suggests strongly that the Misfit destroys the grandmother precisely because they are locked in grotesque positions of gender.

The Misfit's grotesque personality is specifically derived, in his understanding, from the trouble of the son. He cannot comprehend Jesus's sacrifice and so he compulsively returns to murder to explicate through the flesh of others the trope of sacrifice. The content embedded in "Jesus, you ought not to shoot a lady" queers the terms of killing: the Misfit exaggerates the performance of gender by displaying the polite behavior of the Southern gentleman and yet he also abreacts

---

[20] Girard, *The Scapegoat*, 40.

[21] Please see Catherine Clement, "The Guilty One," on the notion of female guilt, in *The Newly Born Woman*, ed. Catherine Clement and Helene Cixous (London: Tauris, 1996), 1–58.

[22] Here I do not imply that O'Connor literally responds to Girard, since her death in the 1960s would rather preclude the possibility of her reading his work that became popular in the 1970s. What I mean is that both the Southern author and the French theorist are concerned with this same problematic of witnessing and scapegoating.

against traditional gender roles by killing whomever he wishes to kill, male and female alike, and indeed, by rehearsing the terms of Christ's sacrificial body through victims of both sex.[23] Because the Misfit is also a parricide, he subverts the Christian paradigm of the sacrifice of the son, and in this gesture queers the notion that the suffering male body purifies the culture. The Misfit himself arguably is queered in the sense that he struggles with and cannot step into the shoes of his father, and of course his name implies his insider-as-outsider status, as if the entire character were drawn to delineate just where normative masculinity exacts a murderous fee.[24] In other words, the grandmother and the Misfit, in the ironic pieta with which the story culminates, face each other as mirrors of the harms of gender, each deformation of masculine and feminine an argument for the beauty of androgyny.

Like Allison's *Bastard Out of Carolina* and O'Connor's "A View of the Woods," O'Connor's "A Good Man is Hard to Find" forges an almost illicit bond with its reader in which we watch the violation of the adolescent, or child, female, or transgender body, in revelation of the very cultural terms that depend upon the *immanence and suppression* of that image of this daughter's body: the broad and broadly suppressed cultural knowledge that the violation of the feminine, transgender, or feminized body codifies the terms of the American South in ways that are both imbricated with racism and that seem to push beyond comprehension within the singular frame of racism. That elided image of the martyred body of the daughter haunts culturally legible images of the cherished, heteronormative daughter. Modernist Southern women writers counter, with significant power, this specter of the daughter who exists to be harmed, for they create the figure of the masculine girl: not the adorable tomboy but the girl whose ferocious lack of charm works, almost, to save her. Recall Bone's mention of her thick skull. Frequently beaten by Daddy Glenn, Bone's masculine-coded and slightly monstrous hard-headedness, her bone-headedness, protects her, even as scars form on her skull. If only Mary Fortune had been so lucky. From such queerly martyred *belles*, I turn, then, to their near cousins for a consideration of the function of female masculinity in some Modernist Southern texts.

Of Saints and Belles

In the introduction to *Female Masculinity*, Judith Jack Halberstam interrogates cultural response to tomboys, arguing that, although some latitude of tomboy play is allowed for young girls, once a girl reaches puberty, feminine behavior and dress are radically, even violently, imposed upon her. Halberstam initiates discussion of our culture's truncation of the tomboy's career at puberty by drawing on the

[23] O'Connor, "A Good Man Is Hard to Find," 152.

[24] When I argue that the character of the Misfit queers stereotypes of gender, I do not suggest that the Misfit is a character drawn as gay. He is placed outside the logic of romance.

literary example of Frankie Addams, also known as F. Jasmine Addams, the main character in Carson McCullers's novel *A Member of the Wedding*.[25] Halberstam's choice of McCullers's novel, on the face of it, is an extraordinary move and one that has gone largely unremarked in scholarly response to Halberstam's work.[26] Halberstam's reading of McCullers's character is an extraordinary move in the light of a critical tradition that has regarded Frankie as a conventional tomboy on the verge of accepting inevitable femininity, a convention that Halberstam refuses. More to the point, Halberstam's decision to choose a character from McCullers's novel of rural Georgia as the exemplification of female masculinity's subversion of traditional femininity seems astonishing, given the strictures that typify the construct of femininity in the traditional, Jim Crow South, both in general and in particular in western Georgia. Although works such as Dorothy Allison's previously discussed *Bastard Out of Carolina* do develop lesbian characters (though Aunt Raylene is hardly presented in erotic connection with any woman, her one great love securely set in the past), my concern, in following Halberstam's *Female Masculinity*, is to return to Modernist Southern women's writing—fiction from the mid-twentieth century, published during the Jim Crow era—and here seek a fuller understanding of how it is that late twentieth-century "female masculinity" finds its patron saint produced from the ranks of mid-twentieth-century Southern Modernist writing by women.

Halberstam's decision to tap McCullers's character Frankie Addams as the impresario of her book *Female Masculinity* may reflect the lurking prevalence of gender ambivalent, queer female characters in Modernist Southern women's writing. Frankie's voice saying "I don't care" becomes Halberstam's rallying cry for how women should respond to our culture's abjuration of female masculinity.[27] If Margaret Mitchell's *Gone with the Wind* overshadows the popular image of Southern women's writing, in the shadows of Scarlett and Melanie's hoop skirts stand androgynous characters—muscular women, intransigent ugly girls, and switchblade toting youths who refuse to grow up into Southern belles, though this may mean they don't grow up at all.[28] In this chapter, I want to look not so much at the role of the cute tomboy but at the bisexual, intersex, and masculine female character in Southern woman-authored Modernist literature—the figure that cannot be made cute and charming, in gender normative terms.

---

[25] Judith Jack Halberstam, *Female Masculinity* (Durham, NC: Duke University Press, 1998), 6.

[26] See Joseph M. Flora, Lucinda MacKethan, and Todd Taylor, eds., *The Companion to Southern Literature: Themes, Genres, Places, People, Movements and Motifs* (Baton Rouge: Louisiana State University Press, 2002), 427. Although Dorothy Allison's work has rightly been interpreted through the prism of queer theory and critical awareness of Ms. Allison's lesbian identity, I am focused here on Modernist texts, and the brilliant *Bastard Out of Carolina* postdates Modernism. Moreover, Bone is not presented as an androgynous child.

[27] Halberstam, *Female Masculinity*, 8–9.

[28] Margaret Mitchell, *Gone with the Wind* (New York: Macmillan, 1936).

The androgynous child or youth centers Flannery O Connor's short story, "A Temple of the Holy Ghost" as well as McCullers's *Ballad of the Sad Café* and *A Member of the Wedding*,[29] and appears in Zora Neale Hurston's auto-ethnography, *Mules and Men*.[30] Despite the rigors of mid-century Southern gender expectations, these mid-century Southern women writers wrote queer texts, often misleadingly grouped under the rubric of the Southern Grotesque, texts that cohere with Halberstam's late twentieth-century theory of female masculinity. But the conceptual framework of the idea of a Southern Grotesque, a critical tradition critiqued by Yaeger's *Dirt and Desire*,[31] works to efface queer readings of Southern women's writing, displacing questions of non-normative sexuality, covering these sexualities beneath a veneer of freakishness.[32] Indeed Flora notes in the encyclopedic *Companion to Southern Literature* that there is a "mutual silence between queer studies and southern studies."[33] The Southern grotesque, as a critical rubric, suggests that individual figures outside heteronormativity are bizarre and pathological. Instead, I will argue that such figures, in the texts under consideration, work primarily as disruptors of gender and it is for this reason that they are depicted as victimized by violence, bearing the mark of the bizarre and pathological.

Although the Southern belle conjures images of vain, bantam-weight beauty queens, that figure itself is produced through excessive inscriptive violence. Laying bare the violent way a *belle* is made, Patricia Yaeger rightly says, "the Southern belle has been eviscerated by the excesses of patriarchy."[34] The belle is created and hollowed by patriarchal codes that effect purposeful or accidental terms of violence. She is made and destroyed by violence. The perfected belle has no interior psyche, only an exterior, a pretty surface to reflect male domination. Southern belle womanhood—as embodied, for instance, in Tennessee Williams's Blanche Du Bois—destroys the subjectivity of its possessor in order to replicate social norms that rely on binaries: black/white, pretty girl/big daddy, teetotaling Baptists/debauched old families. Southern womanhood is propitiatory femininity. And yet, Halberstam introduces the radical concept of female masculinity by quoting a Southern woman writer's Southern character, F. Jasmine or Frankie Addams.

Frankie's feeling of "being a member of nothing in the world … unjoined" becomes an exemplar of a dissociative response to Southern culture's abjuration of

---

[29] Carson McCullers, *The Member of the Wedding* (1946; repr. New York: Bantam Books, 1958).

[30] Hurston, *Mules and Men*.

[31] Patricia Yaeger, *Dirt and Desire: Reconstructing Southern Women's Writing, 1930–1990* (Chicago: University of Chicago Press, 2000).

[32] Recall O'Connor's witty comment that what's considered grotesque in literature is what's most realistically represented, in her *Collected Works*, 819.

[33] Flora et al., *The Companion to Southern Literature*, 247.

[34] Yaeger, *Dirt and Desire*, 221.

female masculinity. Far from happening upon an aberration in Southern women's literature, Halberstam, in depicting McCullers's character Frankie Addams as exemplary of the attitude of female masculinity and androgyny, "[hanging] around in doorways," engages the South as a space of potentially queer resistance.

Halberstam aside, one notes the tradition of reading Southern women's writing as exemplary of freshness and simplicity, a childlike quality.[35] Allying myself with Patricia Yaeger's important work in *Dirt and Desire*, I diverge from dominant critical readings of Southern women's writing as marginal literature, appropriately read only by children and teens or, at best, college girls.[36] Instead, I suggest that Carson McCullers, Flannery O'Connor, and Zora Neale Hurston write literature that mines the territory of adolescence in order to subvert dominant social structures. I suggest that Halberstam's *Female Masculinity* fastens on Southern women's writing not in spite of the South's role as a space of rigid norms and violent gender trauma but because of Modernist Southern women writers' proclivity for producing vivid and troubling characters who embody gender indeterminancy *precisely* because they refuse to grow up to inhabit rigid gender dichotomies.

Southern women's writing published in the 30s, 40s, 50s, and 60s, before Stonewall, excels in its presentation of masculine girls on the brink of puberty, ambiguously sexed persons, and butch, young women. The queerness of Southern Modernist women's writing turns cannily on the trope of this ambiguous social space, adolescence. In other words, Modernist Southern women writers aren't writing adolescent characters because they are themselves like adolescents, their maturity stunted, but rather because this space of adolescence allows them to mine queer terrains of gender ambiguity without seeming to directly question social norms.

Hurston, O'Connor, and McCullers dramatize androgynous adolescents and characters of ambiguous gender not because they can't push themselves into the realm of the adult mind but on the contrary because they write against the grain of stultifying, and as we will see murderous, adult gender expectations. McCullers, O'Connor, and Hurston, in the youthful character of Big Sweet, write about the young and gender indeterminate not because they can't handle adulthood but to dramatize the violence of gender imposition, deploying representation of adolescence as rich terrain in which to engage gender ambiguity, a literary turn that reveals the violence of gender's imposition.

---

[35] Late twentieth- and early twenty-first-century texts such as Susie Mee's anthology *Downhome: An Anthology of Southern Women Writers* (New York: Houghton Mifflin, 1995) and Beth Hoffman's 2010 debut novel, *Saving CeeCee Honeycutt: A Novel* (New York: Pamela Dorman Books-Viking, 2010)—of which Kim Edwards reviews, "This book unfolds like a lush southern garden, blooming with vivid characters, beauty, and surprises"—make clear that Southern women's writing remains fixed in the national psyche as the commonplace of charm and feminine grace, "beauty and surprises."

[36] Yaeger, *Dirt and Desire*, 24.

The Intersex Saint

Consider O'Connor's "A Temple of the Holy Ghost." In this short story, a girl on the brink of puberty regards her slightly older, already pubescent, girl cousins with horror. Her female cousins are completely engrossed in talking about and dressing up for boys. These girls chillingly cede their subjectivity to men and boys, beginning each sentence with the phrase "You know this boy I know well one time he … ."[37] The child, recoiling from the self-negating femininity of her cousins, finds herself without a sex to which to be attracted as she approaches puberty. "The child" views both men and women with horror. Women, who distort themselves primping for men, draw the horror of the child, while men are presented in the short story as naturally or even preternaturally grotesque. In the story, young men are described as "sitting like monkeys" and the child interprets the boys as both "dog-like" and similar to oxen. An older man is described as having a face "like an unpaved road—washed with ruts and gulleys" and he drives a car that "smells like the last circle in hell."[38] In short, heterosexuality and the distortions that it imposes on people repulse the child as she approaches puberty and faces the crisis of having to fit herself into the system of rigid male/female binaries in the traditional South. The child finds herself outside all modes of expressing desire and performing gender that could be viable and visible in her culture.

"A Temple of the Holy Ghost" is infused not only with the problem of becoming a woman but also with the difficulty of being Catholic in the largely Protestant South. The story's title refers to Saint Paul's letters, where the phrase "You are a temple of the Holy Ghost" is used to exhort early Christians against adultery.[39] Here, Paul claims that one's body is a temple in which is housed the Holy Ghost. The older girl cousins jokingly call each other "Temple One" and "Temple Two," referring back to Saint Paul's claim that has been echoed in a nun's admonition to them that if a young man should attempt to take sexual liberties with them they should say to him, "Stop, Sir! I am a Temple of the Holy Ghost."[40]

But the child, on the brink of puberty, finds the phrase "You are a temple of the Holy Ghost" to be no joke. When she hears her older girl cousins make fun of the idea that they should refuse sex with a man based on the nun's repetition of Saint Paul's exhortation, the child does not comprehend what the cousins are laughing about, partly because the child cannot imagine feeling sexual interest in men. Instead, the child finds this idea of the body as a temple of the Holy Ghost to be beautiful, exquisite.

Far from seeing the idea of body and self embedded in the phrase "You are a temple of the Holy Ghost" as a way of properly performing compulsory

[37] O'Connor, "A Temple of the Holy Ghost," in *Flannery O'Connor: Collected Works* (New York: Library of America, 1988), 236.

[38] O'Connor, "A Temple of the Holy Ghost," 240, 237, 239.

[39] 1 Corinthians 3:16.

[40] O'Connor, "A Temple of the Holy Ghost," 238.

heterosexuality, a way of keeping young men from luring one to have sex before marriage, the child of O'Connor's story seizes on the phrase, "You are a Temple of the Holy Ghost," as a way to inhabit her body *outside* of heterosexual norms. She will be holy unto herself, whole unto herself, a temple of the Holy Ghost, neither male nor female, as of course Paul also tells the early Christians that in Christ there is neither male nor female.[41] From her painful rejection of heterosexuality, based on her complete lack of interest in men, the narrator of "A Temple of the Holy Ghost" finds comfort in the idea that her body is a Temple of the Holy Ghost, not an item intended to be sexed.

The visceral arc of O'Connor's short story is that from this idea of androgyny as a viable mode of selfhood, a way for the body to remain not encroached upon by violent, heterosexist gender norms, the story concretizes, makes physical, the gender neutrality for which the child yearns. This concretization occurs in the figure of a true hermaphrodite who enters the story when the elder girls are taken, by their "dog-like" beaus, to the fair.[42] Freak Shows—the parading of biologically rare bodies, or bodies fabricated to appear to be biologically rare, for public consumption as a form of entertainment—were popular and mostly legal in the United States into the twentieth century, and O'Connor's rural Georgia fair boasts a Freak Show tent into which children are not permitted entry.[43] In O'Connor's short story, the child's teenage girl cousins see at the fair's Freak Show an intersex person, who performs in a tent that adults pay to enter, displaying his/her body, including his/her genitals that are both male and female. After the fair, the older girls describe, while the younger girl called "the child" listens, their remembrance of viewing the hermaphrodite. This act of the child listening shapes the drama of "A Temple of the Holy Ghost."

O'Connor writes the Freak Show character as a true hermaphrodite, that is, a person with both male and female sexual attributes—breasts, vagina, and penis—a fully intersex person.[44] The intersex person in O'Connor's story displays him/herself for money against the backdrop of grinding poverty in rural Georgia. He/she has little choice: kept out of the economy of male/female by which he/she

41 "There is neither Jew nor Gentile, neither slave nor free, *nor is there male and female*, for you are all one in Christ Jesus" (emphasis added). Galatians 3:28.

42 The term *intersex person*, rather than *hermaphrodite*, reflects promising cultural shifts in response to intersex identity. Anne Fausto-Sterling movingly describes current medical handling of intersex births and the need for humane change. See *Sexing the Body: Gender Politics and the Construction of Sexuality* (New York: Basic Books, 2000), 45–78, 51–5.

43 For example, please see Diane Arbus's astonishing 1960s photographs of "side show freaks" in *Revelations* (New York: Random House, 2003). Arbus records the gritty reality of these shows. See also Mirja Dauphin, *The Presentation of Gender in Diane Arbus's Work in the Context of the Cold War Era* (Norderstedt, Germany: GRIN Verlag, 2006).

44 Please see Fausto-Sterling for current definitions of biological inter-sex identity, *Sexing the Body*, 45–78.

might either earn a living as a man or marry as a woman, the intersex person earns money by displaying him/herself graphically and erotically. And yet, the hermaphrodite claims a holy discourse, a discourse that queers traditional conceptions of Christianity as a bastion of conservative gender enforcement. For the hermaphrodite while displaying to the paying crowd his/her breasts, vagina, and penis, claims holiness, claims her/his own body as God-made, "God made me thisaway—this is the way God wanted me to be."[45]

O'Connor carefully places the intersex person as a rural Southerner with a deep country drawl and just as carefully chooses his/her discourse of divinity: "God made me thisaway—I don't dispute hit—I ain't disputing God's way."[46] This phrase overheard and reported by the child's elder girl cousins becomes a source of salvation for the child in O'Connor's story. The mode of learning in this story is obsessively set parallel to the priest's position at the confessional: listening without seeing. Just as the child is an interloper on the elder girls' discussion of the nun's admonition to them that their bodies are "Temples" of the Holy Ghost, so also the child learns through a kind of tender eavesdropping the description and story of the intersex person displaying his/her disrobed body at the fair. The child is cast by O'Connor as always already liminal, a listener not a speaker and at that a listener who is not directly addressed but who in effect eavesdrops. This liminal narrative position of "the child" correlates with the child's immense attraction to and valorization of the intersex position, a position that in the culture of the traditional South, where codes of gender performance were rigid, is exemplary of the margins, the limen.

"The child," fearfully approaching adolescence in a culture that promises to deprive her of her subjectivity and self-sovereignty if she becomes a woman, finds salvation in the conversation that depicts this figure of the intersex person: she dreams of the hermaphrodite as a holy figure and believes her own body can be holy also through androgyny, problematically envisioning martyrdom as a route to freedom from repressive gender identity.

But this queerly beatific vision of the holiness of androgyny is summarily cut short by the story's closing movement. At the story's close a man described as having "three folds of fat at the back of his neck, with ears pointed almost like a pig's" verbally desecrates the child's vision of the hermaphrodite, saying of the show: "Some of the preachers from town gone out and inspected it and got the police to shut it on down."[47] As the child listens in, one of the grotesque men who inhabit O'Connor's story tells the child's mother that the preachers and police, the moral and religious arbiters, though not necessarily ethical agents, of the town came in and closed the fair, the Freak Show. The pig-like man's description rhetorically places the hermaphrodite outside the law, and outside morality. This symbolic, and also possibly physical, violence is done to the hermaphrodite by the preachers

[45] O'Connor, "A Temple of the Holy Ghost," 245.

[46] O'Connor, "A Temple of the Holy Ghost," 245.

[47] O'Connor, "A Temple of the Holy Ghost," 248.

and police, traditional male authority figures, and also by the pig-like man, whose authority implicitly resides only in his masculine gender, underscoring the child's sense of despair at the heteronormative culture into which she is coming of age.[48]

In other words, O Connor's short story offers initially a beautifully queer resolution to what Teresa de Lauretis elsewhere has called the "trauma of gender"—the way that women are radically disempowered upon becoming women in our culture.[49] And it is this queer resolution of making the "freak" or the intersex person a holy figure, a figure who follows Saint Paul's injunction to be neither male nor female, that O'Connor singularly offers us. But then the story undercuts that offering through its presentation of the punishment of androgyny, the way that the narrative closes with the closing down of the fair, the shutting down of the visibility of this beatified intersex saint.[50]

Southern women's writing, I want to point out, often strikingly queer, also frequently is punitive of its own queerness. Then again, maybe its queerness is punished no matter what—no matter how O'Connor handles her queer characters, the canon of American literature relegates O'Connor, and her Modernist Southern women writer peers, to a minor tradition.[51] What I mean here is that the punishment of this canonized intersex person in "A Temple of the Holy Ghost" is two-fold. Firstly, O'Connor's text itself dwells on a kind of proxy martyrdom of the intersex body, as the child envisions her path to androgyny through martyrdom. Likewise, the narrative closes with the punishment by the literal *closing down* of the intersex figure. However, it is also the case, as Yaeger makes clear, that as a Southern woman writer, O'Connor herself is vulnerable to critical diminishment, to being closed down should she write too queerly. Highly regarded as she may be in some circles, nevertheless O'Connor is certainly not afforded the deep critical mystique and prestige of a figure like Faulkner.[52] The gentle critical ghetto-ization

---

48 Here I invoke the possibility of physical violence done to the intersex person when the fair is forcibly closed down, for such a possibility is merely reflecting the statistics around violence against intersex persons, which are damning, and O'Connor's story clearly suggests a moment of force when the fair is closed down. As Casey Charles argues, transgender people face a higher risk of violence than those seen to perform gender closer to cultural norms; please see Casey Charles, *Critical Queer Studies: Law, Film and Fiction* (Aldershot, UK: Ashgate, 2012).

49 Teresa de Lauretis, *Technologies of Gender: Essays on Theory, Film, and Fiction* (Bloomington: Indiana University Press, 1987), 29.

50 Here again I must emphasize that "androgyny" does *not* mean a cutely boyish girl but instead literally means between sexes, a union of male and female. As Saint Paul exhorts, and as Tantum Ergo iterates, "To the One proceeding from the Both."

51 Patricia Yaeger, *Dirt and Desire*, 44; Leslie Fiedler, *Love and Death in the American Novel* (Champaign, IL: Dalkey Archive Press, 1960), 475.

52 Here I refer to the Flannery O'Connor as saint movement, emblematized by The Flannery O'Connor Society; for example, this conference on Christianity and Literature: http://theflanneryoconnorsociety.com/upcoming-conferences.html (accessed February 9, 2012).

of Southern women writers ensures that their work, while certainly proving its staying power, encodes a realm of minor literature. This marginalization acts, I suggest, as a second silencing of the queer work done in the stories and novels of the women listed above, shaping a critical discourse in which explosive characters like "the child," the intersex person, Miss Amelia, Big Sweet, and maybe even Bone, are understood as exemplary of specific and narrow concerns, concerns that cannot matter to those not female, Southern, black, awkward teens, or incest-survivors, as the case may be.[53]

While Zora Neale Hurston has enjoyed a well-deserved renaissance in her critical reputation, as an African American writer Hurston is usually not classified as a Southern writer—even though she was born and raised in the deep South, and more importantly considered the north Florida town of Eatonville to be her real home, and set many of her novels in the deep South.[54] Her masterpiece *Their Eyes Were Watching God*,[55] after its revivification by Alice Walker, has achieved broad popularity, placing its author among popular writers. *Mules and Men*,[56] like *Their Eyes Were Watching God*, is set in rural Florida, and also in New Orleans. It originates a style of ethnography containing a weave of personal reflection, ethnography, and original fiction, and it contains a beautiful, powerful female character called Big Sweet. Big Sweet is described by the men who work the rural Florida logging camp where she also works as "uh whole woman and half uh man," a woman with "loaded muscles!"[57] The crew boss is afraid of Big Sweet, afraid of her physical power but also afraid of her fearless and decisive use of her switchblade knife. Hurston vividly describes Big Sweet's willingness to place her body, and her knife, between danger and a feminine woman, Lil' Bit. Big Sweet loves another woman, Lil' Bit, in a manner with homoerotic overtones, insofar as Big Sweet places her body, her fearlessness, and her knife between danger and this pretty and small woman in just the way that traditional gender roles dictate a man should protect a woman.

But Big Sweet would not properly be called a tomboy; though a young woman, she is past childhood. Her female masculinity depicts androgyny as power and beauty but also, like the intersex person in O'Connor's "freak show," a scene of tragedy. Here, I want to unpack further the tendency to tragedy that haunts the queer women in Modernist Southern women's fiction, much as the intersex saint, exorcised from the fair, haunts O'Connor's "child." As Terry Castle has argued, not of the masculine woman or of the androgyne but of the "apparitional lesbian,"

---

53 Patricia Yaeger, *Dirt and Desire*, 297.

54 Notable exceptions include Yaeger's *Dirt and Desire*, which includes extensive readings of Hurston's oeuvre, and Carol S. Manning's essay, "Hurston and Welty, Janie and Livvie," *The Southern Literary Journal* 34, no. 2 (Spring 2002): 64–72.

55 Zora Neale Hurston, *Their Eyes Were Watching God: A Novel* (1937; repr., New York: Perennial Library, 1990).

56 Hurston, *Mules and Men*.

57 Hurston, *Mules and Men*, 112.

"the lesbian ... it seems ... is in the margins, hidden from history, out of sight, out of mind, a wanderer in the dusk, a lost soul, a tragic mistake. She is far away and she is dire."[58] Castle goes on to make the case that the lesbian is "ghosted" in literary representation, but characters like Big Sweet, and McCullers's Miss Amelia, whom I will discuss later in this chapter, aren't so much ghosted as martyred. These characters are less lesbian figures than androgynous figures. Or rather they are both, but figurative emphasis is placed on the characters' androgyny. The price of androgyny, it seems, is not erasure but rather emblematic bodily mutilation, and this suffering, interestingly, crosses racial lines in a Jim Crow era. A "whole woman and half a man" Big Sweet is not a bulldagger but androgynous in Hurston's ethnography insofar as Big Sweet has a boyfriend and is only suggestively attracted to Lil' Bit, whereas Big Sweet's androgyny—her physical body exhibiting both the masculine and feminine in big ways—is demarcated unmistakably androgynous in Hurston's text.

Zora Neale Hurston's depiction of Big Sweet does not repeat racist notions of black women as physically stronger than white women but instead complicates and works against these damaging stereotypes that *Female Masculinity* also debunks.[59] For Hurston's Big Sweet is both truly womanly and truly manly. She is gallant and strong and also erotically tender, if apparently self-destructive. Hurston's *Mules and Men* contains almost no white characters (it is, however, dedicated to a white woman, Hurston's patron for the project). Hurston creates a landscape of African American characters who, in the context of *Mules and Men*, are not performing for a white audience, and consequently are not presented as seen through white power structures. Rather, they create their community and live and act through and for each other. Big Sweet, then, is presented along with other African American female characters: Ella Wall, a sexy vamp, and Lil' Bit herself, Zora Neale Hurston as a character in her book, a gorgeous ethnographer masquerading as a bootlegger of distilled liquor. Ella Wall and Lil' Bit are portrayed by the iconography of traditional femininity while Big Sweet is portrayed as a wild youth, diverging from traditional femininity.

Hurston does not offer the character Big Sweet, then, as a racist depiction of black womanhood, nor as a cute tomboy, but rather as a site of radical gender indeterminacy in flourishing youth. Big Sweet's power is a site of crisis in the traditional South. Big Sweet's probable death in a knife fight functions similarly to the intersex person's probable arrest at the hands of the police in O'Connor's "A Temple of the Holy Ghost": both scenes work to truncate the queer possibilities opened by Hurston's and O'Connor's texts, suggesting that for persons who insist on performing androgyny, or who are androgynous, tragedy, bodily mutilation, or humiliation, await. Importantly, though, this tragedy is the endpoint of intensely desired characters—characters that have drawn the erotic

---

58 Terry Castle, *The Apparitional Lesbian: Female Homosexuality and Modern Culture* (New York: Columbia University Press, 1993), 2.

59 Halberstam, *Female Masculinity*, 29.

longing of the texts' characters. O'Connor's intersex person, like the masculine woman Big Sweet, operates as the focal point of desire—he/she draws others' desire—in the respective texts.

Queer characters presented in Modernist Southern women's writing precede national gay liberation by decades, but such Modernist textual play with the rules of gender and desire has often been interpreted under the rubric of the Southern Grotesque, a critical move that often covers the way that writers like O'Connor, Hurston, and McCullers write texts subversive of heterosexism and heteronormativity.[60] Troublingly, as I've noted, O'Connor's, McCullers's, and Hurston's texts also present characters whose straying from gender norms is met *within the text* by punishment and violence. Textually the punishment of the queer body closes the fate of the queer Southern belle—the androgynous or masculine woman—her career violently abrogated by arrest, disappearance, by social or physical death, by silencing, by loss of livelihood. Or the androgynous figure in text is simply truncated by aphanisis, fading from the text.

Member of No Club

Halberstam's *Female Masculinity* emphasizes Frankie Addams's sense of not belonging—"she belonged to no club"—to point to the young character's gender ambiguity, her female masculinity.[61] Likewise, one could argue that, in writing not only queer characters but also queer characters who embody female masculinity, McCullers, O'Connor, and to a lesser degree Hurston, write themselves out of the "club" of serious consideration as part of the literature of high Modernism.[62] It's not just that Frankie Addams, the girl in *A Member of the Wedding*, "the child" in "A Temple of the Holy Ghost," and Big Sweet *are* masculine female characters—they are characters who to one degree or another desire erotically a body that is not male. And in turn the intersex and androgynous characters of McCullers, O'Connor, and Hurston draw the desire of others. The intersex performer in "A Temple of the Holy Ghost" draws the desire of the child, Big Sweet is presented by Lil' Bit aka Zora Neale Hurston as a frankly romantic figure, and Miss Amelia in *Ballad of the Sad Café* of course is so intensely desired by her husband that he destroys her for rejecting him.

---

60 For a discussion of gender and the Southern Grotesque, please see Sarah Gleeson-White, "Revisiting the Southern Grotesque: Mikhail Bakhtin and the Case of Carson McCullers," *The Southern Literary Journal* 33, no. 2 (Spring 2001): 108–23.

61 Halberstam, *Female Masculinity*, 7.

62 Miss Amelia, in McCullers's *Ballad of the Sad Café*, for example, is visually martyred—a spectacle is made of her being beaten and then she is entombed alive in the town where she once reigned as *de facto* mayor. An uncannily parallel gesture of curtailment occurs in the relegation of Modernist Southern women's "grotesque" writing to a minor literature, closed up in the paternal house of the canon, gazing out with a haunting eye.

Frankie belongs to no club not only because she is tall and boyish and, approaching puberty, becomes gawky and bony rather than curvy but also because, like O'Connor's child in "A Temple of the Holy Ghost," she does not feel heterosexual desire for a man. Likewise Big Sweet, though she has a boyfriend and speaks to him disparagingly while her tender feelings are evinced towards Lil' Bit. O'Connor's "child" apparently finds men and women equally repulsive and conceives of the figure of the intersex person as a site of release that transcends gender. McCullers's Frankie Addams feels desire for both men and women, and wants to be a member of the wedding in the erotic sense of sharing the honeymoon, implicitly the nuptial bed, with both bride and groom at the same time.

The broken body of the masculine or androgynous woman, or the hermaphrodite, that places pathos in the bucolic texts of "A Temple of the Holy Ghost," *Mules and Men*, and *The Ballad of the Sad Café*, functions as a deeply elegiac figure. Where does that leave us, then, in understanding why Halberstam's ground-breaking work of queer theory, *Female Masculinity*, begins its dismantling of gender codes by invoking Southern literature, that is, by invoking a character from Southern women's writing, Frankie Addams? Why is it appropriate for Halberstam to make this move?

I want to close with a reading of McCullers's *Ballad of the Sad Café* framed by the question, pointed towards the location of the South, of what Adrienne Rich calls the "politics of location." But it is significant that these displaced characters are all located by their creators in the South, a significance implicit in Halberstam's invocation of Southern literature in her theoretical dismantling of gender codes. Martin Manalansan uses this conception of the politics of location in *Global Divas* to map differing performances and meanings of queerness according to culture, geography, and more importantly the displacement of cultures across disparate geographies.[63] The *politics of location* to apply Adrienne Rich's phrase and concept to the mid-twentieth-century South are the politics of binaries, of harsh and unjustified divisions: races rigidly and violently separated by Jim Crow segregation laws, born-again Christians aggressively separate from the Southern tradition of dissolution (consider Tennessee Williams's depictions of alcoholism and debauchery amongst the Du Bois).[64] And of course there is the politics of women separated from men, whose subterranean violence echoes the extreme repressiveness of Jim Crow racism. But the figure of the queer woman—the child in "A Temple of the Holy Ghost" who dreams of the hermaphrodite as a beautiful and indeed beatific solution to her own sense of being neither male nor female, the martyred Miss Amelia in McCullers's *Ballad of the Sad Café*, Big Sweet in *Mules and Men*, and emphatically Frankie Addams with whose refrain "I don't care"

63 Martin Manalansan, *Global Divas* (Durham, NC: Duke University Press, 2003), 7–8.

64 Adrienne Rich, "Notes Towards a Politics of Location," in *Women, Feminist Identity and Society in the 1980s: Selected Papers*, ed. Myriam Díaz-Diocaretz and Iris M. Zavala (Amsterdam and Philadelphia: John Benjamins Publishing Company, 1985), 7–22.

Halberstam anchors her important late twentieth-century *Female Masculinity*—not only haunts Modernist Southern women's writing but in some ways stands as the mournful heart of Southern women's Modernist writing. It is as if these women writers who came of age in a radically bifurcated cultural landscape, a landscape where a person was always violently judged as black or white, male or female, religious or dissolute, and never permitted to dwell between categories, decided to rebel against such dichotomies, not so much as activists, but rather, very carefully, in their written texts.[65]

The fact that their rebellions are textual, intertextual, and not activist may have contributed to the lack of connection made by critical theory between queer theory and Southern women's writing until the advent of Dorothy Allison, whose *Bastard Out of Carolina* details a story of incest in a tragedy whose only hero is a lesbian aunt, a tragedy that functions to make Allison the "patron saint of battered women."[66] Classified under the misleading rubric of the Southern Grotesque, Modernist Southern women writers were queer pioneers. The martyr and the belle cohere in the vertiginous space of queering gender in Southern women's Modernist texts. McCullers's *Ballad of the Sad Café*, in particular, predicts the image of the martyred beatific androgyne that O'Connor presents in "A Temple of the Holy Ghost," as Miss Amelia herself is predicted by Big Sweet in *Mules and Men*.

McCullers's Miss Amelia is martyred in her house, and suffers alone. Miss Amelia's suffering, after the battle in which Cousin Lymon betrays her, is hidden and yet also exposed humiliatingly.[67] Even though the fight with Lymon is vividly described, after the fight, Miss Amelia becomes almost instantly hidden. As on the night of her marriage when her virginity was threatened, Miss Amelia, in despair after Lymon's defection, depends on the uncanny architecture of her father's house to hide her defeat. After Lymon leaves her, Miss Amelia turns deeply into, is submerged into, the topos of the father's house, the commonplace of archaic

---

[65] Although I know that here I put a toe in the dangerous waters of conflating author with text, I cannot help but note that while Michelle Abate in *Tomboys: A Literary and Cultural History* (Philadelphia: Temple University Press, 2008) describes McCullers as a woman who acted on bisexual desires and presented as androgynous, this depiction is reductive because it leaves out the heavy price McCullers paid for her very youthful marriage to the tortured and destructive Reeves McCullers, a marriage Carson stuck with long past safety. This early marriage, I would argue, was the sacrifice she made to the appearance of normative femininity, for a Georgia girl in her day, and this marriage to the unstable Reeves (who once asked Carson to commit suicide with him) exacerbated McCullers's fragile health. See Virginia Spence Carr, *Understanding Carson McCullers* (Columbia: University of South Carolina Press, 1990). Also, Claire Rogers Peacock, interview with author, June 1992.

[66] Elisabeth Sherwin, "Patron Saint of Battered Women Writes, Forgives," in *Printed Matter* (Manchester, UK: Manchester University Press, 1998).

[67] Carson McCullers, *Ballad of the Sad Café* (1951; repr., New York: Mariner Books, 2005), 67.

Southern patriarchy. Miss Amelia inhabits this house in a queering of the Southern belle trope of the daughter who is always and endlessly daddy's girl.

Amelia is her daddy's girl at first because she *becomes* her daddy after his death. She becomes the leader of the town but in this transfiguration she is risked, placed at the edge of legitimate culture and her martyrdom re-secures her in the architecture of daddy's house. The near loss of her virginity upon her marriage, as a mere teen, of course predicts the absolute violation of her person and soul when Cousin Lymon betrays her as she fights her erstwhile husband, the once handsome Marvin. And in both violation scenes—the violation averted when Amelia saves her virginity by refusing her husband, securing herself in her father's rooms, and the violation when Amelia cannot save herself because her desire and love have exposed her—the father's house and the daughter's body in the father's house merge. Miss Amelia is not saved, for her body through violence is transfigured into her father's house.

The queer daughter, Miss Amelia, assumes her father's power using her tall, muscular body to convey authority, and also by her dress code of overalls (laid aside for the once-a-week awkward dress). Preeminently she garners to herself her father's power by her willingness to assume power, becoming the de facto mayor of a town eviscerated by poverty.[68] In this way, as the town's leader, Miss Amelia exemplifies the intersex or androgynous person as salvific, as saint. Having assumed her father's power, she preserves it by refusing to give up her virginity in heterosexual congress, and moreover by refusing to be feminized. When Amelia's power is violated, it is through a grotesque rendering of maternity—tiny cousin Lymon, the toddler-sized one human being to whom she is vulnerable. In an instant, Miss Amelia loses her virginity at the level of the symbolic because her baby-sized cousin grabs for her, and her attention immediately goes to him in a self-emptying gesture of love exactly like that of the maternal. Feminized, she is eviscerated.

This asceticism is then echoed in Miss Amelia's anchoritic entombment in her father's house. But the martyrdom does not celebrate traditional female roles. It reveals painfully the destructive character of these roles. The house of the father absorbs the daughter's body not protectively but to annihilate her. Miss Amelia becomes an emblem of the melancholy role accorded gender ambiguous persons, or gender crossing, in the traditional South. Her psyche/soul are eviscerated as she retreats into the supreme position of the Southern daughter, daddy's girl who will not depart from daddy's house, as with Emily and her never materializing rose in Faulkner's story.[69]

Miss Amelia, like Big Sweet and Frankie, is represented as between genders. Miss Amelia's name indicates that she is female but she is not feminine. She is tall and strong and deeply discomfited by subjects to do with female sexuality and

---

[68] McCullers, *Ballad of the Sad Café*, 52.

[69] William Faulkner, "A Rose for Emily," in *Selected Short Stories* (New York: Modern Library, 2012), 47–60.

reproduction. She is marked off from the sphere of the feminine even as she is forced to contend with its strictures. Her body is dressed every Sunday in a dress, a kind of disturbing tokenism, a gesture indicating her inability to escape her sex. Likewise, when Cousin Lymon enters the story, Miss Amelia falls for him partly through the feminine-coded vulnerability of loving the helpless and the childlike. Her desire to protect Cousin Lymon is the desire that leaves her vulnerable and one may say it is depicted by McCullers as a feminine trait, a protectiveness of the small and fragile body that, in this story, represents monstrous unending childish need. The echoed notion that women are trapped in gender roles because of their wish to protect their helpless young, the altricial young of the human, is written as tragedy in the *Ballad of the Sad Cafe*. This feminine trait seals Miss Amelia's doom almost immediately, for it causes her to mistake herself and predict that it is time to slaughter and cook the hogs when in fact the heat returns and destroys all the cooked meat.

A kind of magic adheres to Miss Amelia's androgyny, before the arrival of Cousin Lymon. To her androgyny is attributed an ability to heal others and to protect the town. But that magic, which she protects during her brief early marriage to Marvin Macy, Miss Amelia loses during her love for Cousin Lymon. Whether the hunchback and the androgyne actually have a sexual affair, as some townspeople suspect, or not, the point is that Miss Amelia loses her ability to protect herself because she loses the defense of androgyny as through her love for Cousin Lymon she is feminized.

Like the intersex person in O'Connor's "A Temple of the Holy Ghost," Miss Amelia in *Ballad of the Sad Café* is initially presented as an androgynous person who strongly draws others' sexual desire. Marvin Macy desires her when he cannot desire the tender, young girls whom he easily ruins. Neither male nor female, Miss Amelia attracts him because she transcends gender codes that have destroyed Marvin Macy, insofar as he has been hyper-masculinized, left to fend for himself as a boy. Like the Misfit, Marvin Macy is presented as a figure of inexplicable evil and yet both these men—Macy and the Misfit—can be read as representative of the kind of violent and vicious white masculinity that developed in the Jim Crow South spawning the Klan and the practice of lynching.[70] Notably, the intersex person and Miss Amelia stand in contrast to this figure of violent, white, Southern masculinity; and Miss Amelia is violently punished for her opposition. In this sense, Miss Amelia is a witness—one who sees the sadistic terms of Macy's desire.[71] The novella's close is interestingly concerned with the state of Miss Amelia's eyes: she has gone cross-eyed. Not only has she been closed away, sealed in her father's house, but also Miss Amelia has lost her ability to see

---

70 Dora Apel, *Imagery of Lynching: Black Men, White Women, and the Mob* (New Brunswick: Rutgers University Press, 2004).

71 Marvin Macy's sadism is bluntly suggested by the story's description of his pleasure in torturing animals. McCullers, *Ballad of the Sad Café*, 29.

clearly precisely because she witnessed white male sadism. This too-close-for-safety witnessing has taken away her ability to see.

McCullers hides Miss Amelia's suffering in the hermetic seal of the father's house and yet McCullers also describes that Miss Amelia loses her sight, particularly loses the ability to see depth, becoming fully cross-eyed, just as *Ballad of the Sad Café*'s audience loses its ability to see Miss Amelia in her sealed place. This double blinding, of audience and text, of watcher and watched, shifts the mode of violence as exposition. Here, the androgynous body is exposed in the moment of violation and violation is destruction. While McCullers hides, or sets off-scene, Miss Amelia's death-by-gender, in this immolation, in securing Miss Amelia's martyrdom within the father's house, McCullers makes this invisibility, this ghosting, a form of martyrdom. This violence also is implicitly imposed on the storyteller, even on the writer McCullers, who publicly positioned herself as a storyteller under the sign of androgynous martyr.[72]

What does the example of McCullers's novella clarify about the martyred queer figures this chapter has discussed? A figure more explicitly violated and more blatantly destroyed than Big Sweet, Frankie, and the intersex performance artist, Miss Amelia emblematizes the way that the martyred transgender "belle" also functions as a witness figure in these Southern fictions. The transgender person is representative of an out-of-bounds cultural position through whose perspective the violence of gender restrictions can be revealed. But for this revelation the transgender belle is punished, in narrative, exposing a condition of risk inherent in transgender identity, of course, but also in the position of the witness of gender-based violence in traditional Southern culture.

[72] Brooke Allen, "Emotional Vampire: Review of *Illumination and Night Glare: The Unfinished Autobiography of Carson McCullers*," *The New Criterion* 18 (January 2000): 70. See also, Carson McCullers and Carlos L. Dews, *Illumination and Night Glare: the Unfinished Autobiography of Carson McCullers* (Madison: University of Wisconsin Press, 2002).

Chapter 6
Sadism and the Open Body: Kant, Scarry, and Being in Relation to the Suffering Other

Paul Ricoeur reminds us that the witness is a linking figure, a figure tying the event of violence to veracity, allowing the testimony of the violated to stand as culturally legible truth through this proxy of the witness.[1] The witness figure, in representation, whether literary or photographic, acts as a door between immediate experience of violence and the procedure of thought and time that makes violence a document—a photographic or literary testimony of a violation already done and in the past. At the core of my project on this ethical problematic of the witness figure is the question of how the witness alters the relationship between the violator and the violated. I want in this closing chapter to use the question of how the witness differs from the audience for sadism to leverage an approach for confronting larger issues around witnessing as an action susceptible to ethical judgment. In this chapter, I am defining "witness" as a figure or character that empathetically connects with and absorbs the suffering of the other and "audience" as a figure or character that implicitly (or explicitly as the case may be) gains and/or takes pleasure in the other's pain. For this exploration, I draw on the ethical framework offered by Kant's *Metaphysics of Morals* and Elaine Scarry's *The Body in Pain*.

The gender of the witness is not ethically material: a feminine witness figure may or may not stand as a benign support for the victim, and yet the central figure of the works in this study is the feminine witness figure. I have chosen this focus because when it is a feminine character who watches and/or reports violence, and who may indeed take implicit pleasure in observing the violation of the feminine other, a scandal for feminism arises. And as Maria DiBattista argues, where there is scandal, there is power and interest.[2] My argument is that when the witness takes pleasure in watching the violation of the suffering other, she becomes no longer a witness but instead an audience for whom sadism is performed. In some of the paradigms I have laid bare in this book—in *Beloved*, in *From Here I Saw What Happened and I Cried*—the feminine witness figure, as I have shown, has functioned to assert ethical behavior, manifesting an act of witnessing through the medium of representation. In Morrison's novel and in Weems's photographs the witness figure is a recursive figure, one who sees the sadism of the system in which the victim is locked and yet one who neither takes pleasure in nor turns away from

1 Paul Ricoeur, *Memory, History, Forgetting* (Chicago: University of Chicago Press, 2004).

2 Maria DiBattista, "Scandalous Matter: Women Artists and the Crisis of Embodiment" in *Women Artists at the Millennium*, ed. Armstrong and de Zegher, MIT Press, 2006.

viewing the violation of another woman: a witness who allows truth to become a legible document through inscription. In Morrison's *Beloved*, Sethe's witnessing resists the sadistic pleasure of watching the other suffer, even though Sethe draws on her understanding of the pleasure that schoolteacher takes in watching suffering to guide her virtuoso playing of the terms of the pleasure of sadistic watching. Sethe beats schoolteacher at his own game when she kills her daughter, offering for his sadistic delectation the ultimate taste and barb—a taste for violence that pushes so far it violates even the sadist schoolteacher.

Likewise, Carrie Mae Weems's witness figure in *From Here I Saw What Happened and I Cried* risks the edge of violation, risks violating her subjects and her audience, a choice interpreted by some critics as participating in the pleasurable array of victims for sadistic visual consumption, as noted. To the contrary, I have argued that insofar as Weems's project poses the challenge of witnessing, it necessarily veers close to sadism; yet Weems's work does not participate in the pleasure of watching the victim but rather fuses the position of the artist and audience with that of the victim. Weems insists on a transformed empathetic audience and merges the project of the artist with the place of empathetic witness. Whether Weems always conjures empathy in others is another question—but she works from the premise that she can conjure empathy, deploying witness figures in her photographs to stand for and in effect lead the way to the audience's work of witnessing.

By contrast, the figure of Annie, the mother of the abused daughter in *Bastard Out of Carolina* and the silenced figure of Mark Fortune's daughter, the victim's mother, in "A View of the Woods" function as feminine witness figures who take pleasure in watching/knowing of the violation of a young girl, a violation to which they seem to object and yet in which their pattern of watching/knowing reveals a persistent pleasure in occupying the place of the one who watches the other's violation. They become, in this sense, an audience for whom sadism is enacted.[3] "A Good Man is Hard to Find," too, depicts the pleasure of sadistic watching—the pleasure the Misfit takes in watching those he murders methodically die. The Misfit's courteous display in separating women from men before killing parodies the chivalry of the gallant South and in so doing it implicitly calls up the image of the debased enslaved body and the paradox of the chivalrous Southern gentleman who whips enslaved bodies. In this scene of debauchery through sadism that is inextricably linked to the so-called gallant masculinity of the South, O'Connor's "A Good Man is Hard to Find" poses the figure of the sadist as parodic gentleman (the Misfit states, "ain't no pleasure but in meanness"). While "A Good Man is

[3] In this regard, it is important to recall that Bone comes to long for an audience to her violations, a longing that suggests her strongest link with her mother is through Annie's being the audience of Bone's assaults. Allison, *Bastard Out of Carolina*, 112. Moreover, that Weems, in *From Here I Saw What Happened and I Cried*, does not position the witness figure as a mother, or as a wife, is notable. Embedded in patriarchal structures of wife, daughter, concubine, are the basic building blocks of sadism, so that the only reliable witness to the crimes of gender is the one who has stepped aside from the system, stepped far enough aside to be no one's mother, daughter, lover, or wife.

Hard to Find" does not explicitly raise questions of racism, the story presents the sadism of the white gentleman apocalyptically.

A pattern, then, emerges in my study of the feminine witness figure of sadism in texts invoking the South. Depictions of African American feminine witnesses—Sethe and the witness figures in *From Here I Saw What Happened and I Cried*—present characters who despise the sadism that they witness and present representations of this violence to the audience as a form of testimony and mourning. By contrast, witness figures in *Bastard Out of Carolina* and Flannery O'Connor's short stories are ultimately revealed to take pleasure in watching the suffering of the feminine other. A racial divide emerges that suggests the inheritance of sadism in white femininity—that is, the feminine white character develops from antebellum constraints into a personage who subtly but unmistakably enjoys watching the other suffer. It is worth noting that the figure of the victim, in these representations of white female pleasure in sadism, is also white: the victim a white girl, a daughter significantly vulnerable in her family position.

I suggest that this paradigm of female pleasure in sadism is symbolically true in O'Connor, even as the sadistic actors in these two stories are both males who begin as sadistic watchers. Firstly, the grandfather Mark Fortune is feminized in his role as a man no longer physically powerful, a man who helplessly watches his granddaughter's whippings; likewise, the Misfit's intense rejection of the father (parricide) can be read as a violent abreaction to masculinity. Moreover, in both O'Connor stories, a woman is placed as the watcher of violence: Mary Fortune Pitts's mother knows of her daughter's repeated victimizations and does nothing, while the grandmother, in "A Good Man is Hard to Find," hears the deaths of everyone else in her family insofar as she is last to die. Notably, *after* the Misfit has killed her child and grandchildren, the grandmother reaches towards him and calls him "one of [her] own babies." While she may say this in an effort to recuperate the devastating loss of all her progeny (or she may just be trying to save her own life), the comment also may suggest that the grandmother has enjoyed the violence, and that through this performance of violence the Misfit has found a place in her heart.[4]

---

[4] White women were trained to indirectly observe violations of enslaved women without complaining or intervening. The pattern of white, Southern, slave-holding women having access to no other power but that leveraged over the bodies of enslaved people may explain the arc traced in this study. Southern white women were in effect trained to know of, and in some cases watch, violations done against African American women. The notorious example of Delphine LaLaurie notwithstanding, the evidence from slave narratives as well as WPA former slave testimony makes clear that white women who owned enslaved people were by no means averse to punishing and even torturing the enslaved people over whom the law, and custom, gave them physical power. On Delphine LeLaurie, please see Lorelei Shannon and Victoria Cosner Love, *Mad Madame Lalaurie* (Charleston, SC: The History Press, 2011). See also testimony of former slaves in John W. Blassingame's *Slave Testimony: Two Centuries of Letters, Speeches, Interviews, and Autobiographies* (Baton Rouge: Louisiana State University Press, 1977). For a seminal analysis of the sociology of enslavement, the social figure of the enslaved, please see Patterson, *Slavery and Social Death*.

In this book, I have raised the question of how gender shapes the witness figure in works created by women photographing and writing about the South. I have chosen the South as my field of inquiry because the South stands as the Gothic realm of the national psyche, a psycho-geography of damage and unresolved violations. This landscape also figures in key representations of women watching violence being done to other women. I do not argue that the witness figure in the South is different from the witness figure in other geographies, but rather that she emerges as a critical figure embedded in the violence of the region and the deep residue of its effects. Witnessing sadism and producing a willing audience for sadism are key tropes of the South and yet also, needless to say, are tropes that supersede this geographic region.

The Mean Streets

An aspect of the witness that I have hoped to elucidate in these chapters is the way that the witness is not a person but an act personified. In life, as in representation, the witness is not a subject but an act, and as such changeable: the witness may align herself with the sufferer as in pain and defeat, she may align herself with the violator as a recipient of a bitter triumph. Having established that representation of watching suffering as such is an act that should be theorized, I will here work back through key moments in Immanuel Kant's *Foundations of the Metaphysics of Morals* and Elaine Scarry's *The Body in Pain: The Making and Unmaking of World* to open up the significance of the space of the witness in the ethics of witnessing suffering.[5] In this work I have considered representations of suffering, and representation of the witnessing of these representations, as one group of similar acts, rather than trying to decide how and why photography differs from written text as a conveyor of witnessed pain.

I choose here to consider Kant's ethics, rather than Nietzsche's *Genealogy of Morals*, in order to work through the perimeter moments in ethical decisions that allow us to diverge from Nietzsche's dictum of sadism. Defined by an ethics of witnessing that escapes the Nietzschean imperative of sadism, Kant's system of ethics—that itself has famously been called sadistic by Lacan—I will argue does allow some space for understanding human action in the face of violence that is not itself violent. As Raymond Chandler put it, "Down these mean streets a man must walk who is not himself mean."[6]

Kant insists, in the opening movements of the *Foundations* [or *Groundwork*] *for the Metaphysics of Morals*, that there must be a *metaphysics of morals* in the sense that any moral system must have some recourse to stability: endless

[5] Immanuel Kant, *Groundwork for the Metaphysics of Morals*, ed. and trans. Allen W. Wood (New Haven: Yale University Press, 2002); Scarry, *The Body in Pain*.

[6] Raymond Chandler, *The Simple Art of Murder* (1950; repr., New York: Vintage Books, 1988).

fungibility is the antithesis of ethics.[7] Problematically, Kant allows, the experiential aspect of morality holds in thrall the thinker of ethics. How can we describe an ethical quandary without invoking experience? And yet, Kant insists that just as there is a pure mathematics that justifies applied mathematics, there must also be a pure metaphysics of morals, the ethical that does not depend on circumstance, that overrides and unifies discrete particular circumstance. Kant seeks this register of the absolute in the universalizing structure of the language of the maxim, for it is only in the divvying out and separating of "inclination from duty"[8] that Kant understands some foundation of morals to be possible. Even happiness, asserts Kant, should be sought as a fact of duty not as an aspect of desire or good feeling.[9]

The seeking of a logical structure to happiness that, for Kant, is one's duty (happiness is doing one's duty in Kant's view), as others before me have noted, sounds very odd, counterintuitive.[10] Kant's ultra-rational happiness sounds so odd that Jacques Lacan was inspired to argue that Kant is the cousin, here, of Sade, because Kantian ethics encourage each person to systematically deny his "sympathetic constitution"[11] and instead follow duty because "it alone can be commanded."[12] Surely, argues Lacan, the very premise of such a command is that of violation of will and autonomy.[13] But Kant, in seeking a metaphysics of

---

[7] Kant, *Groundwork for the Metaphysics of Morals*, 1–9. It is important to mention, here, that Kant's record of commentary on race and gender is very problematic. In *Observations on the Feeling of the Beautiful and the Sublime* (1764), Kant argues "The blacks are very vain but in the Negro's way, and so talkative that they must be driven apart from each other with thrashings." Likewise, in this same text Kant asserts that women who engage in laborious or ponderous study and learning destroy the propriety of their sex. Given Kant's obvious and recorded racism, and his avowedly negative attitude toward women's intelligence, how can I use, in this chapter, Kantian ethics to clarify and illuminate the ethical problematic of racism and misogyny? My suggestion is that just as Kant qualifies his remarks on women and on Africans by noting that his assertions cannot hold true in every case because human beings are never uniform, so also we can assert of Kant himself that human variation and fallibility thwarted his ability to apply his own ethical insights to questions of race and gender. But that does not mean that his insights regarding ethics are not ultimately applicable to these issues of race and gender. One could argue that Kant's desire for metaphysics of morals implicitly recognizes individual human fallibility—such as gives rise to misogyny and racism—though perhaps it would strain the point to say that Kant was aware of his own fallibility. But he should have been.

[8] Kant, Groundwork for the Metaphysics of Morals, 14.

[9] Kant, Groundwork for the Metaphysics of Morals, 14.

[10] Robert N. Johnson, *Self-Improvement: An Essay in Kantian Ethics* (Oxford: Oxford University Press, 2011).

[11] Kant, Groundwork for the Metaphysics of Morals, 13.

[12] Kant, Groundwork for the Metaphysics of Morals, 15.

[13] Jacques Lacan, *Ecrits: The First Complete Edition in English*, trans. Bruce Fink (New York: W. W. Norton, 2005); see also Jacques Lacan, "Kant Avec Sade," trans. James B. Swenson, Jr., *October* 51 (1989): 55–75; and Slavoj Zižek "Kant with (or Against) Sade?" *New Formations* 35 (1998): 93–107; see also David Martyn, *Sublime Failures: The Ethics of Kant and Sade* (Detroit, MI: Wayne State University Press, 2003).

morals, is not interested in logistics or even immediate effect. He is interested in separating "ground" from "consequence,"[14] cause from effect, or accidental effect from rational purpose or *will*.

For Nietzsche, will is the guarantor of sadism, the will is sadistic essentially, and Kant's interpretation of will is not radically different from Nietzsche's except in one respect: Kant proposes a superstructure around the will that ultimately is more powerful—because of its inalterable formal qualities—than the will. This superstructure is the extension of rational purpose: desire, for Kant, can only truly long for what will not destroy the subject of desiring and, therefore, logic supersedes will structurally, even though experience tells us that will/desire trumps logic nearly every time. But for Kant, the only true desire (the only desire whose summation would satisfy the longing for it) is desire for the universal good.

Kant's notion of the maxim that will be extrapolated to universality, framed by the question "Can I will that my maxim become a universal law?"[15] functions as a tool to query the difficult space of the witness to violence.[16] For in Kant's formulation of the maxim the will would seem to be suspended not in conceived intent but in active effect. Here is an example of what we might think of as the difference between will and action, and an example of how the maxim in effect suspends the act. Watching my dear friend suffer mortal illness, I have not chosen that she should suffer and it is not in my power to heal her—instead, all I can do is position my mind as ethically as possible to the witnessing of her premature death. Logically, my maxim should not be that she become well through ecologically toxic treatments because, as a universal, this response to illness would, on balance, damage more people. Following Kantian ethics, my maxim should be that she not lose her essential self in suffering, that no one take advantage of her weakened condition, that there be some transcendent meaning to her life, that those who love her be with her at the end. But Kantian ethics do not allow the response that one should desire that environmentally toxic treatments save the life of one's friend, because this desire cannot reasonably become universal law: the environmental damage would be too great. Are these stipulations cold, sadistic? Other options in this situation of *being in relation to the other in suffering* include the option to sadistically enjoy the pain of the other, or to numbly refuse to acknowledge or hear/see the pain of the other, so as to silence the other's pain, to turn away, or to take steps to erase, obscure, or hide the truth of the other's pain. In other words, while Kant's stipulation of the maxim at the core of ethics does seem remote from what might be most people's response to the serious illness of a beloved friend—a desire that everything possible be done to save the beloved—his ethical theory is also not sadistic, that is, it does not center on, and indeed forbids, pleasure in seeing the other suffer.

---

[14] Kant, Groundwork for the Metaphysics of Morals, 400.

[15] Kant, Groundwork for the Metaphysics of Morals, 18.

[16] Johnson argues that Kant's notion of the "universal law" is problematic and must be revised if we are to make use of Kantian ethics. Robert N. Johnson, *Self-Improvement*.

Kant's intense focus on the purity of the will, his idea of disregarding action, has value as a paradigmatic structure for ethics insofar as simply desiring to see the other suffer, even if we do not act on this pleasure, itself is a core problem of ethics. Willing one's thought is related to willing one's desire precisely in the usage of the maxim: by the maxim one wills rational thought to become law. This turn requires not the belief that by magic one's rational decision would effect change; rather it is the rational, necessary antecedent for ethical behavior; that even though the maxim is not positioned with the credulous belief that one's maxim actually will be universalized still one strives to find the right maxim. Kant's ethics, then, in effect are the ethics of witnessing.

Kant asks: how can one will the proper thought; not how can one act the proper act. Here is a question to ask, above all, of the witness who as a witness *cannot* act. The curiously passive aspect of Kant's metaphysics of morals resonates strangely with the omnipotent strategy of the maxim: "Can I will that my maxim become a universal law?" For this maxim is also a way of acknowledging the paradox that nothing of the sort (universal power for the self) ever occurs or should occur and yet the properly ethical maxim can be found only by considering it will be infinitely reiterated. In effect, Kant's ethics are paradigmatically the ethics of the powerless witness.

Maxims

The wrong maxim will destroy itself not through experiential effect but through logical self-negation, argues Kant. The wrong maxim is ultimately nonsense, misshapen. The wrong form manifests as amorality, argues Kant: goodness is formal. If, for example, Mary Fortune's grandfather watching powerlessly as Mary Fortune is beaten by her father, in O'Connor's "A View of the Woods," desires erotically to see the child beaten, indeed desires to become her beater and assert his masculinity thereby, then the maxim asserted as he watches his helpless grandchild being beaten would be something like this: "I enjoy the view, of the woods, because it contains a helpless female body that is being opened by a whip and bleeding." If this were the view of the woods that every man enjoys, then the woods would be bloody indeed, and that's exactly what happens at the close of Flannery O'Connor's story: the woods are drenched in blood-colored light, an apocalyptic space.

Had the grandfather in "A View of the Woods," when watching his ten-year-old granddaughter being beaten, created the maxim, "I cannot bear to see her beaten, I will give away all my land and use all my resources to rescue her to prevent the next beating," it is unclear what would have transpired. Was Mr. Pitts beating the little girl because he wanted Mark Fortune's land? Was the contest over the treasured daughter's body as simple as that? Or was Mr. Pitts beating the little girl because he knew the grandfather was watching? In the latter case, the wrong maxim of the grandfather was pivotal to the continuing abuse of the girl.

What the grandfather in "A View of the Woods" thinks, of course, is that watching Mary Fortune being beaten is like watching himself being beaten (he watches her and feels as if he himself were being beaten). This interchangeability between the witness and the victim in O'Connor's story would seem to generate the wrong maxim. It is the wrong maxim because it does not attempt to deny to the violator a body to violate. Instead, to assume an equivalency between the victim and the witness is to offer the violator an endless supply of bodies, interchangeable bodies, to violate.

Kant's Ethics are the Ethics of the Witness

What is, then, the right, or ethical, maxim for the witness of violence? As the above parable indicates, finding the right maxim for situations in which one is a witness to sadistic violence (in the case of O'Connor's "A View of the Woods," a ten-year-old girl being mercilessly whipped by her father while her grandfather watches) is not easy. For if the grandfather's maxim were that the witness should physically intervene and beat Mr. Pitts because Mr. Pitts beats Mary Fortune, and if the grandfather were to act on this maxim, we might predict an escalation of violent death. But Mary Fortune might not have been the one who died. The place of the witness is a kind of torture in itself. The definition of the witness would be one who cannot effectively override and overturn the violence of the violator but who, unlike the victim, survives the violence, bearing its mark.

Elaine Scarry, in "The Structure of Torture," presents elliptically just such witnesses when she describes one aspect of the "house of open doors" torture program in Argentina, a policy established so that other prisoners could be played tape recordings of the suffering of their fellow prisoners.[17] That is, *hearing* the torture of others becomes part of the prisoners' torture: that they witness is part of their torture. As Scarry makes clear, the victim of torture cannot be held responsible for the actions of his/her body and the words of his/her mouth while under torture. And yet the maxim, what the prisoner can *will*, remains uncannily in his/her possession. But how can there be what Kant asserts must be an "highest and unconditional good" in a wholly good "will"[18] in the mind of a witness to torture who is her/himself a victim of torture?

Kant's idea that there can be an absolutely good will, a holy will—even if no human being might ever have this absolutely good will—slants his ethics to the passive case. For the absolutely good will, materialized in the verbal formalization of the correct maxim, will not in experience be repeated infinitely to become universal law. If I am a prisoner in a "house of open doors" forced to hear the cries of other prisoners as they are tortured, the absolutely good will would generate a maxim, I think, like this: "I will that this prison become in fact a house of open

[17] Scarry, *The Body in Pain*, 40–47.

[18] Kant, Groundwork for the Metaphysics of Morals, 17.

doors, a space from which the imprisoned can walk away." That would be a good maxim, but it would not save anyone. And Kant's ethics, I suggest, accept that their very formal rigorousness makes them impractical.

For the use of Kant's maxims is not in acting but *in witnessing*. For example, if Toni Morrison's Sethe, in *Beloved*, witnesses schoolteacher's abuse of her body through the ironic iconography of his writing a human being into an animal, the maxim of her response would ideally be something like "I will that no human being destroy the dignity of another human being." Indeed, Sethe's ideal maxim would be something very commensurate with Kant's noting that "corrupting the foundation" and "destroying the dignity" of another human being cannot ever be "ultimately good."[19] The destruction of Sethe's dignity, the corruption of her foundation as a human being would be considered unconditionally bad, for Kant, because if this maxim were universalized all human beings would be destroyed. *Beloved*'s Sethe destroys her beloved daughter in order that schoolteacher not "corrupt the foundation" of her child.

And yet what Sethe ceases to be, in the moment she acts and kills her baby girl, is a witness. She ceases to will a maxim and instead acts. The novel depicts Sethe's struggle to come to terms with this moment in which she temporarily stepped out of character—stopped being a witness—and acted. Kant's ethics trend towards *preventing* action because the purity of the maxim tends to be muddied by actual behavior. Far from asserting sadism, as Lacan argued in *Ecrits*, Kant would seem to assert a kind of martyrdom of witnessing, in which Sethe, for example, would witness her daughter's dignity destroyed and would will an outcome in which the dignity of all persons could be held intact *but not act*. The pain of the futile witness is the role of bearing this weight of ethics, a kind of ethical fulcrum point that the one who acts does not bear.

And yet Sethe's departure from her role of witness causes her horrific pain; this act, of killing her daughter, which serves to save all her children from being returned to slavery not to mention protects Sethe herself from return to slavery, puts in place a nodus of pain that only recourse to the supernatural or the psychotic, depending on how one interprets the novel, appeases.

The Futile Witness and the Ethical World

Elaine Scarry's analysis of the structure of torture alludes to just this imprimatur of passivity that separates ethical thought from action when she describes in painful detail the way that "world" is stripped away from the victim of torture. "The disintegration of the contents of consciousness, the contraction and ultimate dissolution of the prisoner's world, acknowledged and objectified in confession, is also objectified in the physical objects the torturer uses as weapons."[20] The

[19] Kant, Groundwork for the Metaphysics of Morals, 19.

[20] Scarry, The Body in Pain, 38.

torture victim is tortured specifically in order to be stripped of world and yet s/he is tortured to give world to the torturer, at least some illusory claiming of world (here, I am following Scarry's usage of the term "world").[21] For example, when Mark Fortune defeats his own image in killing his granddaughter, he very specifically reclaims the territory of "Fortune" from the encroachment of the other, "Pitts." He feels, erroneously but strongly, that by stripping the girl of world he will gain world himself.

The Kantian maxim of not destroying the other lest one destroy oneself O'Connor's and Morrison's works painfully pressure, for in these stories, destroying the other almost seems to save the witness whose pain in witnessing the suffering other has almost caused the witness's demise. One could say that there is not anything redemptive in "A View of the Woods," unlike *Beloved*. And yet O'Connor's claim is that the very nihilistic violence on which her stories center is the redemption, the violent breaking apart of the subject to permit the entering of the deity into the soul.[22] In *Beloved*, Sethe seeks to prophylactically destroy the other—she destroys the corrupted ruined daughter whom schoolteacher would produce were he permitted to take Sethe's child—in order to save her "best thing" the pure and un-enslaved daughter whom she, Sethe, *claims as her world*.

Sethe's world, after the revenant Beloved returns, is her house, with the revenant securely in that house.[23] Sethe states that she needs nothing but this house, this world into which the daughter destroyed has returned. And yet, much as Mark Fortune and Mary Fortune battle each other to the death for world, so also Sethe and Beloved end up in a protracted death struggle over claim of house/world. The difficulty of witnessing is at the core of these deathly struggles for world. In each of these fictional texts a victim dies in order that others—Sethe and Denver and Paul D. in *Beloved*, and the Pitts family in general (without Mary Fortune) in "A View of the Woods"—gain world.

Scarry's argument that language is the barometer of self-possession is so useful an approach to the problem of ethics that one almost doesn't notice, within Scarry's work, the unanswered question: for whom this ethical language is performed. For whom, for what audience, is violence performed might be the one question left unasked in Scarry's magisterial *The Body in Pain*, a work that otherwise answers almost every question that can be raised about the relationship between symbolic structures of embodiment and pain, torture and social/physical victimization. This

---

21 See Scarry, *The Body in Pain*, 146, 234. "World" for Scarry is constituted as the mental space combining intense focus of attention and material culture/experience. For this understanding of "world" she draws from phenomenology, Edmund Husserl defining world as knowable from a process of "eidetic reduction." See, Edmund Husserl, *The Essential Husserl*, ed. Donn Welton (Bloomington: Indiana University Press, 1999).

22 O'Connor, *Mystery and Manners*, 83, 206.

23 "The *World* is in this room" (my italics) muses Sethe, watching her killed daughter returned apparently alive, as an adult revenant, into her house. Sethe's world, unmade by schoolteacher, is made again by the revenant. Morrison, *Beloved*, 183.

question of for whom violence is performed contains the question of the witness. What role does the witness play in shaping ethical structures?

It is of course always possible that violence is performed because the audience wants to watch the violation of the victim: cock-fights and boxing are events performing violence specifically so that someone might watch that violence. Most violence however, as Scarry makes clear in "The Structure of War" and "The Structure of Torture," is firstly enacted *to control the speech of the violated*, to take away that speech or to focus that speech towards one act which in turn will enable the torturer's "side" (country or faction), to all the more effectively silence the other. And yet Scarry's notion of the relationship between language and violence focuses the question of the function of the witness, or the audience, as the case may be.

On a diacritical level, Scarry's whole text—*The Body in Pain*—performs the witness function. Scarry becomes the feminine witness to the atrocities she describes, analyzes, and condemns. Her implicit maxim is Kantian in the sense that Scarry's text performs proof of why torturing the other is unethical: the torture of the other unmakes the world, ultimately unmakes all worlds. But Scarry's text, *The Body in Pain*, creates a world in which voice is reclaimed for the silenced, suffering body. This claim is precisely Kant's claim when he argues that the maxim of ethical behavior must always be that which will not destroy the other, that is, not destroy the world. The universality of every proper maxim means that the witness to another's violation must will that the other not be violated because, for Kant, if one person wills that another be violated that means s/he is willing that everyone, him/herself included, be violated.

The deeply haunting problem of the witness, the problem of whether and where the witness to violence becomes an audience, structures the degree to which we may query whether all violence is not enacted so that the violator may watch the effects of his cruelty, and also give others the pleasure of watching the effects of his cruelty, a profoundly visual turn making of the violator a near cousin to the audience/witness of sadism. And yet clearly the modes of power and powerlessness that differentiate violators from witnesses have some ethical force. It's just that the witness always stands near and the audience often slips into the partaking of the most strongly motivating factor for violence: the desire of the violator to see his work of unmaking the world of the violated, literally to see the interior of the other's body, or to see the other stripped of world, silenced. The role of the audience, its specularity, haunts the urge to commit atrocity. Likewise, the role of the witness veering always riskily close to that of audience makes the usage of Kant's ethics of witnessing an essential compass for the ethics of witnessing.

Consider the paradigm of incest that Allison exposes in *Bastard Out of Carolina*. Bone, the incested daughter, is stripped of world by her stepfather when he penetrates her. He locks Bone in the bathroom or assaults her in the truck hutch, small spaces, exceedingly small spaces, to articulate his claim that she is "his." His sexual use of her chimes with her nickname, "Bone." For she is a girl stripped to the bone of identity, hanging on to the bone of herself against all his efforts to annihilate her identity, to unmake her world. But the little girl's mother, Annie, watches this stripping of her daughter and indeed accedes to the name "Bone" for her girl very specifically in order to hold onto a piece of world: the mother retains her position as a wife, a married woman, *because* she witnesses Bone's stripping and does not object strongly enough to end the abuse. The mother settles into the role of silent witness and from there slides into the position of audience, benefitting from the violence she observes.

The audience for sadism gains pleasure (and heightened social status as a form of pleasure) from watching the other suffer. The mother in *Bastard Out of Carolina* does not, on the surface, seem to enjoy hearing her daughter cry as the young girl is beaten by the stepfather. Rather as in the "house of open doors" the mother listens to the daughter's cries powerlessly. And yet it is surely for her, for the mother, that the stepfather performs violence. He violates the child performatively, to show the mother his masterful penetration of the female body, to show Annie what the female body becomes in his hands.

In this scenario of incest, of a mother hearing a daughter suffer violation, it is surely not that the mother wills her daughter's rape. And yet the mother does gain "world" (a social place in her town society) by dint of being willing to witness her daughter's beatings and molestations. Witnessing the daughter's rape gains world for the mother because she becomes an audience who refuses the inscription of suffering on her own body and instead occupies a Nietzschean space of gaining from the other's pain. The violated other's pain is her gain. Annie ultimately becomes not a witness (on whom suffering is inscribed) but an audience for violence; she benefits from acceding to her daughter's violation.

The ethical problematic of the witness, then, is the way that the witness may be forced to will her own loss of world, if she is not to gain from the fact that some other body has been violated. Otherwise, she risks being the audience, not the witness, for the spectacle of violence—in the case of Sethe and Bone's mother, Annie, the daughter's body is harmed specifically to prevent the witness's body from being harmed. That is, a very knotty exchange takes place in these acts of witnessing, an exchange by which the mother-as-witness, Sethe and Annie in *Beloved* and *Bastard Out of Carolina* respectively, is preserved from violation because the body of the daughter is opened, by murder and rape respectively. And yet how could a witness to violence really will her own loss of world? Surely she would need instead to will the erasure of the violator, as a maxim. Either way, the good witness has to be able to refuse all gains from the violence she witnesses.

The Wound and the Emblem of the Opened Body

Scarry theorizes the opening of the body as that which signifies lack of power in the semiotics of meaning.[24] She argues that this equivalence between the opened body

---

[24] Scarry, *The Body in Pain*, 96, 205–35.

and powerlessness is established, in particular, by the Bible—God's disembodied status, God's unrepresentability, Scarry persuasively argues, denotes God's omnipotence.[25] The disembodied divinity is that which definitively can never be opened. But it is not only the having of body that differentiates humanity and makes humankind vulnerable and God invulnerable. As well the opening of the body is a central trope, argues Scarry, connoting the *vulnerability of embodiment*, a trope that hovers and oscillates between opening the body by a tool and opening the body by a weapon.

Scarry argues that in the Old Testament, God is repeatedly represented as a relation between a deeply embodied suffering human being and wholly disembodied (i.e., immune from pain) principle of creating, mediated by the recurring image of a colossal weapon that transverses the space between them.[26] The weapon, Scarry argues, can at times be indistinguishable from a tool,[27] and it is on this important point that I want to dilate. For the opened body of the daughter represented in *Beloved*, "A View of the Woods," *Bastard Out of Carolina*, is the body opened by tools of varying kinds: the tool of the saw, the primitive tool of the rock, and crudely put the "tool" of the paternal member, Daddy Glenn's oversized phallus.[28] All these tools are represented as easily accessed, always present in the landscape of the narrative, and also mis-used in the moment of ab-use—abused, but at the same time properly used in the sense of generating a sacrificial body the opening of which relieves the witness figure of her own death. The tool then is not only the tool that opens the daughter's body but also the sacrificial daughter *is* the "tool" or *dupe* of other feminine witnesses, who are protected when the violator satiates himself on the sacrificial daughter.

Sethe, opening her daughter's body with the saw, does not intend to save herself but she does indeed save herself by this act. The daughter's opened body—opened with the tool that becomes a weapon, the saw—saves the mother's body from being re-opened, whipped, or raped, by schoolteacher. Sethe is relieved of further whippings and rapes because her daughter's body is catastrophically opened. Sethe's body, the scar sealed on her back, remains sealed when she kills her daughter because she witnesses her daughter's absolute vulnerability to schoolteacher's encroachment and acts on that vulnerability. Likewise, Annie,

---

25 Scarry, *The Body in Pain*, 148–205.

26 Scarry, *The Body in Pain*, 173.

27 Scarry, *The Body in Pain*, 173.

28 *American Heritage Dictionary of the English Language* (Boston: Houghton Mifflin, 2000) offers the following definition of "tool": "A device, such as a saw, used to perform or facilitate manual or mechanical work; A machine, such as a lathe, used to cut and shape machine parts or other objects; The cutting part of such a machine; Something regarded as necessary to the carrying out of one's occupation or profession; Something used in the performance of an operation; an instrument; *Vulgar Slang*. A penis; A person used to carry out the designs of another; a dupe."

witnessing Bone being opened by her husband's whippings, his hands, and then by his penis, is herself left intact.

In all the above instances from *Beloved* and *Bastard Out of Carolina* and "A View of the Woods," one would face extraordinary difficulty in discerning a Kantian maxim for a witness. For Sethe and Annie, *before* they become witnesses to their daughters' violations, are themselves victims of violation, Sethe raped and beaten by schoolteacher's nephews, Annie a victim of statutory rape, the result of which is the birth of Bone, her daughter. Indeed, even Mark Fortune is firstly feminized as he watches little Mary Fortune being whipped by her father, feminized because he cannot fight his son-in-law and stop the whippings, feminized because he initially watches in horror. In other words, the place of the witness in these stories is what Abigail Solomon-Godeau has called the "nightmare of femininity," the feminine as the space of insolvably vulnerable embodiment.[29]

Kant theorizes the problem of ethics as metaphysical, superseding specific instance, and, because metaphysical, curiously disempowered or removed from action. He cannot say what, in any given instance, one necessarily should *do* because that would contaminate the metaphysical or formal premise on which he bases his system of ethics. And yet Kant's *Foundations of the Metaphysics of Morals* does provide an exacting theorization of the place of the witness, for it does speak to the witness's specific *inability to act* and the necessity of framing a correctly ethical will in spite of that powerlessness: to will as if one had power knowing one does not have power.

The nightmare of the cultural feminine Kant's passive metaphysics of morals takes beautifully into account. For here is the will without action and yet capacious of knowing what action should be performed. Argues Kant, "Only a rational being has the capacity of acting according to the conception of laws, i.e., according to principles. This capacity is will … if reason infallibly determines the will, the actions which such a being recognizes as objectively necessary are also subjectively necessary."[30]

Kant theorizes the will as if it had universal effect—for it must have theorizable universal effect to be metaphysical—even though it is clear to Kant, as to any reader of Kant, that a universal effect of each individual's will is impossible. Kant's maxim: one must will that which should have universal effect knowing that one's willing cannot have universal effect. Therefore, one grounds the moral will in an assumption of powerlessness to act. Kant's ethics then turn curiously on feminized (passive) positions of witnessing. I do not mean that femininity is the ultimate moral good. No, I mean that the intense passivity of Kant's ethics show that central to his theory of ethics is the witness.

For Kant, as for Scarry, the question of obedience is central to the symbolic structure of violence. Scarry understands obedience as a structure of belief and

---

[29] Abigail Solomon-Godeau, "Just Like a Woman," in *Catalogue, Hunter College Exhibition of Francesca Woodman Photographs* (New York: Hunter College, 1986).

[30] Kant, Groundwork for the Metaphysics of Morals, 28.

builds her theory from the violent relationship between God and man in the Old and New Testaments (in the New Testament Scarry brilliantly points to the way that Jesus Christ functions as a weapon, a tool).[31] For Scarry, obedience to God causes violence, whereas for Kant, obedience to the divine will ultimately averts violence. Scarry points out the structure of belief, which is the structure of imagination, is also that of the weapon: "In scenes of both reproduction and wounding, the graphic image of the human body substitutes for the object of belief that itself has no content and thus itself cannot be represented."[32] The un-representable quality of the divinity for Kant is not a problem; indeed the position of the ultimately good will as beyond apprehension is precisely what secures its status as holy, and wholly good. For Kant the trauma of this unknowable good will is to be desired.

Belief in God, however, for Scarry the paradigmatic structure of the imagination, is married at every point with the wounding of the body. And yet, paradoxically, Scarry points to numerous places in the Old Testament in which the wounded human body signifies the infinite symbolic potential of belief: "Although an occasion of wounding is often described … as a scene of disobedience and punishment, it is in many ways more comprehensible and accurate to recognize it as a scene of doubt, for it is a failure of belief that continually re-occasions the infliction of hurt."[33] By wounding the body, God as symbol enters the mind. W. T. J. Mitchell has provocatively argued that God and trauma occupy a similar representational axis, both positioned as beyond representation.[34]

The witness to the suffering other, in this paradigm that Scarry introduces, is literally a witness of the truth of God, the witness to trauma is witness to the un-representable. This ethics asks of the witness that she *suffer in the same way as the other*, that she take onto her body the opening of the wound, the plunge of the weapon.[35] But if we confront the representation of violence offered by Morrison, O'Connor, Dickinson, Weems, and Allison from within their texts, that is, if we do not read the authors and photographer as witnesses themselves but rather confine our reading of the problematic of the witness *within the narrative or poem or photograph* then we often are faced with witnesses who do not will that the wounds of the suffering other be inflicted on the body of the witness. However, it is possible that Morrison's Sethe, and Weems's profile witness, take onto their minds if not their bodies the wounds of the suffering other. Is this the paradigm of ethical witnessing that would cohere with Kant's notion of the will as universal maxim, impossible to enact but essential and necessary to discern within the mind of the witness?

---

31 Scarry, *The Body in Pain*, 213.

32 Scarry, *The Body in Pain*, 198.

33 Scarry, *The Body in Pain*, 201.

34 W. J. T. Mitchell, *Cloning Terror* (Chicago: University of Chicago Press, 2012).

35 Scarry, *The Body in Pain*, 16.

For Kant, as well as for Scarry, the nodus of ethics is the structure of belief, and for Kant, belief and obedience are tightly knotted concepts. However, Scarry's notion of God as a created artifact is starkly at variance with Kant's theorization of the divine will as the unknowable and only good. For Kant, the objective law of ethics exists even though we cannot see it.[36] This law's existence necessitates our obedience even as we cannot know its contours: "the relation of objective law to a will which is not completely good is conceived as the determination of the will of a rational being by principles of reason to which this will is not by nature necessarily obedient."[37] Belief, oddly, doesn't much matter to Kant because it is impossible wholly to know in what one believes, Kant admits. The perfectly good will—that for which the witness must strive—is contiguous with the holy will which is the same as the objective law—and is unknowable.[38]

For Kant "imperatives are only formulas expressing the relation of objective laws of volition in general to the subjective imperfection of the will of this or that rational being, i.e. the human will."[39] If the human will can be made coterminous with the holy will, freedom will be achieved because the will needs no constraint when its desire is holy. But as Kant states, there is no formal difference between the poisoner and the physician: other than their differing relationships to the holy will, since an action's result makes no difference to its ethical force.[40] This difference of wills can only be known by some divine viewpoint inaccessible to human knowledge, hence the need for maxims expressing the relational terms between the wounded and the wounding, and expressing this knowledge from the point of view of the witness who may be powerless to act. For Kant, as for Scarry, the divine will is structured like the imagination, but for Kant this place (the imagination) is unknowable because of its quality of noumenality, whereas for Scarry this place is unknowable because it is humanly created. What is important, for my argument here, is to note that both Kant and Scarry understand violence as the failing-place of definition, that place where the weapon and the tool are terrifyingly indistinguishable and where the poisoner and physician are the same.

This place where weapon and tool, poisoner and physician, are the same is the place of torture. In torture, meaning is inscribed in a manner that literalizes power relations and negates the language of the victim, even as the victim's body becomes the testimony of the torturer. Insofar as s/he acts as a torturer, the one who violates only has language by inscription onto the body of the violated while the victim loses language, as Scarry argues, because his/her "world" is unmade. Yet the witness/audience alone can retain some capacity for language or symbolic discourse. Torture describes Sethe's treatment at the hands of schoolteacher's nephews, as it describes the enslavement of African women subject to rape and

---

36 Kant, Groundwork for the Metaphysics of Morals, 28.

37 Kant, Groundwork for the Metaphysics of Morals, 28.

38 Kant, Groundwork for the Metaphysics of Morals, 29.

39 Kant, Groundwork for the Metaphysics of Morals, 30.

40 Kant, Groundwork for the Metaphysics of Morals, 30.

incest without recourse (incest occurring for example when the same master raped an enslaved woman and then raped the daughter that that rape produced, in neither case recognizing himself culturally as the spouse/father *or violator* of either enslaved woman).[41]

Torture may be a correct term for all the violations studied in my book. Torture unquestionably describes the violence that schoolteacher visits on the enslaved people at Sweet Home. Torture as well describes Mr. Pitts's approach to raising his little girl under the whip, and also describes Mark Fortune's attempt to force Mary Fortune to *say* she is all Fortune. The grandfather, just before killing the victim, attempts to force her language to become his language: she must say she is all Fortune or die. As Scarry makes clear, the very point of torture is to get the victim to say what you want them to say, to take over their use of speech.[42] Mark Fortune tries to force his little granddaughter to, as it were, *confess* that she belongs wholly to him, that she is all Fortune. When she will not make this verbal acquiescence, he kills her. Likewise, Bone's mother, hearing Bone's beatings in the bathroom, afterwards forces her daughter to *say* that she will be good from now on—that she will no longer draw the torturer's desire towards her body.

The effort to control the language of the victim is absolutely primary in all these cases of torture and disturbingly it is an effort in which witnesses often collude with the torturer. Certainly Sethe's wish to save her daughter from schoolteacher's deprivation of language is primary: she kills her beloved little girl because she refuses to see her daughter defined linguistically by schoolteacher. And yet Sethe does slit the girl's throat; specifically, she cuts open and destroys the locus of the victim's voice.

Scarry describes the Old Testament God silencing the voices of the people. "Their voices whine and murmur," and God's punishment is to silence these voices.[43] So also Sethe seeks preemptively to silence her daughter before schoolteacher can put corrupting and ruining words of degradation into her infant daughter's innocent mouth. I do not mean here simplistically to argue that Sethe plays God. I mean that the fine line between the witness who wills that the language of the victim be preserved, that the language of the victim survive, and the violator who takes away the victim's language, is a narrow and fraught line, as Morrison surely reveals in her unrelenting depiction of torture in the antebellum South.

---

[41] Christina Sharpe, *Monstrous Intimacies: Making Post-Slavery Subjects* (Durham, NC: Duke University Press, 2010), 14–15.

[42] Hence the use of the bit is central to Morrison's concern with the lost conversation between mother and daughter that haunts Sethe with regards to her ma'am, her mother. Sethe's mother had the bit used on her so many times it deformed her mouth. Scarry, *The Body in Pain*, 47.

[43] Scarry, *The Body in Pain*, 201.

Tawse, the Whipping Strap

In the witnesses I've considered, it is notable that mothers watching daughters being violated is the paradigmatic event of feminine witnessing. Even Mark Fortune in "A View of the Woods" can be read as a stand-in for his silenced daughter, Mary Fortune's mother, who does nothing to stop the husband mercilessly beating her little girl. The disturbingly home-spun settings of the mothers who witness daughters opened by the weapon—the saw, the penis, the rock—shape the texts on which I focus in this book. The domestic scenes of the shed, the kitchen, the woods, do not protect daughters. In *The Body in Pain*, Scarry underscores the paradoxical, home-spun quality of torture when she delineates the usage of home accouterments in the torture chamber as well as the words of hospitality therein: "Called 'guest houses' in Greece and 'safe houses' in the Philippines, the torture rooms are often given names that acknowledge and call attention to the generous civilizing impulse normally present in human shelter."[44] She goes on to describe the inclusion and indeed emphasis of the domestic in torture, the "transition from a refrigerator into a bludgeon."[45] The homeyness of torture may indeed not be paradoxical; rather, if we consider the structure of mother-daughter/witness-victim put forward in Morrison's, O'Connor's, and Allison's texts, we could begin to argue that the structure of torture is preternaturally the structure of the domestic. The whipping strap is a domestic tool.

The Kantian Chill

And here we return to what has been remarked as Kant's inexplicable coldness in the face of domestic or familial emotion, his argument that the parent's natural feeling for his children is the worst basis for ethical action and that instead ethical action must be based on metaphysical principles strictly removed from homey emotion.[46] As Morrison makes clear in naming the scene of Sethe's torture "Sweet Home," schoolteacher's fatherly feeling for his enslaved human "possessions," expressed when he critiques his nephews for *overbeating* Sethe, is precisely the engine of his sadism. What schoolteacher has is homey feeling, paternal care if you will. What he does *not* have is what Kant calls a recognition of every human being as occupying the "realm of ends" as opposed to the realm of means.[47] That is, homey emotion must be extricated from ethical action because it is through the lens of homeyness we view the other as a means—a wife to produce children

---

44 Scarry, The Body in Pain, 40.

45 Scarry, The Body in Pain, 41.

46 Whether Kant himself expressed racist sentiment is not strictly relevant to his theory of ethics. Please see, Marcia W. Baron, *Kantian Ethics Almost Without Apology* (Ithaca, NY: Cornell University Press, 1995); Barbara Herman. *Moral Literacy* (Cambridge, MA: Harvard University Press, 2008).

47 Kant, Groundwork for the Metaphysics of Morals, 49.

and bodily comfort, a child to carry on the name and lineage, a father to provide cultural prestige. The realm of ends, instead, is anti-domestic and indeed rather cold, a little like the ascetic house where Sethe and Paul D. find themselves after their dispossession of Beloved, at the end of Morrison's novel, a little like Dickinson's "bald and cold" universe.[48]

Kant defines the relationship between the rational and the material as one of ethics: "a rational being belongs to the realm of ends as a member when he gives universal laws in it while himself also is subject to those laws."[49] The realm of ends, however, rapidly folds into what can only be understood as a capitalist discourse, for Kant goes on to specify that the realm of ends is not in itself the definition of the human. A human being, Kant stipulates, must always be treated as an end rather than a means; yet even within this realm of ends, capitalism shapes the landscape for "in the realm of ends everything has either a price or a dignity" (and) "Whatever has a price can be replaced by something else as its equivalent; on the other hand whatever is above all price, and therefore admits of no equivalent, has a dignity."[50] In other words, "dignity" for Kant functions in a manner parallel to that of "duty": both "dignity" and "duty" are the boundary conditions of ethics and both at once typify the human and are difficult to ascertain.

Enlightenment Ideology?

While Kant's listing of the distinction between "things" and "persons"[51] at first glance eerily reminds one of schoolteacher's listing of Sethe's "animal" and "human" characteristics, it is important to note that while Kant's methodology may be aped by schoolteacher, schoolteacher's conclusion suggests not Kant but instead an American figure.[52] For Kant further argues that the "practical imperative" is to "act so that you treat humanity, whether in your own person or in that of another, always as an end and never as a means only."[53] Needless to say, schoolteacher does not treat Sethe as an end but as a means.

Yet schoolteacher uses Enlightenment logic to argue that Sethe is not part of humanity.[54] While schoolteacher's use of Kant's methodology of differentiating

48 Caroline Rody has glossed homeyness as too much intimacy in *Beloved* in *The Daughter's Return: African-American and Caribbean Women's Fictions of History* (New York: Oxford University Press, 2001). The problematic of the mother who witnesses her daughter's violation haunts American texts and in particular haunts American texts that contend with the traditional South.

49 Kant, Groundwork for the Metaphysics of Morals, 50.

50 Kant, Groundwork for the Metaphysics of Morals, 51.

51 Kant, Groundwork for the Metaphysics of Morals, 428.

52 Interestingly, schoolteacher's list seems to reflect Thomas Jefferson's musings on race; see, *Notes on the State of Virginia*.

53 Kant, Groundwork for the Metaphysics of Morals, 47.

54 Gilman, Difference and Pathology.

"things" from "persons," like his later separating of "price" from "dignity," is at variance with Kant's ethical demands, we may echo Lacan in raising the question of whether a Kantian ethics is culpable for the distortions of its use. That is, while clearly anyone following the dictum "Act so that you treat humanity, whether in your own person or in that of another, always as an end and never as a means only"[55] could never own slaves, the way that schoolteacher effortlessly co-opts Kantian rational methodology—creating categories, separating "thing" and "person," "price" and "dignity"—could suggest that Kant's method itself is suspect. And yet Sethe follows precisely this method insofar as she is the character who paradigmatically achieves "sublimity and dignity" by "fulfilling (her) duties" that is, by mothering her children with the most extreme seriousness and responsibility imaginable.

The inheritance of Enlightenment methodology, the zeal to distinguish person from thing, *price* from *dignity*, seems in Morrison's exposition in *Beloved* to buttress the project of slavery, to provide a rubric and a paradigm for separating the "animal" from the "human," however specious and hollow the application of those categories.[56] And yet Sethe herself is a paradigmatic Enlightenment subject: she witnesses suffering and reacts to injustice in a way that can only be described as dignified because dutiful: *in extremis* Sethe insists that she and her children be *ends and not means, dignities and not prices*. She follows, in extremis, what Kant calls the principle of autonomy.[57] For the principle of autonomy is "never choose except in such a way that the maxims of the choice are comprehended in the same volition as universal law."[58] Sethe chooses autonomy in the face of tremendous pressure and resistance; she chooses freedom as the universal law.

Indeed, Sethe's behavior is at all points chillingly rational. Who among us could sustain the clear-sightedness to know that schoolteacher's capture of her infant daughter would "dirty [the daughter] so bad" she would forget who she was, and lead to a "gang of whites [who] invaded her daughter's thighs and threw her daughter out of the wagon."[59] But if Sethe's cold, rational performance is not that of Sade, Sethe is Kantian in her logic. For while Sade revels in the degradation of the other, Sethe acts specifically to *not degrade* her daughter, to protect from

---

55 Kant, Groundwork for the Metaphysics of Morals, 47.

56 The contemporaneity of Kant's usage of the terms "price" and "person," "thing" and "dignity," with the upsurge of colonization and enslavement suggests that Immanuel Kant's *Foundations of the Metaphysics of Morals, and What Is Enlightenment?* (New York: Liberal Arts Press, 1959) are in subception responding to the ethical problem of enslaving other human beings. While Horkheimer and Adorno in *Dialectic of Enlightenment* (New York: Herder and Herder, 1972) argued that Kantian ethics were Sadean ethics because of their contemporaneity, I am here making a different argument. My suggestion is that Kant was in principle if not in explicit statement sensitive to, rather than in favor of, the sadistic terms of enslavement.

57 Kant, Groundwork for the Metaphysics of Morals, 53.

58 Kant, Groundwork for the Metaphysics of Morals, 53.

59 Morrison, *Beloved*, 293–4.

degradation at every cost, even becoming the holy sacrifice, the one who does not survive. It is this question of degradation that is hauntingly intangible. (Why some forms of violation, for example sexual violation, degrade the subject is almost beyond theorizing. Kant would argue that to be used as a means rather than an end always degrades the violated subject.)

Sethe's performance as a witness is spurred into crisis by the Enlightenment ideology of the rational that schoolteacher perverts. At the same time, Sethe's performance as a mother and as a witness to violence is arguably rational: anti-emotional, dignified, carrying duty against all resistance—the duty of the mother, not maternal feeling. The materiality of enslavement, that which makes of human beings "price" and tries to separate them from "dignity," Sethe's superlative performance of duty overrides, at great cost, possibly at the cost of everything. Arguably, in killing her daughter, her "best thing," Sethe kills herself. Kant argues that the suicide[60] could further his own happiness by ending a life made miserable and yet this desire to further happiness by material destruction cannot become a universal maxim[61] because it would conflict with the law that every human being treat every human being, him- or herself included, as an end and as a dignity, rather than as a means and as a price. Sethe's act of destruction isn't a witnessing, but an action, and yet is *par excellence* the act of the witness, for Sethe kills her daughter only because she, Sethe, sees what is done to enslaved young girls. She sees that they are dirtied until they have no identity, becoming the living dead.[62]

And yet suicide, if we can say that Sethe's act of killing her daughter is a kind of suicide, moves beyond Kant's ethics. For, to kill yourself, argues Kant, is to treat your self as a means rather than an end. Sethe treats Beloved as an end not a means, even though Sethe's killing of Beloved is like a suicide (the mother killing what is best in herself in the body of her child). Sethe acts violently not because she views her child as a means to an end but rather because she views the child as an end. If Sethe's regarding of her daughter's life as something she has the right to destroy cannot be justified by Kantian ethics, I believe it can be clarified by comparison with Kantian ethics to which it seems to adhere. For Sethe finds herself in an absolutely irrational world, the world of enslavement in which no action can be expected to have rational consequences. Kant's insistence that one treat another human being as an end not a means would in itself obviate slavery, regardless of Kant's pronouncements elsewhere.

The Broken Body

The abject materiality of Beloved's posthumous condition—that Beloved the revenant has a body that is in a state of collapse—illustrates a vulnerability in

---

60 Kant, Groundwork for the Metaphysics of Morals, 47.

61 Kant, Groundwork for the Metaphysics of Morals, 47.

62 Morrison, *Beloved*, 293.

Kant's theory of a metaphysics of morals. For the complete separation of "thing" and "person" cannot be achieved precisely because the objecthood of the body as thing is necessary to perform the duty and dignity of the person: the limits of the embodied ethics are found in slavery.

For Scarry alerts us to the way that the body can itself be made into a tool, an artifact made to suffer by the mechanism of capitalism, or the mechanics of torture.[63] And yet Scarry suggests that the enmeshment of humanity with materiality as artifact is deeper than capitalism. As violent as that system is, the problem is older than nineteenth-century capitalism: "to a vastly greater degree than that of any other animal, [human sentience is] objectified in language and material objects and thus fundamentally transformed to be communicable and endlessly sharable."[64] The structure of tools and the structure of the body as artifact is also the structure of the imagination of torture, suggests Scarry. Scarry reads the misery of the body under capitalism as a kind of flowering of the misery of the body in the structures of symbolic artifact-making. The body in torture, for Scarry, is a body developed to a kind of apogee in capitalism. In capitalism, for Scarry, the materiality of the body prevents ethical action for very Kantian reasons: because the body can itself become a tool.

The Tool and the Child: Maternity as Torture

The body, conceived of as a tool, is open to torture. Beloved's body, as the body of the revenant, is created by her mother's use of the saw, a tool, to open the body of the once-living daughter. Sethe unmakes the world of her daughter with the use of this saw. Then, however, things shift and the revenant returns as a body that is wholly a tool: Beloved comes to her mother's house and Beloved's body echoes the way that Sethe's body has been threatened with becoming only a tool—a tool for sex, a tool for reproduction, a tool for food—Beloved's body functions as a tool for her mother to watch, for her sister to touch, for Paul D. to access sexually. *Beloved*, as Scarry notes of Christ, is at once created by a weapon and becomes a weapon.[65] Her revenant body functions as a tool, for there is no end that Beloved can seek, no appeasement. Sethe and Denver evoke from Beloved the broken voice of the sacrifice.

One's Inner Child

Scarry points out that in the Old Testament, the child, even years after its gestation and birth, represents the interior of the mother's body, and also the interior of the father's body. Beloved sacrificed would represent the interior of her mother, the

---

63 Scarry, *The Body in Pain*, 251.

64 Scarry, *The Body in Pain*, 255.

65 Scarry, *The Body in Pain*, 213.

sacrificed interior space of a self, negated; and yet she also represents the tool *par excellence*. Beloved is the tool by which her mother gains freedom for herself and her other children and Beloved also is the body upon which the tool, the saw, is used. The saw of course opens Beloved's body but it also symbolically opens Sethe's body. The construct of the self collapses under torture. Beloved is a figure for this collapse.[66] In torture, she represents not only her own opened body but also her mother's opened body.

As Kant describes the way that the man who longs for suicide must resist the urge to kill himself based on duty, what he means is that duty must be reconstructed in the face of desolation. The torture victim—Beloved—attempts to reconstitute herself but she cannot, the damage has been too extensive. But what would reconstituting herself mean: the ambiguity about whether or not Beloved is the murdered child returned also makes impossible the healing of the ruined figure that is Beloved; the mother closes her opened body by telling the story.

Witnessing and Capitalism

Kantian ethics stipulate that every human being should be conceived of as an end in her/himself, not a means to an end. But Kant concedes implicitly that many situations leave us without the possibility of right action. It is right thought that must be achieved, for Kant, thus the witness implicitly is the privileged figure in Kantian ethics.

And yet, the witness risks becoming a tool of the torturer. For the presence of the witness inevitably raises the question: does the witness against her will perform the last of the torturer's work, to make public and visible the desecration of the victim? Is the witness paradigmatically a maternal figure, a pieta whose job is to hold up, to hold aloft and make visible, the suffering body of the victim? The figure or character of the woman who witnesses another woman's suffering always risks becoming not only someone who takes pleasure in torture but indeed the very cause of the torturer's performance: for her eyes he opens the body of the victim.

The feminine witness emerges as possibly essential to the structure of torture that Scarry disturbingly and convincingly allies to that of capitalism: the witness is the ghostly third party to scenes of torture. The disembodied figure of the capitalist that Scarry draws she places analogously to the body of the torturer.[67] The capitalist, and here one may read the slaveholder as a paradigm of capitalism, functions as the one who imposes torture on the body of the worker/slave. The disembodied function of the capitalist—disembodied because in capitalism the person who has money is materially represented by his money not his labor, his

[66] Teresa De Lauretis, "Upping the Anti [*sic*] In Feminist Theory," in *Figures of Resistance: Essays in Feminist Theory*, ed. Patricia White (Urbana-Champaign: University of Illinois Press, 2007), 183–99.

[67] Scarry, *The Body in Pain*, 265–70.

money standing in always for his body—extends to the capitalist's inability to see what his program inflicts on the body of the worker.

The witness is the figure of an artifact produced by the torturous structure of capitalism. Marx witnesses capitalism and is himself an artifact, produced by capitalism, in his function as witness, as ghost,[68] oscillating between the body, the maimed body of the worker, and the sadist, the capitalist whose pleasure is the harming of the worker and who indeed produces the artifact par excellence, in Marx's description, that is the maimed body of the worker. More so than pencils, airplanes, or whatever a given factory produces, the capitalist, for Marx, produces the maimed body of the worker.

Let us then reconsider Bone, Mary Fortune, Beloved and Sethe, Weems's *Louisiana Project*, and indeed even Dickinson's "wife": all these pairs of victims and witnesses are marked by their role in capitalism. Annie Boatwright is a working-class woman, a woman who waits tables, who is married to a man from a family of the petite bourgeoisie. Daddy Glenn, although impoverished, is from a family that owns the means for the production of capital, however humble that means (a dairy) may be. Daddy Glenn takes Annie very much because as a member of the bourgeoisie he has access to her. She, as a waitress, is visible to him, he sees her because her body is publicly displayed in the hyper-visible realm of the greasy spoon. Annie is served up to him with the food she brings him, and he can take her because of his position, however much a black sheep, as a member of the bourgeoisie. When Daddy Glenn hugs Annie and her two daughters and says "You're mine" he is not simply expressing a code of gender but as well is arguing the terms of capitalism. They are his because they are the bottom of capitalism (white trash) and he is petit bourgeois. They were his, even before he married Annie; they were his by dint of economic structures.

Similarly, the point of argument between Mary Fortune and Mark Fortune is the land that Mark Fortune owns: he owns the means of the production of capital, and Mary, as Pitts's daughter, does not own the means of the production of capital. Mark Fortune owns Mary Fortune in the sense that he can determine the fate of her view of the woods: he owns her view. Mark Fortune's position as the owner of capital makes him feel that specifically he has the right to beat the one who does not own the means of the production of capital, Mary Fortune.

The very fact that she replicates him—her name, her face—and replicates the possibility that he might lack the means of the production of capital is the grandfather's inspiration in beating and "conquering" his granddaughter. The problem for Annie Boatwright, for her daughter Bone, in relation to Daddy Glenn, as for Mary Fortune in relation to Mark Fortune, is that the torturer, the sadist, owns the means of the production of capital while the victim—the daughter Bone, the daughter Mary—does not.

If we consider Dickinson's witness figure of the "wife" who firstly suffers and then passes the terms of embodied suffering onto an unnamed other, the wife is

---

68 Scarry, *The Body in Pain*, 244.

positioned in capitalism as the one who does not own the means of the production of capital. Indeed, at the time of Dickinson's composing her poem, a wife would not own property independently of her husband. She, a wife, would be defined as property-less and disenfranchised; a wife would be definitively that person who lacked property. Sethe and Beloved suffer because of the peculiarly vicious system of capitalism in slavery. Not only do Sethe and her children lack property if schoolteacher takes them back south, but as well they will *become property*, the property of schoolteacher, if he takes them back. Schoolteacher's viciousness in response to the suffering of Sethe and her progeny is engaged because of their place in capitalism: he views them not as "person" but as "thing," using Kant's distinctions, as means not ends.

Kant then predicts Marx in his development of the distinction between person and thing, Marx who distinguishes between living and dead labor. For Kant, as for Marx, dignity and freedom are Enlightenment concepts that would seem to work against torture. And yet Lacan argues that Kant's system of ethics, because it refuses the role of sentiment, is fundamentally positioned to produce sadism.

As Scarry argues it, the worker suffuses his/her bodily capital with progeny: "the most intimate extension of personhood, the family continually enters bodily into the text, for like all other attributes of the worker, his or her children are present."[69] That is, the body of the worker is both exposed by capitalism, which renders the worker vulnerable to work conditions, and also exposed to the gaze of the capitalist, who functions as if without a body, the body of the one who has money performed by the worker who creates goods. And yet it is not only the body of the worker but also the body of the worker's child that is exposed to harm in capitalism.

Likewise, in her explanation of embodiment and the terms of power in the Old Testament, Scarry makes clear that the child represents the parent's embodiment, the parent's vulnerability. The child represents the interior of the mother's body and also, argues Scarry, the interior of the father's body. The child, in particular the infant, Scarry convincingly argues is the embodied and vulnerable object. The child is vulnerable particularly in relation to those disembodied factors—God (in the Old Testament) and capitalism (in *Das Kapital*). Marx's focus on the image of the child of the worker, the family of the worker, then, gives embodiment to capitalism through the obsessive figuration of the body of the child whose parents are workers, the body of the child vulnerable to being the opened body.

Interestingly the child of the proletariat worker shares his iconography of abused embodiment with the biblical child. In her reading of Abraham and Isaac, Scarry analyzes the child as an object of physical use vulnerable to disembodied sources of power, arguing that Isaac stands for the interior of Abraham's body (child of his loins), and as such the willingness of Abraham to sacrifice Isaac is a willingness to open his embodiment to the force of the disembodied gaze: the pleasure God will take in viewing the sacrifice. That Beloved the child is similarly

---

69 Scarry, *The Body in Pain*, 266.

representative of the opening of her mother's body Morrison makes clear when, in the opening passages of the novel, she describes Sethe's legs "open wide as any grave" to have sex with the gravestone seller and engraver, each letter of her child's name earned by the length of time Sethe has sex with this gravestone seller whose son watches.[70]

Just as the son, standing above, watches Sethe prostituting herself and/or being raped by his father, the son representing the gaze of the father, Beloved stands for and enforces the terms of her mother's most vulnerable embodiment.[71] Sethe labors sexually to buy Beloved a name because Sethe has no other capital. The way that Morrison asks us to watch Beloved, as interior of her mother's body, has uncanny echoes and resemblances to Marx's theorization of the way that watching the suffering body of the worker is implicit in capitalist discourse that needs the body as product for consumption, a means to the end of commerce.

Beloved's body is the made effect of her mother being given to her father to breed; her body is the made effect, as revenant, of captured kidnapped enslaved girls being taken on the Middle Passage; her body is the made effect of young enslaved girls locked up and raped by white masters. Beloved exposes the harms of capitalism, with slavery as capitalism's most violent turn. Her mother, lacking access to other capital, trades on the use she has—her daughter's body which is synecdochically the interior of her own body—and using this interiority Sethe exposes the embodied violation inherent in the abyssal symbolic system of capitalism.

What makes schoolteacher a capitalist is that he owns slaves and owns the means, through the slaves, of turning a profit through his farm, for, *schoolteacher is brought to Sweet Home in order to keep the place profitable*. The structure of torture, then, is the structure by which Sethe is forced to "speak" or articulate her daughter's name as the most interior space of herself. In this enforced articulation, which can only be accomplished by so deeply violating the body of the girl as to empty her of blood and life, the name itself is lost. The silencing force of the capitalist/torturer is completed in the tragedy of *Beloved*, except the novel follows a circular structure bent back towards itself by its coda.

Worker, Child, Woman

The structure of capitalism inscribes a kind of torture onto the body of the worker, which in turn becomes the only body that can be represented in the discursive system of capitalism. The structure of capitalism then works to effectively torture—in the sense of inscribe the capitalist's symbol onto the body—any body that comes to stage of production: the worker, and the child of the worker. By inscribing, of course, I do not mean the capitalist literally writes on the skin of

---

70 Toni Morrison, *Beloved*, 3.

71 Carole Pateman, "What's Wrong with Prostitution," *Women's Studies Quarterly* 57 (1999): 53–64.

the worker but rather that the meaning of the worker, as cultural representation, is inscribed onto the body through labor. That Morrison, Allison, O'Connor, and Dickinson theorize in their texts that this ultimately violated body is that of the daughter, the female child, certainly reflects a problematic of gender, but it reflects a problematic of gender as inscribed, violently, by capitalism. Kant's notion of "dignity" and "price" of "person" and "thing" would seem, when read alongside Scarry's *The Body in Pain*, to signify the affront and threat to ethical structure that capitalism puts in place, as if Kant were predicting the nineteenth twentieth, and twenty-first centuries in which capitalism makes things of persons, *prices* of *dignities*.

The way that Beloved's body is enfolded with her mother's body is not simply Morrison's commentary on the biological mother-daughter bond. Rather and instead, it reflects what must be read through Scarry's theorization of the child as exemplum of the parental body, which also signifies the child as the parent's vulnerability. Beloved stands as both sign and fact of the abroach-able quality of her mother's body. One may follow Sethe's argument that she seeks to put Beloved where none can reach her as also an expression of her desire to put herself where no one can reach her: a way to make both herself and her daughter impenetrable. The sadism of capitalism, in the system of slavery, panics the ethical Sethe who longs to remove her body from place of risk. The interiority of Sethe's body is the daughter whose body she opens with the saw. Morrison's novel's objection to the terms of capitalism, I think, is often lost behind critical concerns with gender and race that center approaches to reading the novel, even as those concerns are of course key.[72]

Self-Denial

But the specter of reading *Das Kapital* returns us to the question raised by Lacan, in writing on Kant, of whether a theorization of ethics can avoid performing as a gaze directed onto the suffering body, that is, whether it can avoid performing sadism. Slavoj Žižek has disputed Jacques Lacan's aligning of Kant and Sade, and my conclusions here will be in agreement with Žižek. Lacan interprets[73] Kant's insistence on the supremacy of a law that cannot cohere with emotion, with sympathy, as a foundation for sadism. Yet it is interesting to note that Kant specifies the "self denial" that guides his approach to theorizing ethics as curiously powerless, a will from which there "never were actions springing."[74] Kant's theory of the metaphysics of morals is to seek a will absolutely good, not despite the fact that it never produces actions but really *because of the fact that it never produces actions*. This passivity is crucial to interpreting Kant.

---

72 Tally, *Toni Morrison's* Beloved.

73 Slavoj Zižek, "Kant and Sade: The Ideal Couple," *Lacanian Ink* 13 (1998): 12–25.

74 Kant, Groundwork for the Metaphysics of Morals, 11.

The sadistic actor is one who acts according to a will or law rather than according to the claims of sympathy, argues Lacan. For Lacan, this rule-bound actor is the creation not only of Sade but also of Kant: *It is this which befalls the executor in sadistic experience when, at its most extreme, his presence is reduced to being no more than instrument.*[75] Lacan argues that "with respect to the coldness of the man, Kant is the turning point."[76] And yet, for Kant, the fact that the ultimate good will may never be known and if known may never become action does not preclude its being universal law. One could, with Lacan, interpret the unreachable remote aspect of this universal law as itself a sadistic turn—indicating a remote, aloof parent who never will help the child.

However, sadism is *not* remote, not aloof. On the contrary, schoolteacher violates Sethe and her daughter when he enters their yard: he is intimate. Had schoolteacher remained remote and aloof and *not* entered Sethe's yard, his sadism could not have been expressed. Kant's idea of an absolutely good will is precisely that which cannot be known in its entirety, that which remains absolutely aloof, that which does not enter the yard, so to speak. Kant's injunction: act as if your behavior were universally repeated. This paradoxical and even uncanny omnipotent powerlessness admittedly makes Kant's metaphysics of morals difficult to fasten on, but the problem of emotion in ethics that Kant highlights would seem to agree with Morrison, not Sade, for it is Morrison who points out precisely that the homey emotion associated with Sweet Home, and with Mr. Gardner who treats his slaves kindly, has nothing to do with ethics. On the contrary, tender emotion covers crime in *Beloved*. Indeed schoolteacher references emotion when he chastises his nephews—emotion, not logic, argues schoolteacher, should have tempered their violence.[77]

At all points in O'Connor, Dickinson, Morrison, and Allison, the tender emotion of paternity and paternalism makes smooth the path of sadism. Žižek points to the possible paternalism of Kant's "sadistic" superego: "is the Kantian Law a superego agency that sadistically enjoys the subject's deadlock, his inability to meet its inexorable demands, like the proverbial teacher who tortures pupils with impossible tasks and secretly savors their failings?"[78] It is worth noting that the super ego, firstly, is a Freudian construct whereas Kant references the idea of an incompletely knowable other—not at all the ego, the self, but the other, the other who is impossible for Freud's system to theorize. What is missed by the structure of Freudian thought is the possibility of the other who in no way is part of the self.

---

75 Jacques Lacan, *Le seminaire, Livre VII: L'éthique de la psychanalyse* (Paris: Seuil, 1986), 115–34; Jacques Lacan, "Kant avec Sade," in *Écrits* (Paris: Seuil, 1966), 765–90.

76 Lacan, "Kant avec Sade."

77 Morrison, *Beloved*, 174.

78 Žižek, Slavoj. "Kant and Sade: The Ideal Couple." *Lacanian Ink* 13 (1998): 12–25.

The Other and the Audience

Kant argues that this absolutely respected other—a dignity and a person who is *not* part of the self—is necessary for a metaphysics of morals: there must be an absolutely good will, argues Kant, for there to be any good in the world. There must be an other, wholly autonomous, for there to be a self. Even if that goodness is never seen or experienced in the actions of the other or the actions of the self it must yet exist in an Augustinian sense for the world to exist. Likewise, for the self to exist as autonomous, a dignity, the other must also exist as a dignity.[79]

Schoolteacher, Daddy Glenn, Mark Fortune, and the "they" who husband Dickinson's speaking "wife," share in common a position of fatherliness. "They" are fathers who assert a will that sadistically pleasures itself by opening the other, the daughter in nearly every case, the daughter who stands for and stands as the opening of the mother's body, the closing of the mother's body secured only by the mother's willingness to witness the daughter's sacrifice. In parallel structure, Sethe, Annie, and Pitts's wife all share a position of motherliness, bent by the sadism of the fathers.

In the most sadistic system possible, the mother survives because she watches the daughter—Beloved, Bone, Mary Fortune—be eviscerated by paternal desire (I interpret schoolteacher as a paternal figure, reflecting the history of rape and incest common between slave-owners and enslaved women). Here, we are not merely in the realm of anti-Oedipus but approach the exposure of the problematic of paternal desire for the daughter that functions as sadism across the boundary of capitalist exchange—the body of the slave, the body of the woods, the body of waitress-offering-food, the body that the paternal figure takes under his control, takes for himself. This taking is the recurrent figuration of sadism.

Kant's metaphysics of morals turn on the assumption of shared vulnerability while the structure of sadism does not reflect mutual vulnerability. The father figure's desire to open the body of the daughter repeats itself in the sadistic paradigms revealed by Morrison, Allison, O'Connor, and Dickinson. Kant's metaphysics, frustratingly remote though they be, offer a path *away* from the torture of the other, that system of symbolization that functions to annihilate the victim's language. That these pairs of women—watcher and watched—in the texts I've considered seem to generate the victimization of the other woman rather than stop it is a problem I address by returning to Scarry's superlative reading of the structure of torture. The mother's body, as Scarry persuasively argues in her analysis of biblical scenes of sacrifice, is represented in its openness and vulnerability by the child. Scarry articulates that the having of body is a sign of powerlessness and vulnerability. Scarry's analysis of torture also describes ways that the body can be used by the violator to violate the victim by turning her own body against herself.[80]

---

[79] Oliver Sensen, *Kant on Human Dignity* (Berlin: De Gruyter, 2011).

[80] Scarry describes, for example, the Greek torture of "swallowing knots" as a form of torture that only turns the body against itself. But one may carry Scarry's paradigm of "swallowing knots," or turning the body against itself, to the mother/daughter configuration or to the woman/woman configuration.

Indeed, in the scenes in literature and photography representing sadism that have been the focus of this study, the interior of the woman's body—represented by her child or, in Dickinson, by her beloved—is the trope of paternal violence, the mark that signifies violation.[81]

The turning of the mother against the daughter, insofar as she can only watch as her daughter performs as object violated, typifies the scenes of mother-daughter, witness and sacrificial victim, that I have studied in this book. The body used against itself that Scarry magisterially describes as the knot of torture—the way that torture uses the body to erase its own capacity to speak—is also a description of the paradigm of the mother-daughter/witness-victim structure. For if the daughter represents, as Scarry elsewhere argues, the interior of the mother's body, the exposure site, the daughter also functions as that place where the mother's vulnerability in capitalism, or in slavery as an intensification of the degrading terms of capitalism, finds its terrible extension.

Likewise, when Dickinson describes her beloved, the woman to whom she is "wife," this beloved becomes the physical and psychical interior of the speaker. The victim occupies the interior space, the space without language and importantly the space where the witness is asked to violate herself, to violate a female figure or character who represents, as Morrison puts it, "her best." This violated feminine other represents the space of absolute interiority: the feminine witness figure is forced to turn against herself.

And yet this enforced witnessing, in some instances that I have considered, becomes a form of pleasure. What's important about the Kantian field of ethics is that it constitutes the *possibility* of ethical response to situations in which no ethical *action* may be possible. It permits the possibility of an ethical will even when the action of ethical rightness cannot take place. In this sense, Kantian ethics would condemn mothers like Annie in *Bastard Out of Carolina*. The position of the witness leaves the witness in an ethical no man's land: she cannot act. But she could have a good ethical will, and I have tried to tease apart different modes of witnessing, feminine witnessing, of feminine sacrificial victims—modes of witnessing that in some cases, studied in this book, are ethical and in some cases are deeply problematic in terms of ethics.

Seeing the Other

Insofar as Kant specifies that what he means by obedience to the good will is almost impossible to execute, Kant's notion of obedience entails giving up one's instinctive desires. It is this almost impossible relinquishing of desire that allows

81 Dickinson's astonishing claim that "when my hands are cut her fingers will be found inside" asserts that Susan Dickinson literally occupies the interior of Emily Dickinson. "When my Hands are Cut, Her fingers will be found inside," in Ellen Louise Hart and Martha Nell Smith, eds., *Open Me Carefully: Emily Dickinson's Intimate Letters to Susan Huntington Dickinson* (Ashfield, MA: Paris Press, 1998).

one to see the suffering of the other as if it were one's own. For Kant makes clear that this universally good will, although it must exist for a foundation of morals, is unknowable in its entirety for a finite being. The absolutely good will must in principle be obeyed but cannot in fact be obeyed, according to Kant, just as the other must be fully respected in her ultimate unknowability. Kant's point is that we must remain alert to every possible, fractionary aspect of knowing the wholly good will, even though in our finite lives we can never act on this will, because circumstance will cloud our knowledge of the good and as well will very often prevent our capacity to do the good.

Kant's metaphysics of morals appeals to me because, far from asserting a sadistic doctrine of obedience, Kant maps the circumstantial parameters of action that nevertheless must link to some unknowability of a wholly good will. Because the other—the holy other—Kant allows, is unknowable, and yet also must be paid attention to as much as possible, Kant's metaphysics of morals establishes a framework for seeing the other with dignity, as a person. The idea that the other might be holy, that is, unknowable, contained in Kant's abstract metaphysics, implies as well that the structure of seeing the other as merely a replica of the self, an extension of the self in time, is a foundation of sadism. Scarry's interpretation of the sacrifice as the interior of the self, along these lines, is powerful in that she writes exposing a patriarchal framework. What the patriarch cannot do is see beyond his own desire. Kant insists that we see beyond our desires; in this sense he negates the patriarch whose law is desire, even as Kant himself is legible as a "father" of Enlightenment philosophy.

As Scarry argues, the way for many torturers to train themselves to inflict suffering on the other is to be aware only of how inflicting suffering on the other causes the *torturer to suffer*. Some of the texts I've considered in this book push towards revelation of the problem of seeing the other's suffering in a way that might save rather than sacrifice the other. Morrison, as I've noted, ends *Beloved* on the tragic note of describing how everyone forgets the sacrificial victim, her sacrifice complete because all trace of her is erased after she has been used. Allison can only envision Bone's survival by effectively giving her her walking papers: Annie gives Bone a falsified birth certificate, and Bone is free to give birth to herself, very much elsewhere, very much away from her mother, away from South Carolina, cast adrift in the magical American landscape of reinvention. Dickinson's "wife" speaker, after undergoing hypothetical dismemberment, turns the beloved other into the ultimate sacrificial figure, while O'Connor's Mark Fortune destroys and tears apart the sacrificial other. But as these sacrifices occur, the witness figure sees the suffering other and, feminized utterly in this moment of seeing, crucially decides what and how to *think*.

By Way of a Conclusion: What I Have Done in Your Name

The universal good will for which Kant longs, needless to say, does not govern all of the witness figures I've considered in this study. And yet Carrie Mae Weems's positioning of the witness figure in *From Here I Saw What Happened and I Cried* may expose violence without producing a replication of that violence, a representational move that may be likened to an ethical maxim. And it's interesting to note that in her deployment of the witness figure, in the *Louisiana Project*, Weems claims to take on the abject embodiment of the whore and the chamber maid: the witness who is abject.[1] Only the witness who has already come through suffering, in Weems's paradigm, offers some way of seeing the suffering of the other, and willing an end to that suffering rather than taking pleasure in the vision of the other's abjection. That Weems does not position this admittedly hypothetical witness figure as a mother, or as a wife, suggests that embedded in patriarchal structures of wife or favorite daughter are possible building blocks of sadism. The true witness to the crimes of gender is the one who has stepped aside from the system of gender. Here, one reaches back to Kant's notion of the universally willed maxim, and finds that the farther from love the closer to goodness we arrive.

Kant's notorious example of the gallows as that which should be visited upon a man who is considering enjoying illicit sexual congress could support a view of Kant as sadist, insofar as here Kant conjures the juxtaposition of suffering, in fact torturous death, and eroticism. The gallows example asks, "Suppose that someone says his lust is irresistible when the desired object and opportunity are present … would [he] not control his passions if, in front of the house where he has this opportunity, gallows were erected on which he would be hanged immediately after gratifying his lust."[2] Kant states that violence should be visited *not* on the body of the other but rather return recursively to be visited on the powerful desiring (because desire is a form of power) subject, and in this notion of punishing the powerful self who desires rather than the powerless other who is desired Kant displaces rather than invokes sadism. In other words, unlike Kant, Freud and Lacan are concerned with what Žižek aptly calls the "Big other" rather than the other as fellow being. But Kant is concerned with the other as fellow being (interestingly, he is even concerned when the other fellow being is a woman) whose objectification and misuse should be punished. The Big other, Žižek's term, supervises and controls. The other as fellow being by contrast emerges as focal point of Kant's ethics.

Kant's concern is not with the performance of power but the proper renunciation of power; he is not concerned with the way the Big other may deny the desire of

---

1 Carrie Mae Weems, *Carrie Mae Weems: The Louisiana Project*.

2 Immanuel Kant, *Critique of Practical Reason*, trans. Thomas Kingsmill Abbott (Chicago: Encyclopædia Britannica, 1952), 30.

the implicitly masculinized self (desire exclusively is accorded to a masculine subject in a Kantian/Freudian/Lacanian paradigm). Instead, Kant is concerned with the way that the Big other *should constrain his will*. The trope of the gallows in the bedroom that Kant posits in his *Critique of Pure Reason* ultimately is a balancing trope.

And this possibility of equality reemerges in the linguistic analysis that Scarry offers in *The Body in Pain*. Indeed, one can say that the point of distinction between the witness and the torturer is only and solely this difference in the access to language, access to the language of the sufferer: the witness brings forward the scene of torture as articulation of the victim's right to be released from torture by speaking while the torturer brings forward torture as articulation of the enforced impossibility of the victim's voicing of self. Language and image as metaphors of witnessing become the gallows for the Big other. When Sethe witnesses her daughter's unspeakable vulnerability before schoolteacher's desire to take the enslaved female body and humiliate and degrade the person connected to that body, she inscribes and indeed articulates on her daughter's body the mark of the witness. She opens her daughter's throat, literally, fusing her daughter's body with a speech of nearly unbearable power. Beloved is cast as a figure of the universal witness to the atrocity of enslavement, as Morrison indicates by inscribing her book's dedication to all those killed during the centuries of American enslavement of West African peoples, "To the Sixy Million and More." Beloved, the killed daughter, becomes the emblematic witness whose suffering in witnessing is so extreme it annihilates her (the character's persistence in Morrison's text is the one way she is not annihilated). The act of this killing of the baby girl makes of the baby girl the supreme witness to all the suffering of the enslaved.

Notably, in Kantian terms Sethe's will is pure: she purely wills her daughter's salvation. In *Bastard Out of Carolina* Annie Boatwright gets caught in a muddier paradigm of witnessing. Hearing Bone being beaten through the bathroom door Annie Boatwright decides to take up the will of the torturer, Daddy Glenn, to some degree, as her will. For after Bone is beaten by her stepfather, Annie tells Bone not to anger him again, and of course Annie horrifyingly reconciles with Daddy Glenn after discovering him raping her 12-year-old daughter. This reconciliation is not forgiveness but alliance. This reconciliation is the vanishing point of witnessing, the collapse of seeking to see and articulate the other's suffering, and the beginning of torturing, the taking up the point of view of the sadist. Annie allies herself with the power of the torturer.

What Kant offers in his metaphysics of morals is the endless possibility that the "I" is not necessarily in a position of power. To formulate the right maxim, the witness must retain some capacity of articulation, either words or image, to witness. This capacity is what Eduardo Galeano calls "a luminous mystery that redeems the human adventure in the world."[3] And yet Galeano's lyrical remarks

[3] Sebastião Salgado, Eduardo H. Galeano, and Fred Ritchin, *An Uncertain Grace* (San Francisco: San Francisco Museum of Modern Art; New York: Aperture Foundation, 1990), 8.

on the work of Salgado also beg the question of how one might witness without gaining pleasure from the suffering other. Salgado, writes Galeano, "does not violate but penetrates the human spirit in order to reveal it."[4] What is the difference between violating and penetrating?

Galeano also quotes a witness figure, Davison Budhoo, who resigns from witnessing saying that "There has been too much blood … it befouls me completely. I sometimes feel that there isn't enough soap in the world to wash away what I have done in your name."[5] The witness gets soaked in blood. Sethe gets soaked in her daughter's blood and, really, it never comes off despite the reemergence of beautiful Paul D. at the novel's close. The woods whose view is fought for get soaked in blood in O'Connor's "A View of the Woods." Bone's mother is an audience for Bone's blood-soaked legs after her whippings in *Bastard Out of Carolina.* And the emblematic witness ceaselessly watching the suffering of enslaved Americans in Carrie Mae Weems's *From Here I Saw What Happened and I Cried* stares at those images through the blood-red tinting that Weems imposes on the nineteenth-century original photographs.

The witness who comes close enough (to paraphrase Robert Capa) gets bloodied. None of the good or bad witnesses I've considered in this study were witnesses by choice. All initially were forced to watch the whipping, beating, rape, silencing, and humiliation of the other. But the photographer who re-photographed figures, and the authors who wrote characters of witness did choose to become witnesses. The risk of witnessing is the risk of repeating the torturer's gesture of putting words in the victim's mouth. Weems, Morrison, O'Connor, Dickinson, Allison, and McCullers handle this risk differently but all face it—the risk of revictimizing the victim in representing her—with fresh and powerful torque.

Morrison leaves us with fractured words and vanishing images to stand for Beloved's lost self. The waif who disappears into the woods at the end of *Beloved* eerily coheres with the haunted space of the woods evoked in O'Connor's "A View of the Woods." The novel *Beloved* closes not with Sethe but with a narrator's omniscient voice: Morrison implicitly places herself as the last witness. Similarly, Weems takes upon herself the position of the abject witness, the "whore, the chambermaid," when she mourns for enslaved women of the nineteenth century.[6] O'Connor gives to her figure of sacrificial killing her own name and initials, Mary F., while Allison writes about herself as a child in what she calls an autobiographical novel, thereby re-inscribing her earlier status as victim even as she, the author, becomes a literary success. Dickinson generates the power of her poetry in part arguably because Dickinson's speaker also becomes the victim, performatively; indeed, Dickinson's long sojourn as an unpublished poet puts in place the textual abject that draws on metaphors of suffering and redemption. The position of the witness, then, has to be willed as that which takes no pleasure in the suffering of

4 Salgado et al., *An Uncertain Grace*, 8.

5 Salgado et al., *An Uncertain Grace*, 14.

6 Carrie Mae Weems, *Carrie Mae Weems: The Louisiana Project*.

the other and also as that which refuses to put words in the mouth of the victim but instead strives to open a rhetorical space in which the victim can be seen and heard, and redeemed. The witness accedes to fracturing of language, fracturing of image, enigmatic boundaries of erasure, to draw as true a form of suffering as possible, as true as possible an image, of the victim whose suffering must be redeemed by the witness, not enjoyed by the audience, if we are to inhabit the proper realm of the ethical.

Appendix

The Jacket Of Gray

Fold it up carefully, lay it aside;
Tenderly touch it, look on it with pride;
For dear to our hearts must it be evermore,
The jacket of gray our loved soldier-boy wore.

Can we ever forget when he joined the brave band
That rose in defense of our dear Southern land,
And in his bright youth hurried on to the fray,
How proudly he donned it—the jacket of gray?

His fond mother blessed him and looked up above,
Commending to Heaven the child of her love;
What anguish was hers mortal tongue cannot say,
When he passed from her sight in the jacket of gray.

But her country had called and she would not repine,
Though costly the sacrifice placed on its shrine;
Her heart's dearest hopes on its altar she lay,
When she sent out her boy in the jacket of gray.

Months passed and wars thunders rolled over the land,
Unsheathed was the sword and lighted the brand;
We heard in the distance the sound of the fray,
And prayed for our boy in the jacket of gray.

Ah, vain, all in vain, were our prayers and our tears,
The glad shout of victory rang in our ears;
But our treasured one on the red battle-field lay,
While the life-blood oozed out of the jacket of gray.

His young comrades found him, and tenderly bore
The cold lifeless form to his home by the shore;
Oh, dark were our hearts on that terrible day,
When we saw our dead boy in the jacket of gray.

Ah! spotted and tattered, and stained now with gore,
Was the garment which once he so proudly wore;
We bitterly wept as we took it away,
And replaced with death's white robes the jacket of gray.

We laid him to rest in his cold narrow bed,
And graved on the marble we placed o'er his head
As the proudest tribute our sad hearts could pay—
"He never disgraced it, the jacket of gray."

Then fold it up carefully, lay it aside,
Tenderly touch it, look on it with pride;
For dear must it be to our hearts evermore,
The jacket of gray our loved soldier-boy wore!

While God He Leaves Me Reason, God He Will Leave Me Jim

"Soldier, say, did you meet my Jimmy in the fight?
You'd know him by his manliness, and by his eye's sweet light."
"I fought beside your gallant son—a brave, good fellow he;
Alas! he fell beneath the shot that should have taken me."
"And think you that my Jimmy cared about a little fall?
Why make a great ado of what he would not mind at all?
When Jimmy was a little boy, and played with Bobby Brown,
He always played the enemy, and Bob he shot him down.
"I've seen him fall a hundred times, the cunning little sprite;
He can't forget his boyish tricks though in an earnest fight.
But never mind about the fall; I want to hear of him;
Perhaps you've heard the Captain speak of what he thinks of Jim."
"I've often heard the Captain say Jim was a splendid lad,
The bravest and the handsomest of all the boys he had.
And here's a lock of Jimmy's hair, and here's a golden ring;
I found it tied around his neck upon a silken string."
The mother took the matted tress, she took the ring of gold,
But shook her head, and laughed aloud at what the soldier told.
"Soldier," said she, "where is my boy? Where is my brave boy Jim?
I gave the others all to God, but God he left me him.
"Hush, there is Uncle Abraham a-knocking at the door;
He calls for other mother's sons, 'Three hundred thousand more!'
Be still, Old Uncle Abraham; 'twill do no good to call:
You think my house is full of boys; ah, Jimmy was my all."

Works Cited

Abate, Michelle Ann. *Tomboys: A Literary and Cultural History*. Philadelphia: Temple University Press, 2008.

Adams, Rebecca, and René Girard. "Violence, Difference, Sacrifice: A Conversation with René Girard." *Religion & Literature* 25, no. 2 (Summer 1993): 9–33.

Adorno, Theodor W., and Max Horkheimer. *Dialectic of Enlightenment*. London: Verso, 1979.

Agamben, Giorgio. *Remnants of Auschwitz: The Witness and the Archive*. Brooklyn, NY: Zone Books, 1999.

Alexandre, Sandy. "From the Same Tree: Gender and Iconography in Representations of Violence in *Beloved*." *Signs* 36, no. 4 (2011): 915–40. Accessed online April 10, 2012.

Allen, Brooke. "Emotional Vampire: Review of *Illumination and Night Glare: The Unfinished Autobiography of Carson McCullers*." *The New Criterion* 18 (January 2000): 70.

Allison, Dorothy. *Bastard Out of Carolina*. New York: Plume, 1992.

———. *The Women Who Hate Me*. Hanover, NH: Smith and Kraus, 2006.

American Heritage Dictionary of the English Language. Boston: Houghton Mifflin, 2000.

Angelo, Bonnie. "The Pain of Being Black: An Interview with Toni Morrison." *Time Magazine* 133, no. 21 (May 22, 1989): 120–23.

Apel, Dora. *Imagery of Lynching: Black Men, White Women, and the Mob*. New Brunswick, NJ: Rutgers University Press, 2004.

Appiah, Kwame Anthony. "Race, Culture, Identity: Misunderstood Connections; The Tanner Lectures on Human Values." Lecture, University of California at San Diego, October 27 and 28, 1994.

Arbus, Diane. *Revelations*. New York: Random House, 2003.

Armstrong, Nancy, and Leonard Tennenhouse. *The Violence of Representation: Literature and the History of Violence*. London and New York: Routledge, 1989.

Ashcraft, Karen Lee, and Lisa A. Flores. "'Slaves with White Collars': Persistence Performances of Masculinity in Crisis." *Text and Performance Quarterly* 23, no. 1 (2003): 1–29.

Barnes, Elizabeth. *Love's Whipping Boy: Violence and Sentimentality in the American Imagination*. Chapel Hill: University of North Carolina Press, 2011.

Baron, Marcia W. *Kantian Ethics Almost Without Apology*. Ithaca, NY: Cornell University Press, 1995.

Barrett, Faith, and Cristanne Miller, eds. *"Words for the Hour": A New Anthology of American Civil War Poetry*. Amherst: University of Massachusetts Press, 2005.

Barthes, Roland. "The Death of the Author" (1968). In *Image, Music, Text*, ed. and trans. Stephen Heath. London: Fontana, 1977.

———. "The World of Wrestling." In *Mythologies*, trans. Annette Lavers, 15–26. New York: Farrar, Straus and Giroux, 1972.

Benjamin, Jessica. *The Bonds of Love: Psychoanalysis, Feminism, and the Problem of Domination*. New York: Pantheon Books, 1988.

Benjamin, Walter. "A Small History of Photography." In *One Way Street and Other Writings*, trans. Edmund Jephcott and Kingsley Shorter. London: New Left Books, 1979.

Berlant, Laurent. *Cruel Optimism*. Durham: Duke University Press, 2011.

Bernier, Celeste-Marie. *African American Visual Arts: From Slavery to the Present*. Chapel Hill: University of North Carolina Press, 2009.

Bernstein, Susan. *Confessional Subjects: Revelations of Gender and Power in Victorian Literature and Culture*. Chapel Hill: University of North Carolina Press, 1997.

Bey, Dowould. "Carrie Mae Weems." *BOMB* 108 (Summer 2009): 60–67.

Beya, Abdennebi. "The Question of Regarding Traumatic Testimony: Jones's *Corregidora* and Morrison's *Beloved*." *Alif: Journal of Comparative Poetics* 30 (2010): 85–108. Accessed online April 10, 2012.

Blanchot, Maurice. *The Writing of the Disaster*. Trans. Ann Smock. Lincoln: University of Nebraska Press, 1996.

Blassingame, John W. *Slave Testimony: Two Centuries of Letters, Speeches, Interviews, and Autobiographies*. Baton Rouge: Louisiana State University Press, 1977.

Bordo, Susan. *Unbearable Weight: Feminism, Western Culture, and the Body*. Berkeley: University of California Press, 1993.

Boxwell, D. A. "'Sis Cat' as Ethnographer: Self-Presentation and Self-Inscription in Zora Neale Hurston's *Mules and Men*." *African American Review* 26, no. 4 (1992): 605–17. Accessed online April 13, 2012.

Bronfen, Elisabeth. *Over Her Dead Body: Death, Femininity, and the Aesthetic*. New York: Routledge, 1992.

Browning, Elizabeth Barrett. *Selected Poems*. Ed. Marjorie Stone and Beverly Taylor. Peterborough, Ontario: Broadview, 2009.

Burke, Edmund. *A Philosophical Enquiry into the Origin of our Ideas of the Sublime and Beautiful. Reissue Edition*. New York: Oxford University Press, 2009.

Butler, Judith. *Gender Trouble: Feminism and the Subversion of Identity*. New York: Routledge, 1999.

———. "Hegel's Unhappy Consciousness." In *The Psychic Life of Power: Theories in Subjection*. Palo Alto, CA: Stanford University Press, 2007.

Cahill, Ann J. "Sexual Violence and Objectification." In *Overcoming Objectification: A Carnal Ethics*. New York: Routledge, 2011.

Califia, P. *Public Sex: The Culture of Radical Sex*. Pittsburg, PA: Cleis Press, 1994.

Canning, Susan. Review of *Carrie Mae Weems: Projects*, by Carrie Mae Weems, Museum of Modern Art, New York, and *From Here I Saw What Happened and I Cried*, by Carrie Mae Weems, P.P.O.W., New York. *Art Papers* 20, no. 2 (1996): 50.

Carawan, Guy, and Candie Carawan, eds. *Ain't You Got a Right to the Tree of Life: The People of Johns Island South Carolina—Their Faces, Their Words and Their Songs*. 1966. Reprint, Athens: University of Georgia Press, 1989.

Carby, Hazel V. *Reconstructing Womanhood: The Emergence of the Afro-American Woman Novelist*. New York: Oxford University Press, 1987.

Carden, Mary Paniccia. "Models of Memory and Romance: The Dual Endings of Toni Morrison's *Beloved*." *Twentieth Century Literature* 45, no. 4 (Winter 1999): 401–27.

Carnes, Mark. *Meanings for Manhood: Constructions of Masculinity in Victorian America*. Chicago: University of Chicago Press, 1990.

Carr, Virginia Spence. *Understanding Carson McCullers*. Columbia: University of South Carolina Press, 1990.

Caruth, Cathy. *Unclaimed Experience: Trauma, Narrative, and History*. Baltimore, MD: Johns Hopkins University Press, 1996.

Cash, W. J. *The Mind of the South*. New York: A. A. Knopf, 1941.

Castle, Terry. *The Apparitional Lesbian: Female Homosexuality and Modern Culture*. New York: Columbia University Press, 1993.

Chambers, Eddie. Review of *Carrie Mae Weems*, by Carrie Mae Weems, Café Gallery Projects, London. *Art Monthly* 288 (2005): 30–31.

Chandler, Raymond. *The Simple Art of Murder*. 1950. Reprint, New York: Vintage Books, 1988.

Charles, Casey. *Critical Queer Studies: Law, Film and Fiction*. Aldershot, UK: Ashgate, 2012.

Clarke, Erskine. *Dwelling Place: A Plantation Epic*. New Haven, CT: Yale University Press, 2005.

Clement, Catherine. "The Guilty One." In *The Newly Born Woman*, ed. Catherine Clement and Helene Cixous, 1–58. London: Tauris, 1996.

Coffman, C. "Lyric Queerness." *Journal of Modern Literature* 34, no. 1 (2010): 185–9.

Collins, Joseph. *Taking the Literary Pulse: Psychological Studies of Life and Letters*. New York: George H. Doran, 1924.

Cook, Carol J. "Emily Dickinson: Poet as Pastoral Theologian." *Pastoral Psychology* 6 (2011): 421–35. Accessed online March 23, 2012.

Cooks, Bridget R. "See Me Now." *Camera Obscura* 12, no. 36 (1995): 66–83.

Copeland, Huey, and Krista Thompson. "Perpetual Returns: New World Slavery and the Matter of the Visual." *Representations* 113, no. 1 (2011) 1–15. Accessed online April 10, 2012.

Coryell, Janet, Thomas H. Appleton, Jr., Anastasia Sims, and Sandra Gioia Treadway. *Negotiating Boundaries of Southern Womanhood: Dealing with the Powers that Be*. Columbia and London: University of Missouri Press, 2000.

Coughlin, Ann. "Representing the Forbidden." *California Law Review* 90, no. 6 (2002): 2143.

Crawford, Nicholas, "An Africanist Impasse: Race, Return, and Revelation in the Short Fiction of Flannery O'Connor." *South Atlantic Review* 68, no. 2 (Spring 2003): 1–25.

Crouch, Stanley. "Aunt Medea." In *Notes of a Hanging Judge: Essays and Reviews, 1979–1989*. New York: Oxford University Press, 1990.

———. "Literary Conjure Woman." *The New Republic* 194 (1987): 43.

Crouch, Stanley, and Ted Gioia. "*Beloved* by Toni Morrison." *The New Canon*, July 26, 2008. Accessed online March 3, 2011.

Cullinan, Colleen. "A Maternal Discourse of Redemption: Speech and Suffering in Morrison's 'Beloved.'" *Religion & Literature* 34, no. 2 (2002): 77–104.

Danto, Arthur C. *The Abuse of Beauty: Aesthetics and the Concept of Art*. Chicago: Open Court, 2003.

———. "The Naked Truth." In *Aesthetics and Ethics: Essays at the Intersection*, ed. Jerrold Levinson, 257–82. Cambridge: Cambridge University Press, 2001.

———. *Playing with the Edge: The Photographic Achievement of Robert Mapplethorpe*. Berkeley: University of California Press, 1996.

Dauphin, Mirja. *The Presentation of Gender in Diane Arbus's Work in the Context of the Cold War Era*. Norderstedt, Germany: GRIN Verlag, 2006.

Davis, Rod. *American Voudou: Journey into a Hidden World*. Denton: University of North Texas Press, 1946.

De Lauretis, Teresa. *Figures of Resistance: Essays in Feminist Theory*. Ed. Patricia White. Urbana-Champaign: University of Illinois Press, 2007.

———. "Sexual (In)difference and Lesbian Representation." In *Figures of Resistance: Essays in Feminist Theory*, ed. Patricia White, 48–71. Urbana-Champaign: University of Illinois Press, 2007.

———. *Technologies of Gender: Essays on Theory, Film, and Fiction*. Bloomington, IN: Indiana University Press, 1987.

———. "Upping the Anti [*sic*] In Feminist Theory." In *Figures of Resistance: Essays in Feminist Theory*, ed. Patricia White, **183–99.** Urbana-Champaign: University of Illinois Press, 2007.

———. "The Violence of Rhetoric: On Representation and Gender." In *Gender/ Sexuality Reader: Culture, History, Political Economy*, ed. Roger N. Lancaste and Micaela Di Leonardo. New York: Routledge, 1997.

Derrida, Jacques. *The Gift of Death*. Chicago: University of Chicago Press, 1995.

———. *The Margins of Philosophy*. Chicago: University of Chicago Press, 1982.

———. *Of Grammatology*. Trans. Gayatri Chakravorty Spivak. Baltimore and London: Johns Hopkins University Press, 1976.

Dickinson, Emily. *Emily Dickinson: Selected Letters*. Ed. Thomas H. Johnson. London: The Belknap Press of Harvard University Press, 1986.

———. *The Master Letters*. Ed. R. W. Franklin. Amherst, MA: Amherst College Press, 1986.

———. *The Poems of Emily Dickinson: Reading Edition*. Ed. R. W. Franklin. Cambridge, MA: Belknap Press of Harvard University Press, 1998.

Dickinson, Susan Huntington. "Obituary of Emily Dickinson." *Digital Amherst*, Item #904. http://www.digitalamherst.org/items/show/904. Accessed August 5, 2012.

Didion, Joan. *The Year of Magical Thinking*. New York: Random House/Vintage International, 2007.

Diehl, Joanne Feit. *Dickinson and the Romantic Imagination*. Princeton, NJ: Princeton University Press, 1981.

———. "The Poetics of Loss: Erotic Melancholia in Agamben and Dickinson." *American Imago* 66, no. 3 (2009): 369–81.

———. "Selfish Desires: Dickinson's Poetic Ego and the Rites of Subjectivity." *The Emily Dickinson Journal* 5, no. 2 (Fall 1996): 100–106.

Dubois, Diane. "'Seeing the Female Body Differently': Gender Issues in *The Silence of The Lambs*." *Journal of Gender Studies* 10, no. 3 (2001): 297–310.

DuBois Shaw, Gwendolyn. "The 'Rememory' of Slavery: Kara Walker's *The End of Uncle Tom and the Grand Allegorical Tableau of Eva in Heaven*." In *Trauma and Visuality in Modernity*, ed. Lisa Saltzman and Eric Rosenberg. Hanover, NH: Dartmouth College Press, 2006.

Dutton, Wendy. "The Problem of Invisibility: Voodoo and Zora Neale Hurston." *Frontiers: A Journal of Women Studies* 13, no. 2 (1993): 131–52. Accessed online April 13, 2012.

Dworkin, Andrea. *Pornography*. New York: Perigee Books, 1981.

Erkkila, Betsy. *The Wicked Sisters: Women Poets, Literary History, and Discord*. New York: Oxford University Press, 1992.

Faulkner, William. "A Rose for Emily." In *Selected Short Stories*, 47–60. New York: Modern Library, 2012.

Fausto-Sterling, Anne. "Gender, Race, and Nation: The Comparative Anatomy of Hottentot Women in Europe, 1815–1817." In *Feminism and the Body*, ed. Londa Schiebinger, 203–34. Oxford: Oxford University Press, 2000.

———. *Sexing the Body: Gender Politics and the Construction of Sexuality*. New York: Basic Books, 2000.

Felman, Shoshana, and Dori Laub. *Testimony: Crises of Witnessing in Literature, Psychoanalysis, and History*. New York: Routledge, 1991.

Fiedler, Leslie. *Love and Death in the American Novel*. Champaign, IL: Dalkey Archive Press, 1960.

Finnerty, P. "Queer Appropriations: Shakespeare's Sonnets and Dickinson's Love Poems." *The Journal of Shakespeare and Appropriation* 3, no. 2 (2008): 1–25.

Flora, Joseph, Lucinda MacKethan, and Todd Taylor, eds. *The Companion to Southern Literature: Themes, Genres, Places, People, Movements and Motifs*. Baton Rouge: Louisiana State University Press, 2002.

Foucault, Michel. *Discipline and Punish: The Birth of the Prison*. 2nd ed. Trans. Alan Sheridan. 1977. Reprint, New York: Vintage-Random House, 1995.

———. *The History of Sexuality, Volume I: An Introduction*. Trans. Robert Hurley. New York: Vintage-Random House, 1979.

———. "The Thought of the Outside." In *Aesthetics, Method, and Epistemology*. Vol. 2 of *Essential Works of Foucault, 1954–1984*, ed. James Faubion, trans. Robert Hurley et al. New York: The New Press, 1998.

Franklin, Donna L. *Ensuring Inequality: The Structural Transformation of the African-American Family*. New York: Oxford University Press, 1997.

Frei, Christian, James Nachtwey, Christiane Amanpour, Hans-Hermann Klare, Christiane Breustedt, Des Wright, Denis O'Neill, Peter Indergand, E. Karaindrou, Arvo Pärt, David Darling, and Schweizer Fernsehen. *War Photographer*. Brooklyn, NY: First Run Features, 2003.

Freud, Sigmund. "A Child Is Being Beaten." *The Journal of Nervous and Mental Disease* 56, no. 4 (1922): 405–6.

_______. "Freud, Sigmund. "A Note upon the 'Mystic Writing Pad.'" 1925. Trans. James Strachey. *General Psychological Theory*. Ed. Philip Rieff. New York: Touchstone-Simon & Schuster, 1963, 1997. 207–12.

———. *Three Essays on the Theory of Sexuality*. 1962. Reprint, New York: Basic Books, 1975.

Freyd, Jennifer. *Betrayal Trauma: The Logic of Forgetting Childhood Abuse*. Cambridge, MA: Harvard University Press, 1996.

Fuller, Randall. *Battlefields Rising: How the Civil War Transformed American Literature*. New York: Oxford University Press, 2011.

Gearhart, Suzanne. "The Taming of Michel Foucault: New Historicism, Psychoanalysis, and the Subversion of Power." *New Literary History* 28, no. 3 (1997): 457–80.

Gerald, Kelly. "Flannery O'Connor and the Habit of Art." *Paris Review Daily*, April 30, 2012. http://www.theparisreview.org/blog/2012/04/30/flannery-o%E2%80%99connor-and-the-habit-of-art/. Accessed August 1, 2012.

Gilman, Sander L. "Black Bodies, White Bodies: Toward an Iconography of Female Sexuality in Late Ninetieth-Century Art, Medicine, and Literature." In *"Race," Writing, and Difference*, ed. Henry Louis Gates, Jr. and Kwame Anthony Appiah, 223–61. Chicago: University of Chicago Press, 1986.

———. *Difference and Pathology: Stereotypes of Sexuality, Race and Madness*. Ithaca: Cornell University Press, 1985.

Ginzburg, Carlo. "Killing a Chinese Mandarin: The Moral Implications of Distance." *Critical Inquiry* 21, no. 1 (Autumn 1994): 46–60.

Girard, René. *Sacrifice*. Trans. Matthew Pattilo and David Dawson. East Lansing: Michigan State University Press, 2011.

———. *The Scapegoat*. Palo Alto, CA: Stanford University Press, 1986.

———. *Violence and the Sacred*. Baltimore, MD: Johns Hopkins University Press, 1977.

Gleeson-White, Sarah. "Revisiting the Southern Grotesque: Mikhail Bakhtin and the Case of Carson McCullers." *The Southern Literary Journal* 33, no. 2 (Spring 2001): 108–23.

Gordon, Avery F. *Ghostly Matters: Haunting and the Sociological Imagination.* Minneapolis: University of Minnesota Press, 2008.

Gordon, Linda. *Heroes of Their Own Lives: The Politics and History of Family Violence: Boston, 1880–1960.* New York: Viking, 1988.

Gosselin, Chris, and Glenn Wilson. *Sexual Variations: Fetishism, Sadomasochism, and Transvestism.* New York: Simon & Schuster, 1980.

Green, Mitchell. "Empathy, Expression, and What Artworks Have to Teach." In *Art and Ethical Criticism*, ed. Garry L. Hagberg, 95–122. Oxford: Blackwell, 2008.

Griffiths, Jennifer. "Uncanny Spaces: Trauma, Cultural Memory, and the Female Body in Gayl Jones's 'Corregidora' and Maxine Hong Kingston's the 'Woman Warrior.'" *Studies in the Novel* 38, no. 3 (2006): 353.

Grimwade, Robert. "Between the Quills: Schopenhauer and Freud on Sadism and Masochism." *The International Journal of Psychoanalysis* 92, no. 1 (2011): 149–69. Accessed online January 30, 2012.

Hahn, Steven. "Divine Rights." *New Republic* 234, no. 4 (2006): 28–33.

Halberstam, Judith. *Female Masculinity.* Durham, NC: Duke University Press, 1998.

———. *In a Queer Time and Place: Transgender Bodies, Subcultural Lives.* New York: New York University Press, 2005.

Hale, Grace E. *Making Whiteness: The Culture of Segregation in the South, 1890–1940.* New York: Pantheon Books, 1998.

Hammond, Jeffrey A. *The American Puritan Elegy: A Literary and Cultural Study.* Cambridge, UK: Cambridge University Press, 2000.

Hardy, Donald E. "Politeness in Flannery O'Connor's Fiction: Social Interaction, Language, and the Body." *Style* 44, no. 4 (2010): 524–48.

Hart, Ellen Louise, and Martha Nell Smith, eds. *Open Me Carefully: Emily Dickinson's Intimate Letters to Susan Huntington Dickinson.* Ashfield, MA: Paris Press, 1998.

Hart, Stephen M. "Magical Realism in the Americas: Politicized Ghosts in One Hundred Years of Solitude, The House of the Spirits, and Beloved." *Tesserae: Journal of Iberian and Latin American Studies*, 2003 Dec; 9 (2): 115–23.

Heberle, Renee, and Victoria Grace. *Theorizing Sexual Violence.* London: Routledge, 2009.

Hegel, Georg Wilhelm Friedrich. *Hegel's Phenomenology of Spirit.* Trans. A. V. Miller. New York: Oxford University Press, 1977.

Hennenberg, Sylvia. "Neither Lesbian nor Straight: Multiple Eroticisms in Emily Dickinson's Love Poetry." *Emily Dickinson Journal* 4, no. 2 (1995): 1–19.

Herman, Barbara. *Moral Literacy.* Cambridge, MA: Harvard University Press, 2008.

Herman, Judith Lewis. *Father Daughter Incest.* Cambridge, MA: Harvard University Press, 1981.

Hertz, Robert. *Death and the Right Hand.* Trans. Rodney and Claudia Needham. Glencoe, IL: Free Press, 1960.

Hirsch, Marianne. “Projected Memory: Holocaust Photographs in Personal and Public Fantasy.” In *Acts of Memory: Cultural Recall in the Present*, ed. Mieke Bal, Jonathan Crewe, and Leo Spitzer, 3–23. Hanover, NH: Dartmouth College Press, 1999.
Hirsch, Susan F. *In the Moment of Greatest Calamity: Terrorism, Grief and A Victim's Quest for Justice*. Princeton, NJ: University Press, 2006.
Hoffman, Beth. *Saving CeeCee Honeycutt: A Novel*. New York: Pamela Dorman Books-Viking, 2010.
Holland, Sharon P. *Raising the Dead: Readings of Death and (Black) Subjectivity*. Durham, NC: Duke University Press, 2000.
Hollywood, Amy. “Kill Jesus.” In *Mel Gibson's Bible: Religion, Popular Culture, and the Passion of the Christ*, ed. Timothy K. Beal and Tod Linafelt, 159–68. Chicago: University of Chicago Press, 2006.
hooks, bell. “Carrie Mae Weems: Diasporic Landscapes of Longing.” In *Inside the Visible: An Elliptical Traverse of 20th-Century Art in, of, and from the Feminine*, ed. Catherine de Zegher, 173–80. Cambridge, MA: MIT Press, 1996.
Horvitz, Deborah M. *Literary Trauma: Sadism, Memory, and Sexual Violence in American Women's Fiction*. Albany: State University of New York Press, 2000.
“How Testimony Communicates.” *Poetics Today* 26, no. 2 (Summer 2005): 171–3.
Hurston, Zora Neale. *Mules and Men*. 1935. Reprint, New York: Harper Perennial, 1990.
———. *Their Eyes Were Watching God: A Novel*. 1937. Reprint, New York: Perennial Library, 1990.
Husserl, Edmund. *The Essential Husserl*. Ed. Donn Welton. Bloomington: Indiana University Press, 1999.
Irigaray, Luce. *The Speculum of the Other Woman*. Ithaca, NY: Cornell University Press, 1985.
Johnson, E. Patrick, and Mae G. Henderson, eds. *Black Queer Studies*. Durham, NC: Duke University Press, 2004.
Johnson, Robert N. *Self-Improvement: An Essay in Kantian Ethics*. Oxford: Oxford University Press, 2011.
Jones, Anna Maria. *Problem Novels: Victorian Fiction Theorizes the Sensation Self*. Columbus: Ohio State University Press, 2007.
Jones, E., L. Trilling, and S. Marcus. *The Life and Works of Sigmund Freud*. New York: Basic Books, 1961.
Jones, Maxine D. “The Rosewood Massacre and the Women Who Survived It.” *Florida Historical Quarterly* 76 (1997): 193–208.
Jordan, Ervin L., Jr. “Sleeping with the Enemy: Sex, Black Women, and the Civil War.” *Western Journal of Black Studies* 18 (1994): 55–63.
Juhasz, Suzanne. “Amplitude of Queer Desire in Dickinson's Erotic Language.” *Emily Dickinson Journal* 14, no. 2 (2005): 24–33.
Kant, Immanuel. *Critique of Judgement*. Ed. Nicholas Walker and James C. Meredith. New York: Oxford University Press, 2007.

———. *Critique of Practical Reason*. Trans. Thomas Kingsmill Abbott. Chicago: Encyclopædia Britannica, 1952.

———. *Foundations of the Metaphysics of Morals, and What Is Enlightenment?* New York: Liberal Arts Press, 1959.

———. *Fundamental Principles of the Metaphysics of Morals*. Trans. Thomas Kingsmill Abbott. Raleigh, NC: Alex Catalogue, 1999.

———. *Groundwork for the Metaphysics of Morals*. Ed. and trans. Allen W. Wood. New Haven, CT: Yale University Press, 2002.

Kennedy, V. Born *Southern: Childbirth, Motherhood, and Social Networks in the Old South*. Baltimore, MD: Johns Hopkins Press, 2012.

Kinnell, Galway. "The Deconstruction of Emily Dickinson," *The Poetry Ireland Review* 43/44 (Autumn–Winter 1994): 177–8.

Lacan, Jacques. "Kant avec Sade." In *Écrits*, 765–90. Paris: Seuil, 1966.

———. "Kant Avec Sade." Trans. James B. Swenson, Jr. *October* 51 (1989): 55–75.

———. "Kant with Sade." In *Écrits: The First Complete Edition in English*, trans. Bruce Fink. New York: W. W. Norton & Company, 2007.

———. Le seminaire, Livre VII: L'éthique de la psychanalyse. Paris: Seuil, 1986.

LaCapra, Dominick. *Writing History, Writing Trauma*. Berkeley: Parallax, 2001.

Lamothe, Daphne. "Vodou Imagery, African-American Tradition and Cultural Transformation in Zora Neale Hurston's 'Their Eyes Were Watching God.'" *Callaloo* 22, no. 1 (1999): 157–75. Accessed online April 13, 2012.

Landry, Jordan H. "The Touched, the Tasted, and the Tempted: Lesbianizing the Triangles of Puritan Conversion Narratives in Emily Dickinson." *Women's Studies: An Interdisciplinary Journal* 33, no. 7 (2004): 875–906.

Larsen, Ernest. "Between Worlds." *Art in America* 87, no. 5 (1999): 122–9.

Laub, Dori. "Truth and Testimony: The Progress and the Struggle." In *Trauma: Explorations in Memory*, ed. Cathy Caruth. Baltimore, MD: Johns Hopkins University Press, 1995.

LeMahieu, Michael. "An Interview with Dorothy Allison." *Contemporary Literature* 52, no. 4 (Winter 2010): 650.

Levesque, George, and Nikola Baumgarten. "A Monstrous Inconsistency: Slavery, Ideology and Politics in the Age of the American Revolution." *Contribution in Black Studies* 8 (1986): 20–34.

Linfield, Susie. *The Cruel Radiance: Photography and Political Violence*. Chicago: The University of Chicago Press, 2010.

Liss, Andrea. "Facing History." *Afterimage* 23 (1995): 21–2.

Lockride, Aisha Damali. "Toni Morrison's *Beloved*: Origins." *Callaloo* 33 (Summer 2010): 892–4.

Long, Carolyn M. "Perceptions of New Orleans Voodoo: Sin, Fraud, Entertainment, and Religion." *Nova Religio: The Journal of Alternative and Emergent Religions* 6, no. 1 (2002): 86–101.

MacKenzie, Cynthia J. "'Heavenly Hurt': Dickinson's Wounded Text." *Emily Dickinson Journal* 9, no. 2 (2000): 55–63.

MacKinnon, Catharine. *Only Words*. Cambridge, MA: Harvard University Press, 1993.
Malson, Helen. *The Thin Woman: Feminism, Post-Structuralism, and the Social Psychology of Anorexia Nervosa*. New York: Routledge, 1998.
Manalansan, Martin. *Global Divas*. Durham, NC: Duke University Press, 2003.
Mandel, Naomi. "'I Made the Ink': Identity, Complicity, 60 Million and More." *Modern Fiction Studies* 48, no.3 (Fall 2002): 581–613.
Manning, Carol S. "Hurston and Welty, Janie and Livvie." *The Southern Literary Journal* 34, no. 2 (Spring 2002): 64–72.
Martinich, A. P. *The Two Gods of Leviathan: Thomas Hobbes on Religion and Politics*. Cambridge: Cambridge University Press, 1992.
Martyn, David. *Sublime Failures: The Ethics of Kant and Sade*. Detroit, MI: Wayne State University Press, 2003.
"Martyr." *The Oxford English Dictionary Online*. http://www.oed.com/. Accessed online June 4, 2011.
Mason, Gail. *The Spectacle of Violence: Homophobia, Gender, and Knowledge*. London: Routledge, 2002.
Massé, Michelle A. *In the Name of Love: Women, Masochism, and the Gothic*. Ithaca, NY: Cornell University Press, 1992.
Mazlish, Bruce. *Psychoanalysis and History*. Englewood Cliffs, NJ: Prentice-Hall, 1963.
McCullers, Carson. *The Ballad of the Sad Café*. 1951. Reprint, New York: Bantam Books, 1983.
———. *The Member of the Wedding*. 1946. Reprint, New York: Bantam Books, 1958.
McCullers, Carson, and Carlos L. Dews. *Illumination and Night Glare: The Unfinished Autobiography of Carson McCullers*. Madison: University of Wisconsin Press, 2002.
McNally, Richard J. "What is Psychological Trauma?" In *Remembering Trauma*, 78–104. Cambridge, MA: Belknap Press of Harvard University Press, 2005.
Mee, Susie, ed. *Downhome: An Anthology of Southern Women Writers*. New York: Houghton Mifflin, 1995.
Megan, Carolyn E. "Moving Toward Truth: An Interview with Dorothy Allison." *The Kenyon Review* 16, no. 4 (Autumn 1994): 71–83.
Miller, Nancy K. "Men's Reading, Women's Writing: Gender and the Rise of the Novel." *Yale French Studies* 75 (1988): 40–55.
Miller, Richard W. "Three Versions of Objectivity: Aesthetic, Moral, and Scientific." In *Aesthetics and Ethics: Essays at the Intersection*, ed. Jerrold Levinson, 26–58. Cambridge, UK: Cambridge University Press, 2001.
Mills, Catherine. "An Ethics of Bare Life: Agamben on Witnessing." Review Essay. *Borderlands e-journal* 2, no. 1 (2003). http://www.borderlands.net.au/vol2no1_2003/mills-agamben.html. Accessed January 4, 2013.
Mitchell, Angelyn. *The Freedom to Remember: Narrative, Slavery, and Gender in Contemporary Black Women's Fiction*. New Brunswick: Rutgers University Press, 2002.

Mitchell, Margaret. *Gone with the Wind*. New York: Macmillan, 1936.

Mitchell, W. J. T. *Cloning Terror*. Chicago: University of Chicago Press, 2012.

Mohanty, Chandra Talpade. "Under Western Eyes: Feminist Scholarship and Colonial Discourses." *Feminist Review* 30 (1988): 61–88.

———. "'Under Western Eyes' Revisited: Feminist Solidarity through Anticapitalist Struggles." *Signs* 28, no. 2 (2003): 499–535.

Morrison, Toni. *Beloved*. New York: Knopf, 1987.

———. *The Bluest Eye*. New York: Plume, 1994.

———. *Playing in the Dark: Whiteness and the Literary Imagination*. Cambridge, MA: Harvard University Press, 1992.

Morton, Clay. "Southern Orality and 'Typographic America': *I'll Take My Stand* Reconsidered." In *Themes of Conflict in the Nineteenth- and Twentieth-Century Literature of the American South*, ed. Ben P. Robertson, 227–40. Lewiston, NY: Edwin Mellen Press, 2007.

Mulvey, Laura. "Visual Pleasure and Narrative Cinema." In *The Sexual Subject: A Screen Reader in Sexuality*. New York and London: Routledge, 1992.

Murray, Aife. *Maid As Muse: How Servants Changed Emily Dickinson's Life and Language*. Durham, NH: University of New Hampshire Press; Hanover, NH: University Press of New England, 2009.

Naef, Weston. *Hidden Witness: African American Images from the Dawn of Photography to the Civil War*. Los Angeles: The J. Paul Getty Museum, 1995.

Nietzsche, *Beyond Good and Evil*. Trans. Helen Zimmern. Lexington, KY: Aeterna Press, 2010.

Noble, Marianne. *The Masochistic Pleasures of Sentimental Literature*. Princeton, NJ: Princeton University Press, 2000.

———. "The Revenge of Cato's Daughter: Dickinson's Masochism." *Emily Dickinson Journal* 7, no. 2 (1998): 22–47.

O'Connor, Flannery. *The Complete Stories*. New York: Farrar, Strauss, Giroux, 1971.

———. *Flannery O'Connor: Collected Works*. Ed. Sally Fitzgerald. New York: Library of America, 1988.

———. "A Good Man is Hard to Find." In *Flannery O'Connor: Collected Works*. New York: Library of America, 1988.

———. *The Habit of Being: Letters*. Ed. Sally Fitzgerald. New York: Farrar, Straus, Giroux, 1979.

———. *Mystery and Manners: Occasional Prose*. Ed. Sally Fitzgerald and Robert Fitzgerald. New York: Farrar, Straus & Giroux, 1969.

———. "A Temple of the Holy Ghost." In *Flannery O'Connor: Collected Works*. New York: Library of America, 1988.

———. "A View of the Woods." *Partisan Review* 24 (Fall 1957): 475–96.

The Online Etymology Dictionary. Ed. Brian Harper. http://www.etymonline.com/. Accessed June 4, 2011.

Paglia, Camille. *Sexual Personae: Art and Decadence from Nefertiti to Emily Dickinson*. New Haven, CT: Yale University Press, 1990.

Pateman, Carole. *The Sexual Contract*. Palo Alto, CA: Stanford University Press, 1988.

———. "What's Wrong with Prostitution." *Women's Studies Quarterly* 57 (1999): 53–64.

Patterson, Orlando. *Slavery and Social Death: A Comparative Study*. Cambridge, MA: Harvard University Press, 1982.

Phelan, Peggy. *Unmarked: The Politics of Performance*. London and New York: Routledge, 1993.

Plath, Sylvia. *Ariel*. New York: Harper & Row, 1966.

———. "Witch Burning." In *The Collected Poems*, 135. New York: Harper Perennial, 1980.

Plummer, Ken. *Telling Sexual Stories: Power, Change, and the Social Worlds*. London and New York: Routledge, 1995.

Powers, Peter K. "Gods of Physical Violence, Stopping at Nothing: Masculinity, Religion, and Art in the Work of Zora Neale Hurston." *Religion and American Culture: A Journal of Interpretation* 12, no. 2 (2002): 229–47. Accessed online April 13, 2012.

Ransom, John Crowe. "Emily Dickinson: A Poet Restored." In *Emily Dickinson: A Collection of Critical Essays*, ed. Richard B. Sewell, 88–100. Upper Saddle River, NJ: Prentice Hall, 1963.

———. "Reconstructed but Unregenerate." In *I'll Take My Stand: The South and the Agrarian Tradition*, ed. Lewis P. Simpson, 1–27. Baton Rouge: Louisiana State University Press, 1977.

Rape, Abuse & Incest National Network. "Who are the Victims?" http://www.rainn.org/get-information/statistics/sexual-assault-victims. Accessed June 20, 2012.

Rath, Sura P., and Mary Neff Shaw, eds. *Flannery O'Connor: New Perspectives*. Athens: University of Georgia Press, 1996.

Raymond, Claire. *Aftermath: The Trope of the Posthumous Voice in Women's Writing*. Ann Arbor, MI: University Microfilms International, 2001.

———. *The Posthumous Voice in Women's Writing from Mary Shelley to Sylvia Plath*. Aldershot, UK; Burlington, VT: Ashgate, 2006.

Reed, Roxanne. "The Restorative Power of Sound: A Case for Communal Catharsis in Toni Morrison's 'Beloved.'" *Journal of Feminist Studies in Religion* 23, no. 1 (2007): 55–71.

Reinhardt, Mark, Holly Edwards, Erina Dugganne, et al. *Beautiful Suffering: Photography and the Traffic in Pain*. Chicago: University of Chicago Press, 2007.

Rich, Adrienne. "Notes towards a Politics of Location." In *Blood, Bread, and Poetry: Selected Prose, 1979–1985*, 210–31. New York: Norton, 1986.

Ricoeur, Paul. *Memory, History, Forgetting*. Chicago: University of Chicago Press, 2004.

Rody, Caroline. *The Daughter's Return: African-American and Caribbean Women's Fictions of History*. New York: Oxford University Press, 2001.

———. "Toni Morrison's *Beloved*: History, 'Rememory,' and a 'Clamor for a Kiss,'" *American Literary History* 7 (Spring 1995): 92–119.

Rosenberg, Eric. "Walker Evans's Depression and the Trauma of Photography." In *Trauma and Visuality in Modernity*, ed. Lisa Saltzman and Eric Rosenberg, 28–47. Hanover, NH: Dartmouth College Press, 2006.

Rosenblum, Naomi. *A World History of Photography*. 4th ed. New York: Abbeville Press, 1984.

Rudnytsky, Peter, and Andrew Gordon. *Psychoanalyses/feminisms*. Albany: State University of New York Press, 2000.

Rustin, Susanna. "Predicting the Past." *The Guardian*, October 31, 2008. http://www.guardian.co.uk/books/2008/nov/01/toni-morrison. Accessed August 4, 2012.

Salgado, Sebastião, Eduardo H. Galeano, and Fred Ritchin. *An Uncertain Grace*. San Francisco: San Francisco Museum of Modern Art; New York: Aperture Foundation, 1990.

Sapphire. *Push*. New York: Alfred A. Knopf, 1996.

Scarry, Elaine. *The Body in Pain: The Making and Un-making of World*. New York: Oxford University Press, 1987.

Scheier, Claus-Artur. "The Rationale of Nietzsche's *Genealogy of Morals*." In *Nietzsche, Genealogy, Morality: Essays on Nietzsche's Genealogy of Morals*, ed. Richard Schacht, 449–59. Berkeley: University of California Press, 1994.

Schopenhauer, Arthur. *The World as Will and Representation*. Trans. E. F. G. Payne. New York: Dover Publications, 1969.

Schroeder, Alan, Augusta Savage, and JaeMe Bereal. *In Her Hands, The Story of Sculptor Augusta Savage*. New York: Lee & Low Books, 2009.

Sebold, Alice. *The Lovely Bones*. Boston: Little, Brown, 2002.

Sekula, Allan. *Photography Against the Grain: Essays and Photo Works 1973–1983*. Halifax: Press of the Nova Scotia College of Art and Design, 1984.

Sensen, Oliver. *Kant on Human Dignity*. Berlin: De Gruyter, 2011.

Seremetakis, C. Nadia. *The Last Word: Women, Death, and Divination in Inner Mani*. Chicago: University of Chicago Press, 1991.

Serrano, Julia. *Whipping Girl: A Transsexual Woman on Sexism and the Scapegoating of Femininity*. Berkeley, CA: Seal Press, 2007.

Shannon, Lorelei, and Victoria Cosner Love. *Mad Madame Lalaurie*. Charleston, SC: The History Press, 2011.

Shapiro, Barbara. "The Bonds of Love and Boundaries of Self in Toni Morrison's *Beloved*." *Contemporary Literature* 32, no. 2 (Summer 1991): 194–210.

Sharpe, Christina. *Monstrous Intimacies: Making Post-Slavery Subjects*. Durham, NC: Duke University Press, 2010.

Shaw, Gwendolyn DuBois. "The 'Rememory' of Slavery: Kara Walker's *The End of Uncle Tom and the Grand Allegorical Tableau of Eva in Heaven*." In *Trauma and Visuality in Modernity*, ed. Lisa Saltzman and Eric Rosenberg, 158–88. Hanover, NH: Dartmouth College Press, 2006.

Sherwin, Elisabeth. "Patron Saint of Battered Women Writes, Forgives." In *Printed Matter*. Manchester, UK: Manchester University Press, 1998.

Simpson, J. A., and E. S. C. Weiner, eds. *Oxford English Dictionary*. New York: Oxford University Press, 1989.

Singerman, Howard. *Art History, After Sherrie Levine*. Berkeley: University of California Press, 2011.

———. "Sherrie Levine's Art History." *October* 101 (2002): 96–121.

Singerman, Howard, Catherine Ingraham, and Sylvia Lavin, eds., *Sherrie Levine: Sculpture*. New York: Galerie Jablonka, 1996.

Smith, Adam. *The Theory of Moral Sentiments*. 1759. Reprint, Indianapolis, IN: Liberty Fund, 1984.

Smith, Cherise. "Fragmented Documents: Works by Lorna Simpson, Carrie Mae Weems, and Willie Robert Middlebrook at the Art Institute of Chicago." *Art Institute of Chicago Museum Studies* 24 (1998): 244–59, 271–2.

———. "Rethinking Carrie Mae Weems's Historic Appropriations." Address delivered at the conference Pictures and Progress: Early Photography and the Making of African American Identity, Duke University, Durham, NC, March 2–3, 2007.

Smith, Lindsay. *The Politics of Focus: Women, Children, and Nineteenth-Century Photography*. Manchester, UK: Manchester University Press, 1998.

Smith, Martha Nell, and Mary Loeffelholz. *A Companion to Emily Dickinson*. Malden, MA: Blackwell Publications, 2008.

Smith, Robert McClure. *Dickinson and the Masochistic Aesthetic*. Baltimore, MD: John's Hopkins Press, 1998.

Smith, Robert McClure. "Dickinson and the Masochistic Aesthetic." *Emily Dickinson Journal* 7, no. 2 (1998): 1–21.

Snediker, Michael D. *Queer Optimism: Lyric Personhood and Other Felicitous Persuasions*. Minneapolis: University of Minnesota Press, 2009.

Sollors, Werner, ed. *Interracialism: Black White Intermarriage in American History, Literature, and Law*. Cambridge MA: Harvard University Press, 2000.

Sollors, Werner. "Presidents, Race, and Sex," in *Sally Hemings & Thomas Jefferson: History, Memory, and Civic Culture*, ed. Jan Ellen Lewis and Peter S. Onuf. Charlottesville: UP of Virginia, 1999.

Solomon-Godeau, Abigail. "Just Like a Woman." In *Catalogue, Hunter College Exhibition of Francesca Woodman Photographs*. New York: Hunter College, 1986.

———. "Taunting and Haunting: Critical Tactics in a 'Minor' Mode." In *Women Artists at the Millennium*, ed. Carol Armstrong and Catherine de Zegher, 371–402. Cambridge: MIT Press, 2006.

Sontag, Susan. *On Photography*. New York: Farrar, Straus and Giroux, 1977.

———. *Regarding the Pain of Others*. New York: Farrar, Straus and Giroux, 2003.

Spelman, Elizabeth. *Fruits of Sorrow: Framing Our Attention to Suffering*. Boston: Beacon, 1997.

Tal, Kalí. *Worlds of Hurt: Reading the Literatures of Trauma*. New York: Cambridge University Press, 1996.

Tally, Justine. *Toni Morrison's* Beloved*: Origins*. New York: Routledge, 2009.

Tanner, Laura E. *Intimate Violence: Reading Rape and Torture in Twentieth-Century Fiction*. Bloomington: Indiana University Press, 1994.
Taylor, Gary, and Jane Ussher. "Making Sense of S&M: A Discourse Analytic Account." *Sexualities* 4, no. 3 (2001): 293–314.
Tirrell, Lynn. "Aesthetic Derogation." In *Aesthetics and Ethics: Essays at the Intersection*, ed. Jerrold Levinson, 284–314. Cambridge: Cambridge University Press, 2001.
Travis, M. A. "Beyond Empathy: Narrative Distancing and Ethics in Toni Morrison's *Beloved* and J. M. Coetzee's *Disgrace*." *Journal of Narrative Theory* 40, no. 2 (2010): 231–50.
Ussher, Jane. *Fantasies of Femininity: Reframing the Boundaries of Sex*. New Brunswick, NJ: Rutgers University Press, 1997.
von Kleist, Heinrich. "On the Marionette Theatre." In *Essays on Dolls*, trans. Idris Parry. London: Penguin/Syrens, 1995.
Walker, Alice. *In Search of Our Mothers' Gardens: Womanist Prose*. San Diego, CA: Harcourt Brace Jovanovich, 1983.
Wallis, Brian. "Black Bodies, White Science: Louis Agassiz's Slave Daguerreotypes." *American Art* 9, no. 2 (Summer 1995): 38–61.
———. "Black Bodies, White Science: The Slave Daguerreotypes of Louis Agassiz." *The Journal of Blacks in Higher Education* 12 (1996): 102–6.
Weaver, A. M. "Carrie Mae Weems: History and Dreams." *Aperture* 197 (2009): 24–31.
Weems, Carrie Mae. Carrie Mae Weems and Deborah Willis: INSight Conversation. LOOK3 Festival of the Photograph, Charlottesville, Virginia, June 13, 2013.
———. *Carrie Mae Weems: The Louisiana Project*. Ed. Erik Neil, Susan Cahan, and Pamela R. Metzger. New Orleans, LA: Newcomb Art Gallery, 2004.
———. *Carrie Mae Weems: Three Decades of Photography and Video*. Ed. Kathryn E. Delmez. New Haven: Yale University Press, 2012.
———. *From Here I Saw What Happened and I Cried*. In *Out of Time: A Contemporary View*. Photographic Exhibit, New York, Museum of Modern Art, August 30, 2006–April 9, 2007.
———. *Sea Islands Series*. In *Carrie Mae Weems: Bodies of Work*. http://carriemaeweems.net/galleries/sea-islands.html. Accessed July 1, 2011.
Westley, Robert. "First-time Encounters: 'Passing' Revisited and Demystification as a Critical Practice." *Yale Law and Policy Review* 18, no. 2 (2000): 297–349.
Weston, Kath. *Families We Choose: Lesbians, Gays, Kinship*. New York: Columbia University Press, 1991.
———. *Traveling Light: On the Road with America's Poor*. Boston, MA: Beacon Press, 2008.
Willis, Deborah. "Photographing Between the Lines: Beauty, Politics, and the Poetic Vision of Carrie Mae Weems." In *Carrie Mae Weems: Three Decades of Photography and Video*, ed. Kathryn E. Delmez. New Haven: Yale University Press, 2012.
Wriggins, Jennifer. "Rape, Racism and the Law." *Harvard Women's Law Journal* 6 (1983): 103–41.

Wu, Yung-Hsing. "Doing Things with Ethics: Beloved, Sula and the Reading of Judgment." *Modern Fiction Studies* 49, no. 4 (2003): 780–805.

Wyatt, Jean. "Giving Body to the Word: The Maternal Symbolic in Toni Morrison's *Beloved*." *PMLA* 108, no. 3 (1993): 474–88.

Yaeger, Patricia. "Consuming Trauma; or, the Pleasures of Merely Circulating." In *Extremities: Trauma, Testimony, and Community*. Urbana: University of Illinois Press, 2002.

———. *Dirt and Desire: Reconstructing Southern Women's Writing, 1930–1990*. Chicago: University of Chicago Press, 2000.

Young, Jason R. *Rituals of Resistance: African Atlantic Religion in Kongo and the Lowcountry South in the Era of Slavery*. Baton Rouge: Louisiana State University Press, 2007.

Žižek, Slavoj. "Kant and Sade: The Ideal Couple." *Lacanian Ink* 13 (1998): 12–25.

———. "Kant with (or Against) Sade?" *New Formations* 35 (1998): 93–107.

———. *Looking Awry: An Introduction to Jacques Lacan through Popular Culture*. Cambridge, MA: MIT Press, 1991.

———. *The Sublime Object of Ideology*. New York: Verso, 1989.

Index

Note: An 'n' following a page number indicates a footnote; 'f' indicates a figure.